MW00785508

BOOTS ON THE GROUND

OSPREY
PUBLISHING

BOOTS ON THE GROUND

MODERN LAND WARFARE
FROM IRAQ TO UKRAINE

LEIGH NEVILLE

OSPREY PUBLISHING
Bloomsbury Publishing Plc
Kemp House, Chawley Park, Cumnor Hill, Oxford OX2 9PH, UK
29 Earlsfort Terrace, Dublin 2, Ireland
1385 Broadway, 5th Floor, New York, NY 10018, USA
E-mail: info@ospreypublishing.com
www.ospreypublishing.com

OSPREY is a trademark of Osprey Publishing Ltd

First published in Great Britain in 2025

A catalogue record for this book is available
from the British Library.

ISBN: HB 9781472846846;
eBook 9781472846853;
ePDF 9781472846822;
XML 9781472846839

25 26 27 28 29   10 9 8 7 6 5 4 3 2 1

Cover, page design and layout by Stewart Larking
Index by Zoe Ross
Printed by Repro India Ltd.

Osprey Publishing supports the Woodland Trust, the UK's leading
woodland conservation charity.

To find out more about our authors and books visit
www.ospreypublishing.com. Here you will find extracts, author
interviews, details of forthcoming events and the option to sign up
for our newsletter.

CONTENTS

INTRODUCTION
CURRENT AND FUTURE LAND WARFARE

'It makes no difference what men think of war, said the judge. War endures. As well ask men what they think of stone. War was always here. Before man was, war waited for him. The ultimate trade awaiting its ultimate practitioner.

Cormac McCarthy, *Blood Meridian* (Picador, 2010)

The aim of this book is to provide a brief, and hopefully readable, non-technical overview of land warfare in the 21st century and what the immediate future may hold. To do so, it looks back to the wars following 9/11 in Afghanistan and Iraq, and examines important factors from other conflicts including the civil war in Libya, the war against Islamic State in Iraq and Syria, Russia's seizure of the Crimea, the Second Nagorno-Karabakh War, Israeli operations in Lebanon and Gaza and, of course, most recently, and most deeply, the Russo-Ukrainian War.

It takes lessons and observations from these conflicts and uses them to posit what land warfare will likely look like in the next decade or so. Some of these predictions will naturally be wrong as new information or capabilities present themselves; others will only be partly correct. Every war teaches us lessons: some are recognized at the time; others only become apparent in the fullness of time.

ABOVE A Ukrainian BTR-82A firing at the range. Its dual-feed capability, much like the 25mm Bushmaster of the Bradley, allows the 30mm 2A72 cannon to switch between High Explosive –Tracer and Armour Piercing – Tracer rounds. (Photo by Kostiantyn Liberov/ Libkos/Getty Images)

FUTURE BATTLEFIELDS

Before we consider how war has been fought in the past 20 years, and how it will be fought in the next decade or two, we should consider what wars are likely to flare up in the immediate future. Terrain and geography are both vitally important factors influencing how wars are physically fought and how military technology is employed. We will focus here primarily on larger-scale, so-called peer or near-peer conflicts.

What is *peer* or *near-peer*? These two terms get bandied around in most discussions of future warfare. Remarkably for such popular buzzwords, the US Department of Defense (DoD) does not have an agreed definition of either. Most understand the term 'near-peer' to relate to Russia and China – state actors that approach the US in terms of military capability. Others have termed Russia and China as 'peer' adversaries, and nations such as Iran and North Korea as 'near-peer'.

Despite the lack of a common definition by DoD, the terms have generally come to be known as a description of state entities or large non-state entities that approach US or NATO military capabilities in some areas. For convenience's sake, in this book we will use 'near-peer' to denote countries such as Iran and large non-state actors such as Islamic State, and 'peer' as Russia and China.

Each potential future theatre of war throws up its own unique challenges. Let's look at each of the most probable and highlight how a war would likely play out.

A wonderful image of a gathering of Libyan National Transitional Council technicals in 2011. Note the range of weapons, including recoilless rifles, DShK heavy machine guns, and ZPU cannon. (Photo by John Cantlie/Getty Images)

ABOVE Chinese PLA Type 95 self-propelled anti-aircraft artillery with quad 25mm guns which are guided by an integral radar. The Type 95 can also mount four QW-2 infrared homing surface-to-air missiles. (Photo by Costfoto/ NurPhoto via Getty Images)

BELOW Taiwanese ground forces exercise with outdated M60A3 main battle tanks and CM-32 Clouded Leopard wheeled infantry fighting vehicles. (Photo by Walid Berrazeg/SOPA Images/LightRocket via Getty Images)

Taiwan or the South China Sea

Any action against Taiwan would likely first include a significant naval blockade to strangle the island, denying it reinforcement, before an invasion landing would occur. The US Navy and US Marine Corps (USMC) would be the primary combatants against the Chinese People's Liberation Army (PLA). Initially at least, a war over Taiwan would be a largely maritime affair, with US and Chinese submarines being a key weapons system.

Whether the US would attempt to lift a blockade by force is a political decision, but any such effort would see large-scale loss of life and ships, and the PLAN (People's Liberation Army Navy) go head-to head with the US Navy. As far as US involvement in land warfare would be concerned, operations would be limited in most scenarios to US training teams and/or special operations forces (SOF) on the island fighting alongside the Taiwanese.

Attempting to repel an invasion would be costly; however, recent wargaming studies predict an eventual success by the Taiwanese Armed

Forces. Indeed, one recent (2023) wargame developed by the Center for Strategic and International Studies (CSIS) highlighted the physical and political losses to both sides of any such campaign: 'The United States and its allies lost dozens of ships, hundreds of aircraft, and tens of thousands of servicemembers. Taiwan saw its economy devastated. Further, the high losses damaged the U.S. global position for many years. China also lost heavily, and failure to occupy Taiwan might destabilize Chinese Communist Party rule.'[1]

Another scenario might see Chinese forces attempt an expansionist grab against island states in the Indo-Pacific, likely after an escalation of tensions in the South China Sea. Again, this would be predominantly an air/sea engagement, but US, Japanese and Australian ground forces might well be involved in terms of sea-lane and area denial. The USMC, as we shall see later in this book, is realigning its entire force structure towards operations in the Indo-Pacific.

US Marines and their Japanese and Australian allies could well be deployed among the narrow chokepoints of the Indonesian archipelago to deny access to PLAN surface craft with the employment of armed drones and anti-shipping missiles (including the Naval Strike Missile, with a range of some 185km mounted on the menacingly named NMESIS, or Navy Marine Expeditionary Ship Interdiction System). This could lead to conventional ground combat, with PLA forces despatched to clear the islands and the Marines planning on deploying light anti-aircraft platforms to defend these far-flung outposts.

These operations are known as Expeditionary Advanced Base Operations (EABO) and will become a key feature of any future conflict in the Indo-Pacific region, establishing ad hoc bases on land and sea and advancing from these temporary bases in a leapfrog movement, or maintaining a presence to deter or deny enemy freedom of movement.

The US Marines' manual on EABO defines them as:

> . . . a form of expeditionary warfare that involves the employment of mobile, low-signature, operationally relevant, and relatively easy to maintain and sustain naval expeditionary forces from a series of austere, temporary locations ashore or inshore within a contested or potentially contested maritime area in order to conduct sea denial, support sea control, or enable fleet sustainment.[2]

AREA AND SEA-LANE DENIAL

Area and sea-lane denial are related to the strategic concept of anti-access, area denial, or A2AD. A2AD is anything that attempts to limit the freedom of movement of enemy units within or through the battlespace. In relation to a potential conflict in the Indo-Pacific, this would entail limiting the free movement of PLAN surface and subsurface craft through key sea lanes. It could also represent an integrated air defence network denying ground and/or air movement through a particular region.

Officially, the US DOD defines A2 and AD as follows: 'Anti-Access (A2) is an action, activity, or capability, usually long-range, designed to prevent an advancing enemy force from entering an operational area. Area Denial (AD) is an action, activity, or capability, usually short-range, designed to limit an enemy force's freedom of action within an operational area.'

Source: *Department of Defense Dictionary of Military and Associated Terms*, November 2021

Western or Northern Europe

The potential exists for Russia, particularly after even a partial success in Ukraine, to invade (or 'annex', as Russia would likely term it) one or more European states. The then-German Defence Minister noted in early 2024, 'We hear threats from the Kremlin almost every day… so we have to take into account that Vladimir Putin might even attack a NATO country one day.'[3]

A possible scenario could see Russia conducting a regional 'stabilization operation' against Moldova in support of the breakaway Russian-backed region of Transnistria. Moldova is not a NATO member and thus represents easy pickings for Russia while supporting a nationalistic narrative of preserving the Slav identity.

BELOW A Ukrainian T-64BV with ERA blocks and additional slat armour fitted around the turret, pictured in March 2023. Note the worn 'friend or foe' identification marking and the camouflage net wrapped around the barrel to help break up the shape. (Photo by ARIS MESSINIS/AFP via Getty Images)

RIGHT One of the iconic images of the Russo-Ukrainian War: Ukrainian farmers towing away immobilized or bailed-out Russian armour using their farm tractors. In this case, an MT-LB – note the 'Z' invasion markings, which were crudely applied to decrease the potential for fratricide, particularly with both combatants using primarily Russian AFVs. (Photo by GENYA SAVILOV/AFP via Getty Images)

The Baltic states – Estonia, Latvia and Lithuania – are the other most plausible flashpoint, with Russia invading to claim that it is pushing back NATO 'expansionism'. A successful Russian operation to seize the Suwalki Gap, a corridor along the Lithuanian–Polish border, would see the three Baltic states isolated from direct reinforcement from NATO and essentially encircled by Russia.

Any such invasion risks a full-scale confrontation between NATO states and Russia. So-called 'tripwire forces' – NATO elements forward deployed into at-risk countries – would bear the brunt of the initial attack. NATO partners such as Poland, Germany and France would be forced to attempt to hold back the Russian advance until reinforcements from the US could arrive. The increased deployment of rotational heavy US Army units, including tanks and infantry fighting vehicles, into Europe acknowledges the threat and goes some way to deter Russian aggression.

ABOVE A Russian 30mm AGS-17 automatic grenade launcher. The AGS-17 and its successor the AGS-30 can be used in direct or indirect fire mode as seen here. (Photo by Vladimir Aleksandrov/Anadolu Agency via Getty Images)

Nagorno-Karabakh

Tensions continue between Armenia and Azerbaijan, with open combat again breaking out in late 2023, which saw Azerbaijan retake the region of Armenian-controlled Nagorno-Karabakh, located inside Azerbaijani territory, ending a 30-year dispute. The offensive saw some 100,000 Armenians leave the region. Future conflict may still be triggered by Azerbaijan attempting to secure a land corridor to its disputed exclave, the Nakhchivan Autonomous Republic. It is unlikely that any such war would escalate beyond its borders.

LEFT A fascinating image of a field expedient tank destroyer platform deployed by Armenian forces during the 2020 Nagorno-Karabakh War. The gun appears to be the Russian 100mm smoothbore T-12 anti-tank gun while the carrier is the ubiquitous MT-LB. Similar designs have been seen in Syria. (Photo by Aziz Karimov/Getty Images)

Islamic State Resurgence

While Islamic State (ISIL) was largely destroyed by the US-led Coalition in Iraq and Syria, remnants survive and are still active in both nations. The US and their Kurdish allies continue to prosecute kill/capture raids against ISIL in an effort to deny the organization any opportunity of a resurgence. The greater Syrian Civil War continues apace, although Syrian government forces have largely taken the upper hand.

A return of Islamic State, perhaps enabled by a withdrawal of US forces and a regional conflict elsewhere that distracts the US and partners, could end in an open civil war within Iraq between ISIL and Iranian forces. This could quickly become a regional conflict and draw in additional Gulf states.

Iran

After becoming the predominant political player in Iraq, a long-held ambition, Iran is controlling and financing numerous non-state actors to conduct operations in Iran's strategic interest. The Houthis in Yemen continue to threaten shipping in the Red Sea and Gulf of Aden after fighting an Arab coalition led by Saudi Arabia to a standstill. Iran continues to threaten Israel via Hezbollah, who have become the predominant Shia Islamist terror group in the region. There are also claims that the Iranian Revolutionary Guard Corps (IRGC) may have been involved in the planning of the 7 October 2023 attacks on Israel.

Some commentators posit the perfect storm of three concurrent regional conflicts all involving the US military. Certainly, if the US became embroiled in one regional conflict, for instance with Iran, China and Russia could, in concert or independently, launch offensives against Taiwan and the Baltics. This would lead to a three-front war that would stretch US capabilities to bursting and force NATO nations to take up some of the slack – a task many are not yet capable of doing. Such a three-front 'perfect-storm' war is unlikely but certainly not outside the realms of possibility.

Australian defence academic Dr Albert Palazzo, in his book *Land Warfare*, describes the domains of war that the Australian military identifies:

> [There are] five broad domains in which war takes place. They are air, land, sea, space, and information/cyberspace. Other militaries use similar terms to identify these domains. For example, the United States calls its domains land, sea, air, space, and cyber, whereas the United Kingdom uses cyber, space, maritime, land, and air. As technology advances, it is highly likely that the military will define additional domains. Indeed, arguments are already being made for the identification of sub-surface and the human as domains.[4]

CSIS posits two likely scenarios for future war: the 'slow smolder' and the 'hot blast': 'The slow smolder is geared towards victory without firing a shot. Intelligence activities, competitive behaviors, and hybrid war result in a slow shift of the adversary's mindset until there is no will to fight', while the hot blast would 'involve overwhelming precision-strike capability, domination of communications, and a decapitation attempt, in addition to well-hidden preparations for war.'[5]

On the slow-smolder side of the equation is the Grey Zone, a term popularized when discussing Russian attempts at operations 'other than war'. Major James Athow-Frost of the British Parachute Regiment offers the following definition(s):

> The Idea of 'Grey Zone' is ill-defined, and many definitions are so broad (including conflicting alignment with irregular or unconventional warfare, economic activity, cyber-attacks and misinformation) that it seems all interstate activity could be considered grey zone activity. For some, grey zone activity is a new phenomenon rooted in Russian Chief of Staff General Gerasimov's [at the time of writing in 2024] theory of 'non-contact warfare'. For others, sub threshold conflict is as old as war itself, and was effectively exploited throughout the Cold War.[6]

Houthi technical seen outside Sanaa in late 2016. Among the mass of fighters carrying AKs and RPGs is a gunner manning what looks to be a Chinese QJC88 12.7mm heavy machine gun. (Photo by MOHAMMED HUWAIS/AFP via Getty Images)

RIGHT Russian Orthodox priests demonstrating in support of 'Little Green Men' (or 'Polite People', as they were known in Russia) in a cordon around a Ukrainian Frontier Guard base in Balaklava, near Sevastopol in March 2014. The 'Little Green Men', likely Spetsnaz or VDV Recce, were a concrete example of 'Grey Zone' operations that skirt but do not breach the threshold for war. Note the Russian GAZ Tigr protected mobility vehicle in the background. (Photo by VIKTOR DRACHEV/AFP via Getty Images)

BELOW Well-equipped Russian soldiers, possibly special operations forces, seen in Mariupol, Ukraine, in 2022. Note the optics and sound suppressors on what appear to be 5.45mm AK-12s. (Photo by OLGA MALTSEVA/AFP via Getty Images)

Certainly, Grey Zone activity has been seen historically as soft power diplomacy mixed with the cultivation of intelligence assets and the occasional use of paramilitary or military resources to telegraph intentions or warn adversaries. It is not a new phenomenon, and one could argue that the classic Cold War period was one of extended Grey Zone activity by the major powers.

CASUALTIES

Any future peer or near-peer war will be very casualty intensive. Most deaths and wounds will be caused by indirect fire; the 'God of War', artillery, will be dominant but with the full gamut of both guided and unguided rockets and missiles also adding to the toll. The ratio of fatalities to wounded will also narrow, and a greater percentage of wounds will prove fatal as forces struggle to evacuate their wounded.

During the GWOT (Global War on Terror) era in 2001–21, improvised explosive devices (IEDs) were the principal casualty-causing weapon: 'Explosive mechanisms of injury made up the largest portion of combat wounds in the GWOT, accounting for approximately 79% of battlefield injuries.' Some '60 percent of all American fatalities in Iraq and half of all American fatalities in Afghanistan, more than 3,500 in total, were caused by IEDs.'[7]

The vast majority of those wounded, however, survived due to several factors. In the immediate aftermath of the IED contact, access to advanced first aid, with most NATO soldiers trained and equipped to use tourniquets and blood-clotting products to stem catastrophic bleeds such as those caused by traumatic amputation, increased survivability and increased the window of opportunity to evacuate the wounded.

In a non-peer conflict environment such as Afghanistan and Iraq, total air supremacy meant that medical evacuation by air was consistently available. Soldiers knew this and operated in the field under the belief that should they be wounded, they would be evacuated. Generally, aeromedical evacuation would see the wounded transported back to a surgery-capable hospital within the so-called 'Golden Hour'.

The *Journal of the American College of Surgeons* noted the following:

> Compared with insurgent/terrorist forces, NPAs [near-peer adversaries] have much heavier and longer-range weaponry, with a resultant increase in morbidity and mortality among combat casualties... Ukrainian physicians demonstrate that over 70% of all Ukrainian combat casualties are due to artillery and rocket barrages from Russian forces, which has resulted in significant polytrauma to multiple organ systems.

An IED initiator using a mobile/cell phone recovered by US Marines in Fallujah. IEDs are typically composed of an initiator, switch, main explosive charge and power source. (Photo by Scott Peterson/Getty Images)

The grim reality of urban combat as 1st Battalion, 3rd Marines negotiate a rubble-filled street with downed power lines and other hazards in Fallujah, Iraq, 2004, following a firefight with four insurgents that killed one Marine and wounded several others. (Photo by Scott Peterson/Getty Images)

These same experts in combat medicine predict 'mortality rates in this and future NPA conflicts may be 5 times greater than in the GWOT.'[8]

The belief that should they be wounded, they would be evacuated was all-pervasive across US ground forces; however, in a future conflict, 'U.S. service members who are injured in combat may consequently not reach definitive care until days later'.[9] Aircrew who are downed over enemy-held territory face an even longer wait for rescue – something we will return to in Chapter 3.

Even when medically evacuated, the challenges continue as the nature of the battlefield changes due to the development of sensors and deep fires:

> The practices of opposition forces jamming the electronic spectrum used by US forces to communicate will impair these processes during future NPA conflicts. In Ukraine, responding medical personnel and receiving medical installations frequently have no advance notice as to the nature or extent of the injuries of the incoming patients from the front line for fear of Russians intercepting the communications and then attacking the location of the casualty collection point.[10]

TECHNOLOGY AND THE UNBLINKING EYE

Rapid advances in technology, including quantum processing, will alter the field of future battle to an almost unrecognizable extent. The Office of the Director of National Intelligence (DNI) in the United States recently noted the following, in terms of the potential changes we will see in the 2020–40 period, and where defence research and development is focusing its energies:

> During the next two decades, new and emerging technologies could change and potentially revolutionize the battlefield in four broad areas – connectivity, lethality, autonomy, and sustainability.
>
> Connectivity: the ways in which combatants detect and locate their adversaries, communicate with each other, and direct operations; Lethality: the damage that new weapons and weapon systems can inflict on battlefields; Autonomy: the ways in which robotics and AI can change who (or what) fights and makes decisions; Sustainability: the ways that militaries supply and support their deployed forces.[11]

In terms of connectivity, we are already seeing Western armies operating legacy battlefield management systems, such as Blue Force Tracker, which has enabled US and allied forces to plot their own location, see the location of other friendly forces plotted, and mark suspected and confirmed enemy units, all in real time.

As ISR (intelligence, surveillance and reconnaissance) platforms have gained prominence over the first two decades of the 21st century, battlefield management systems have become increasingly complex and increasingly capable, disseminating the feeds from multiple ISR types to the on-the-ground commanders.

According to the US Armed Forces publication *Joint and National Intelligence Support to Military Operations*, ISR is 'an activity that synchronizes and integrates the planning and operation of sensors, assets, and processing, exploitation, and dissemination systems in direct support of current and future operations. This is an integrated intelligence and operations function.'[12]

The fusion of ISR feeds will only increase in speed, as will their dissemination to the lowest tactical level; the US, for example, has been developing (and fielding) smart night-vision/augmented reality goggles (Integrated Visual Augmentation System, or IVAS), which includes a head-up display that can show vision from networked ISR platforms, mapping, locations of friendly and enemy units, and even a chat function.

Incidentally, the IVAS platform has faced some criticism from users, with complaints of headaches and eyestrain caused by the goggles (a common complaint with most night-vision goggles). Others mentioned the light emitted by the head-up display potentially giving away their position. Such

NEXT PAGES Ukrainian infantry seen in the blasted landscape of Donetsk Oblast in early 2024. The lead soldier appears to be carrying the domestically produced 5.56mm UOR-15 fitted with an aftermarket drum magazine. (Photo by Diego Herrera Carcedo/ Anadolu via Getty Images)

teething issues are faced by all emerging technology. On the positive side, the reliability of the IVAS has increased, and a version of the platform will likely be issued to all combat arms personnel.

Additionally, artificial intelligence (AI) enabled battlefield management technologies will use algorithms and machine learning (ML) to predict enemy courses of action and assist in everything from fuel management of individual vehicles to identifying targets and providing a firing solution faster and more accurately than any human operator could.

CSIS notes that 'AI/ML-enabled systems will eventually be able to take much of the command-and-control burden off a battlefield commander – they can send a UAV [unmanned aerial vehicle] swarm to collect information, identify targets and "decide" whether those targets need more investigation, and flag items of highest concern, leaving the commander more time to focus on more pressing priorities.'[13]

This revolution in data will cause tactical and strategic change on the battlefield. Again, the DNI points out:

> The future of warfare is likely to focus less on firepower and more on the power of information and the way it connects a military's forces through the concepts of command, control, communications, computers, intelligence, surveillance, and reconnaissance (C4ISR). More than ever, the advantage will lie with whichever side can collect the most vital information, accurately and quickly analyze it, and then rapidly and securely disseminate the information and associated instructions to forces.[14]

This fusion of data creates its own problems, with the very real danger of data overload as the products from innumerable feeds compete for the human commander's attention. Until the AI/ML systems have matured to become a reliable disseminator of actionable data (turning the raw product into actual intelligence), this will remain an issue as more and more systems are joined together.

ELECTRONIC WAR

Conversely, this revolution in connectivity will also see concerted efforts to disrupt and degrade such systems with battlefield jamming and electronic warfare (EW), along with offensive cyber operations (the fancy term for hacking or introducing a virus into an opponent's computer network) becoming the norm. We have seen this already occurring in Ukraine.

Russian cyber and EW was initially somewhat underwhelming, leading some observers to question the quality and extent of their capabilities; analysts have now identified that Russian EW units are not equipped to support

UNMANNED SYSTEMS
DON'T BLEED

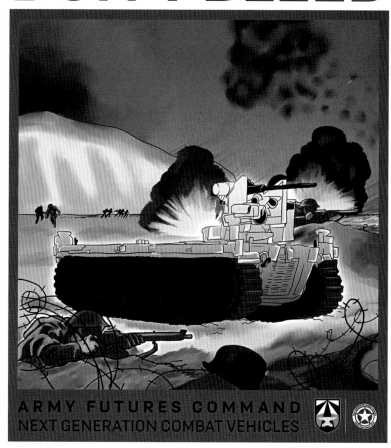

ARMY FUTURES COMMAND
NEXT GENERATION COMBAT VEHICLES

An amusing 1930s-style promotional poster from the US Army's Next Generation Combat Vehicles Cross-Functional Team, promoting the benefits of manned-unmanned teaming using RCVs. (Photo by Dan Heaton, DVIDS)

fast-moving offensive operations and require a more static presence to be effective. However, the Russians are learning, and this will be a key lesson for their EW fraternity.

Where Russia did succeed within a few weeks of the invasion was in jamming Ukrainian UAVs. The Royal United Services Institute (RUSI) analysis observed, 'The average life-expectancy of a quadcopter remained around three flights. The average life-expectancy of a fixed-wing UAV was around six flights… in aggregate, only around a third of UAV missions can be said to have been successful.'[15]

Indeed, after a year of the war, most frontline EW units were tasked with 'controlling and defeating UAVs'.[16] In 2023, reliable estimates indicated

Ukrainian mobile air defence group using technicals mounting M2 .50cal heavy machine guns with optics to shoot down Russian drones. (Photo by Zinchenko/ Global Images Ukraine via Getty Images)

approximately 10,000 Ukrainian UAVs were lost each month (this number includes loitering munitions, otherwise known as 'kamikaze' or 'one-way attack' drones). This may seem an astonishing number, but it tells a story of just how widely the Ukrainians are employing UAVs and how many the Russians are downing, primarily through EW.

Russian EW also managed to disrupt Ukrainian Air Force operations, as the RUSI report describes: 'As Russian EW complexes began to be deployed systematically, Ukrainian pilots found that they often had their air-to-ground and air-to-air communications jammed, their navigation equipment suppressed, and their radar knocked out.'[17]

EW has become an all-pervasive factor on the modern battlefield, and its importance will only increase. Coupled with the unblinking eye of persistent ISR from crewed, uncrewed, electronic and space-based assets, signature management has become a new buzz-term for military planners. Simply put, units will have to minimize their signature – be that electronic, physical, thermal or otherwise. To be seen is to be hit.

Historian Bruce W. Menning noted sagely, 'Despite the requirement to achieve mass and concentration for decisive results, the greater lethality of weapons dictated a contradictory need for dispersion. Much of the history of modern warfare can be written as a function of attempts to reconcile these seemingly contradictory elements.'[18]

The US Army is taking this lesson very seriously indeed:

Specifically, command posts are targeted because they have become easily targetable. Contemporary tented command posts – with their radio frequency emitting antennas, dozens of generators and vehicles, and extensive support requirements – are easily targetable to even the untrained eye. During large-scale combat operations, these command posts can be easily seen by an ever-expanding array of sensors and just as easily struck by complementary effects throughout the depth and breadth of the battlefield.

To fight and win on the modern battlefield in large-scale combat operations, Army command posts can and must become more flexible, agile, and resilient while not sacrificing effectiveness. Otherwise, our command posts will be a place our leaders go to die.[19]

ORDER OF BATTLE

Before we move into examining specific capabilities and discussing how they have operated throughout the first two decades of the decade and how they will likely operate in the next 20 years or so, let's spend a moment discussing organization. The following illustrates how a land force is composed, at least for the combat arms or 'teeth arms' as they are known.

OPPOSITE A Russian 122mm D-30 artillery piece manned by Ukrainian gunners. Note the elaborate camouflage net to break up the shape of the gun from the air and the wire net to counter attacks by FPV (first-person view) drones. Such nets/cages will likely become standard practice for artillery units. (Photo by Jose Colon/Anadolu via Getty Images)

Forces are typically classed as heavy, medium or light. The New Zealand Army's *Future Land Operating Concept 2035* document explains the differences rather well:

> A 'heavy force' is a force possessing a full range of combat and combined-arms capabilities, enabling sustained and high intensity close combat. Heavy forces possess armoured forces for close combat (including Main Battle Tanks and Mechanised Infantry) and high levels of firepower, including artillery such as Self-Propelled 155mm and rocket artillery systems, and close attack aviation (attack helicopters).
>
> Light forces, on the other hand, trade off the full spectrum of combat capabilities and lack the logistically demanding but powerful armour and fire-power of heavy forces for a more strategically mobile force.[20]

All of the combat arms only function due to an extensive logistics and support structure. The tooth-to-nail ratio, as it is known, denotes how many soldiers are required in support roles to keep one soldier in combat. During Operation *Iraqi Freedom*, the ratio was around eight to one.

An Iraqi Lion of Babylon (Asad Babil) T-72M1 variant destroyed in April 2003. Note local modification of the searchlight added to the turret, while Coalition armour used thermal optics. (Photo by US Army)

We do not specifically cover these support roles or logistics in general in this book, as to do so would require a far larger volume to attempt to do the subject justice, but bear in mind that these soldiers are often exposed to similar levels of risk within peer and near-peer conflict, with adversaries specifically targeting sustainment and logistics nodes.

Even in counterinsurgency or other 'operations other than war', these personnel are required to risk life and limb crewing convoys open to ambush or providing critical services at forward bases under rocket and drone attack (see 2024 casualties at US facilities in Iraq and Syria from kamikaze drones).

Armies are organized in reasonably common ways. For the infantry, at the lowest tactical level is the fire team of typically four soldiers or Marines. Several of these fire teams, two in most armies but three in the USMC, comprise a squad (US terminology) or a section (UK terminology). Three or four squads/sections make up a platoon.

A British Army Warrior IFV pictured in Helmand Province, Afghanistan, in 2013. Most Warriors had been fitted with WRAP-2 reactive armour by this time; however, this vehicle appears only to be fitted with the slat armour cage. (PA Images/ Alamy Stock Photo)

A platoon will have a small headquarters element and may have its own vehicles, either light platforms like Humvees, GAZ Tigrs or JLTVs (joint light tactical vehicles) or armoured vehicles such as MRAPs (Mine Resistant Ambush Protected) or tracked or wheeled IFVs (infantry fighting vehicles).

Three or four platoons make up a company: this will often see two to three infantry platoons supported by a support or weapons platoon typically equipped with medium machine guns, light mortars and anti-tank weapons. Three to four of these companies comprise the next level up – the battalion. Dependent on the army, the battalion may have a support company which groups battalion assets, including snipers and reconnaissance, anti-tank weapons and medium mortars.

The same basic structure is seen in tank and artillery units; however, the naming conventions often differ. A tank troop, for instance, may include three to five main battle tanks (MBTs), with three to four troops making up a squadron or company in most armies. A similar structure is seen with cavalry units, which are usually equipped with light reconnaissance vehicles (although US cavalry units include MBTs and attack helicopters and their squadrons are battalion-sized groupings).

Artillery companies are called batteries and have three to four gun sections that comprise two to three towed artillery guns, self-propelled guns, or MLRS (Multiple Launch Rocket Systems) each.

At the next level up from battalion come the regiments and the brigades: regiments comprise one type of unit, while brigades are a combined-arms force with normally a mixture of infantry, tank, cavalry, aviation, air defence, electronic warfare, UAV and artillery formations with requisite supporting and logistics arms. Two to three brigades are organized into a division. Two to four of these divisions are a corps; three to four corps form the highest organizational level – the army.

Although this is the theoretical structure of most armies, it is further confused by task-organized structures such as Battalion Combat Teams, Battle Groups and Battalion Task Groups at nominal battalion to brigade level and, further down, with combined-arms teams at the company level. Many Western armies are able to 'task organize' an array of units together for a specific task or mission.

The Russian BTG (Battalion Tactical Group) of Ukraine infamy is a good example of this. The Australian Army Research Centre explains exactly how one is organized:

The typical contemporary BTG is based on either a Motorized Rifle or Tank Battalion. In Russian parlance, any infantry equipped with vehicles are referred to as 'Motorized Rifles'. These may be equipped with armoured personnel carriers (APCs) such as the

wheeled BTR or tracked MT-LB or tracked infantry fighting vehicles (IFVs) such as the BMP series.

Given the significant differences in capability between APCs and IFVs, fighting approaches differ between these units, as do the tasks they are expected to perform. Motorized Rifle Battalions contain three Motorized Rifle Companies which are supported by a self-propelled Mortar Company and Grenade Launcher, Signal, Medical and Support Platoons. In comparison, Tank Battalions lack the organic fire support assets that Motorized Rifles Battalions have. Tank units are equipped with T-72B3M, T-80BVM or T-90M series main battle tanks (MBT). Notably, Tank Battalions in MRB may include a fourth company.[21]

Russian operators seen at Ukraine's Belbek Airbase in 2014. Note the VANT-VM ballistic shield with LED lights to disorient opponents and what appears to be an AK-12 with red dot optic carried by the centre soldier. (Photo by Oleg Klimov/ Epsilon/Getty Images)

We will examine the question of how armies organize their forces in some of the later chapters, particularly as it relates to the success of combined-arms operations, bringing together artillery, armour, infantry, engineers and attack aviation to provide both flexibility and depth in operational capability. What becomes clear is that combined arms, and mass, are still of vital importance, even in the era of the drone.

So, what will near-future land warfare look like? As we will examine in the following chapters, recurring themes point to possible answers:

- longer-ranged, more accurate and autonomous artillery and rocket systems;
- the demise of manned close air support to be replaced by UAS (Unmanned Aircraft Systems);
- swarms of UAVs, each one an ISR node and flying bomb;
- manned-unmanned teaming;
- renewed focus on GBAD (Ground-based Air Defence) to include lasers and microwaves;
- a concurrent adoption of counter-UAS systems across combat and logistics vehicles;
- UGVs (uncrewed ground vehicles) conducting frontline resupply, medical evacuation, counter-UAS and acting as overwatch for manned elements;
- APS (Active Protection System) on all AFVs (armoured fighting vehicles) with renewed focus on counters to top-down attack ATGMs (anti-tank guided missiles), sabot penetrators and loitering munitions;
- thermal shielding across vehicle fleets to reduce signature;
- dispersed and mesh connected command posts;
- an electromagnetic battlespace of constant war between competing EW (including completely GPS denied battlefields) and countermeasures where an element's invisible 'signature' can cause its doom;
- unparalleled real-time ISR feeds to ground commanders that will be distributed down to the individual soldier.

What will not change? Ultimately, as Field Marshal Earl Wavell famously declared, 'all battles and all wars are won in the end by the infantryman.' Now, with that little teaser, let's move on to the main event and start by looking at that iconoclast of land warfare, the main battle tank.

CHAPTER ONE
MAIN BATTLE TANKS

'A tank is like a dinner jacket: you don't need them very often, but when you do, nothing else will do.'

Major General Kathryn Toohey,
Australian Army,
RUSI Land Warfare Conference 2019[1]

If artillery is the god of the battlefield, the tank is the armoured workhorse – an eminently lethal but conspicuous array of armour, sensors and, quite simply, very big guns. The tank was first employed during World War I to break the stalemate of the trenches and allow a return to manoeuvre warfare, using its armoured might to punch through fixed defensive lines.

In the modern era, MBTs remain a key capability in ground warfare. They protect more thinly skinned armoured personnel carriers (APCs) and infantry fighting vehicles (IFVs) by engaging enemy tanks and AFVs, while also enabling ground offensives through contested areas. They have also proven their worth in counterinsurgency warfare, both as a battering ram into fortified insurgency strongholds and due to their typically advanced sensors.

For example, tank optics proved useful in Afghanistan in identifying insurgents from civilians at range and scanning for IEDs and insurgent firing positions. The coaxial machine gun (the coax) was also prized due to its accuracy when slaved to the tank's optics. Despite these advantages,

ABOVE A captured T-72B3 fitted with Kontakt-5 ERA being crewed by Ukrainian tankers. The B3 is also seen in the B3M variant that adds skirts with Relikt ERA and additional UPH ERA bags. (Photo by Roman Petushkov/Global Images Ukraine via Getty Images)

WHY 'TANK'?

Why the name 'tank'? The term dates to British attempts at counterespionage during World War I to disguise the vehicles' development from the Germans as innocuous 'water tanks' rather than armed and armoured behemoths. During trials, these first tanks were also known internally as 'landships'.

A British Army Challenger 2 of the 7th Armoured Brigade seen in Basra, Iraq, 2003. Note the canvas skirts fitted below the Chobham/Dorchester L2 composite armour to reduce the ingestion of dust, and the prominent Combat Identification Panel (CIP), which can be seen under infrared or thermal to reduce fratricide. (Photo by Mirrorpix/Getty Images)

there was an understandable school of thought that saw the use of tanks in COIN (counterinsurgency) environments as counter-productive to the winning of hearts and minds.

For generations, the dictum was that the best defence against a tank was another tank. With developments in both modern top-attack ATGMs and armed drones, that dictum has taken something of a battering. The tank now faces a wider range of capable threats than ever before.

Has the ATGM led to the end of the tank? No, far from it. As we will see in this and other chapters, this panoply of complex anti-armour threats means adaption both technologically and in terms of tactics, but the tank is far from dead.

First, let's look at the main element that distinguishes a tank from any other AFV, namely a large-calibre main gun. Tank main guns are either smoothbore or rifled. Smoothbore guns allow the firing of ATGMs via the main gun, a feature primarily seen on Russian MBT designs, along with facilitating the use of a greater range of ammunition types and reduced barrel wear from firing.

Traditionally, rifled barrels also offered greater accuracy. Relatively few modern in-service MBTs still use rifled guns, however, the British Army's Challenger 2 being one of these few outliers. The British use a type of main gun ammunition called the high-explosive squash-head or HESH, a dual-use round that can be used against both armoured targets and infantry and soft-skins (when striking armour, it flattens before detonating, causing spalling inside the enemy tank – literally sending pieces of superheated metal flying around inside the crew compartment).

The German Rheinmetall 120mm rifled tank gun is the most commonly encountered type on Western tanks such as the M1A2 Abrams. The Rheinmetall 120mm is available in both a standard and a long-barrel version which improves velocity with certain types of ammunition.

Modern anti-armour tank ammunition can be grouped into primarily two types: chemical energy (CE) penetrators and kinetic energy (KE) penetrators. Chemical energy penetrators use a shaped charge to detonate a penetrator (typically a copper cone) that is superheated by the explosion into a liquid copper jet to punch through armour. CE penetrators are typified by both the HESH and traditional high-explosive anti-tank (HEAT) designs.

Kinetic energy penetrators instead use a subcalibre penetrator (known as a rod) that is fired at high velocity from either rifled or smoothbore guns. KE penetrators include older APDS (armour-piercing discarding sabots) that carry their rods within a sabot casing that falls away in flight. Rifling was required to stabilize earlier types of APDS, but with modern ammunition, APDS is as effectively fired from smoothbore as it is rifled main guns.

APDS was further refined into today's standard anti-tank round type, the armour-piercing fin-stabilized discarding sabot (APFSDS). This adds a set of fins to further stabilize the round in flight, increasing accuracy.

The British Challenger 2 main battle tank in Ukrainian service with the 82nd Separate Air Assault Brigade. The performance of the Challenger has been marred by its propensity to become bogged (71-ton weight); its vulnerability, as it was not supplied with the same TES (theatre entry standard) up-armouring as used in Iraq; and the short operational life of the main gun barrel. Ukrainian crews have added slat armour and cope cages to guard against FPVs. (Photo by GENYA SAVILOV/AFP via Getty Images)

Characteristic of the APFSDS was the US M829 series, which employs a depleted uranium penetrator.

Modern Western rounds are often dual use for employment against infantry in cover and light to medium armoured targets. For instance, Rheinmetall offers a programmable 120mm HE round called the DM 11 which incorporates an 'electronic module [which] programs the time-delay fuse to detonate at a specific point in the projectile's flight path: the round can be timed to explode for maximum effect either above, in front or inside of a target (e.g. after penetrating a wall)'.[2]

The Rheinmetall DM 12A1, another dual-use round, was adopted by the US Army as the M830A1 MPAT or Multi-Purpose Anti-Tank, which was widely employed in Iraq and could be used against aerial targets by a manually set fuse. Today, the US Army issues the M1147 AMP or Advanced Multi-Purpose round along with the M829A4 Armor Piercing, Fin Stabilized, Discarding Sabot – Tracer (APFSDS-T), which is its primary tank-killing round. It also wins a prize for the longest acronym in current service!

The AMP round can be set for airburst out to 2,000 metres to combat the likes of enemy ATGM teams. It can also be set for traditional point detonation for use against vehicles or point detonation – delay, which can be used against buildings and bunkers, allowing the round to penetrate before detonating. This latter fuse setting is also useful in conducting breaching into buildings for accompanying infantry or reducing obstacles such as concrete barricades.

Russian-designed ammunition still trails that of the West; however, the 125mm 3VBM17 Mango-M APFSDS is similar to more modern Western designs but has thus far not seen widespread issue. Russian tanks mainly rely upon the 3BM60 Svinets-2, which employs a 'long rod' penetrator made of tungsten alloy, and the 3BM59 Svinets-1, which uses a depleted uranium penetrator. HEAT-T ammunition is also in use. There is no known Russian equivalent to multi-use rounds like the AMP.

Despite advances in fire control, tanks still fire using line of sight, meaning they need to see the target to be able to engage it; although thermal sensors and similar optics may be able to detect concealed armour, a line of sight is still required. Indirect fire techniques for tank main guns have long been in the armoury, but traditionally, without an observation of the fall of shot, this has been employed as an area effect weapon using high-explosive rounds.

In 2024, Ukrainian tank crews have employed indirect fire to some significant success; their accuracy has been guided by the employment of UAVs to correct the fall of shot (watching where the rounds land and then providing corrective guidance to improve accuracy). Although a technique that exists in training manuals (but never employed), Western crews will likely begin drills incorporating these Ukrainian lessons. The Ukrainians use specially developed software called ARMOR that develops firing solutions to allow tanks to fire in indirect mode.

For the Russians, this indirect fire mode is conducted mainly by older model tanks such as the T-55 and T-62, whose armour, sensors and main gun capabilities leave it at a severe disadvantage against more modern Ukrainian armour. These T-55s and T-62s have also been pressed into action as assault guns supporting infantry assaults in a manner not dissimilar to that of the German StuG of World War II.

Sergio Miller, analyst and author, makes a clear distinction between Russian tank models in theatre in Ukraine, with only the T-72B3/B3M, T-80BVM and T-90A/M considered to be relatively modern:

An ageing T-55 in action with Southern Transitional Council (STC) separatists in Yemen, 2020. Russia has deployed numbers of T-55s to Ukraine to act as assault and self-propelled guns (firing indirectly). (Photo by NABIL HASAN/AFP via Getty Images)

They are modern because they are fitted with an advanced gunner's sight (the Sosna-U) with night capability and boast modern fire control systems (FCSs). The commander's station sight in the 'modern' tanks remains an inferior sight, but the commander shares a flat screen display with the gunner.

The older variant tanks are fitted with Soviet-era sights and fire control systems that are no match for Western tanks. As such, Russia invaded Ukraine with a tank force that was outdated and ageing; a tank force which had failed to address key vulnerabilities and to equip their tanks with an array of battle-winning capabilities.

Further, he notes the vulnerabilities of Russian armour:

> YouTube videos show Russian tanks with ERA [explosive reactive armour] correctly fitted have proved vulnerable to anti-tank systems (the indigenous Stugna, NLAW, and Javelin); other tank fire; and artillery fire. The latter has been especially noteworthy with splinters from 152mm/155mm calibre shells quite capable of provoking catastrophic kills...
>
> It is important to understand ERAs are not intended to fully defeat threats (although in some cases they may). They degrade threats. This means some penetration may occur. In the case of Russian-designed tanks that penetration can be catastrophic.[3]

Coming back to more modern designs, arguably the most recognized modern MBT is the American Abrams. Rising to prominence during the 1991 Gulf War and the famous battle of 73 Easting, the Abrams has since seen action with US tankers in Afghanistan and Iraq.

Export models have been deployed by the Saudis to Yemen and the Iraqi Army during their war against Islamic State (although these fared far less well – a factor we will consider later in this chapter). It is simply the standard by which all other MBTs are measured. So, what makes it so good?

The Abrams manages to combine high speed, superbly efficient armour, and a deadly 120mm main gun. It's also very survivable, with numerous technologies built in to aid crew survivability. Most telling of these is how main gun ammunition is stored.

In contrast to Russian designs which store their ammunition in the underside of the turret, the Abrams carries its ammunition at the rear of the turret, protected by armoured doors with external blow-out panels. At least

Former deputy of Ukrainian Parliament Tetyana Chornovil operates a Stugna-P ATGM control interface. The domestically produced Stugna-P has performed well, with a tandem warhead capable of defeating ERA and remote firing to improve the survivability of the crew. (Photo by GENYA SAVILOV/ AFP via Getty Images)

one Abrams suffering an otherwise catastrophic kill in Ukraine appeared to have spared the lives of the crew thanks to these blow-out panels.

If a catastrophic hit is inflicted, the ammunition is designed to detonate outwards via these panels, channelling the blast away from the crew compartment. Readers will likely have witnessed the effects of catastrophic hits on Russian armour during the Russo-Ukrainian War – such spectacular, and deadly, catastrophic explosions are rare with Western-designed platforms.

The autoloader carousel used in Russian MBTs is largely responsible for the phenomenon of tank turrets being launched into the air when a catastrophic penetration occurs. Sergio Miller writes, 'Any penetration of a Russian tank (HEAT, long rod penetrator or shell splinter) is potentially catastrophic. Ignition of an unprotected charge bag sets off the entire carousel. The energy release is sufficient to fling turrets weighing over ten tons.'[4]

Western tanks have proven far more survivable than their Russian counterparts in terms both of human crews surviving and of the tanks themselves being recoverable and repairable. Catastrophic kills that entirely destroy a Western tank are rare. Far more commonly, the tank is immobilized, allowing the crew to escape and the tank to eventually be recovered.

One of the biggest reasons is the design, or, more accurately, the design of their Russian counterparts. By storing ammunition in the base of the turret, typically without any specialist survival measures such as blow-out panels which channel the blast from exploding ammunition away from the crew, Russian tanks often exhibit catastrophic kills that see the turret explode into the air.

The Abrams has benefited from a number of major upgrades over the years, increasing survivability and lethality. The latest version in widespread service within the US Army is the M1A2 SEPv3 (System Enhancement Package, Version 3).

A pair of US Army M1A1s fitted with TUSK 1, which includes extra machine guns, gun-shields, improved under body armour and XM19 ARAT-1 (Abrams Reactive Armour Tiles) ERA armour. (US Air Force photo by Staff Sergeant Jason T. Bailey)

An urbanized variant of the Abrams was also introduced during the later years of operations in Iraq – the TUSK and TUSK 2 (Tank Urban Survival Kit). These kits were developed based on crew feedback from the urbanized and semi-urbanized Iraqi environment and the threats that such urban geographies presented. Tanks were contacted by insurgents armed with a range of RPG (rocket-propelled grenade) variants (including the deadly RPG-29) and an even wider range of RPG warheads, while insurgents also targeted exposed crew members with small-arms fire.

The additional threat in Iraq was of course the IED. For the MBT, this meant two principal IED types: a large device or daisy-chained network of devices buried under the road (incredibly, sometimes these were even tarred over with bitumen by the insurgents to decrease the odds of detection) and often employing multiple artillery rounds; and the EFP or explosively formed projectile or penetrator.

The EFP was introduced into theatre by the Iranian backers of Shia insurgents, but the technology soon spread as its success was appreciated. The EFP uses a copper plate which is positioned like a shaped charge against the main charge of the IED, meaning that as the EFP detonates, the copper plate becomes super-heated and strikes the unfortunate target as a high-velocity copper slug.

The TUSK is an applique kit that adds additional armour in the form of a type of explosive reactive armour (ERA) to increase protection, particularly against later-generation RPGs; an increase in belly armour to counter large IEDs; the option of a CROWS (Common Remote Operated Weapon Station) and an armoured shield for the loader's external machine gun; additional racks of grenade dischargers that can be loaded with both chemical smoke and anti-personnel munitions; and additional thermal cameras to improve the situational awareness of the crew.

At the time of writing, US Army Abrams are undergoing the installation of the Israeli Trophy Active Protection System (APS). Like all APS kits, Trophy adds both additional weight and energy requirements. It will be intriguing to see how quickly the Israelis can modify Trophy to defend against FPV (first-person view) drones, which have become the scourge of Russian and Ukrainian armour in Ukraine.

The standard Russian hard-kill APS, called Arena, works on the same principles as Trophy. Radar detects the incoming threat and launches a barrage of explosives to interdict the missile or rocket. It can defeat top-attack profile missiles, although the famed Javelin is impervious to Arena due to its extreme angle of attack (current-generation Arena also has a vulnerability to the rear of the vehicle, hence the addition of slat or bar armour to cover those areas not protected by the APS).

Afghanit is the name of the planned replacement for Arena and was designed for use on the Armata series of vehicles. There have been unverified

An M1A2 SEPV2 fitted with TUSK 2, which adds XM32 ARAT-2 tiles over XM19 ARAT-1 ERA to further increase protection, particularly against EFP IEDs, advanced tandem projectiles and multiple strikes from tank main guns. (US Army photo by Chaplain (Captain) Malcolm Rios, 3rd ABCT Public Affairs, 4th Infantry Division)

claims that Afghanit can intercept APFSDS, which as we will see in a moment, is a significant challenge for APS.

The PLA have an equivalent APS called the GL5 produced by NORINCO, which appears to be roughly modelled on Trophy. It uses a radar system to detect threats before engaging with launched high-explosive fragmentation grenades. The GL5 does not appear to be able to destroy top-attack munitions.

WHAT IS APS?

An APS is an Active Protection System that provides a level of protection against incoming projectiles. All APSs operate in a similar manner: a radar detects a threat, and the APS responds either kinetically (with cannon fire or explosives, for instance) to destroy the projectile, or non-kinetically, through electronic means (jamming the guidance) or using lasers to knock the threat off target.

Following the disastrous experiences against Hezbollah's ATGM and RPG-29 capability during the 2006 Second Lebanon War, the Israelis accelerated efforts to deploy an APS, with Trophy being the result. It uses radar to detect and categorize threats before engaging said threats with Multiple Explosively Formed Penetrators (MEFPs), which spread out like a shotgun blast to destroy or disable the incoming missile.

Trophy is intelligent enough to prioritize incoming threats, including judging those which will result in near misses (in which case they will not be engaged by the MEFP launchers). It has proven very successful operationally, defeating the RPG-29, the RPG-7, SPG-9 recoilless rifles and ATGMs, including the AT-14 Kornet. It has also been tested against top-attack platforms including the Javelin.

Latest-generation Western ATGMs, such as the TOW 2B Aero, employ a countermeasures system that effectively jams Trophy's radar system, but no similar Russian or Chinese capability is currently known.

The Chinese PLA latest-generation ZTZ-99 or Type 99 main battle tank. Equipped with a smoothbore 125mm main gun that can also fire the Russian-licensed 9M119 beam-rider ATGM, the Type 99 is protected by a mix of composite and reactive armour. (Photo by Getty Images)

APS has a significant disadvantage in terms of electromagnetic signature, as the radar is detectable and thus APS-equipped vehicles may be targeted by their signature alone. Israel's Elbit have developed a fix to this challenge with the Iron Fist Light Kinetic (IFLK) system. IFLK has also reportedly partly solved the issue of APS defeating sabot main tank gun rounds.

Sabot rounds – the APFSDS – also cause a significant challenge to APS. This is because of the speed of the typical sabot main gun round (travelling at circa Mach 5). Instead of seeking to destroy the APFSDS penetrator (which may result in simply several smaller extremely high-velocity projectiles striking the target), current thinking is to disrupt the path of the round by damaging the fins that stabilize the penetrator in flight.

Technology will eventually find a solution that defeats (or at least disrupts, affecting accuracy) an APFSDS round (and, as noted above, perhaps Elbit have managed a partial solution), but for now, a combination of reactive armour (such as Rafael's Armor Shield technology) and APS is the best protection for an AFV, allowing it to engage rockets, missiles and recoilless rifles with APS and leaving the sabot tank rounds to (hopefully) be defeated by a reactive armour package.

APS designers are also attempting to counter loitering munition UAVs with coverage that could engage such aerial threats (and potentially at least certain types of top-attack ATGMs). Whether current-generation APS can protect against a swarm of dozens of loitering munition UAVs remains to be tested in combat, although this is another likely capability to defeat APS. Near-future AFVs will require an APS that can protect against ATGMs and loitering munitions (and ideally APFSDS tank gun rounds) to survive in an increasingly UAV-heavy environment.

In an article for the Modern War Institute in 2020, Captain Vincent Delany noted that 'the critical weaknesses of an APS are an upper limit on its ability to handle volume of fire, its vulnerability to degradation by external forces, and the arc of its detection system and countermeasures'.[5]

A fourth potential avenue of attack will be using electronic warfare to degrade the radar or sensors on the vehicle. Destroying the radars and sensors by more kinetic means – by mortars or artillery which may not necessarily destroy the vehicle itself – could be employed as preparatory fires before the now APS degraded vehicle is engaged by ATGMs.

In comparison with the US, Russian tank design has largely stalled with the T-72 and T-80. A smaller number of T-90s are also in inventory (although some have been confirmed destroyed in Ukraine). The T-90 was touted as the next generation between the T-80 and the prototype T-14 Armata; however, in reality the T-90 is essentially an upgraded T-72 with improved optics (including thermal imaging) and armour.

When Moscow intervened in Syria in 2015 on behalf of the beleaguered regime of Bashar al-Assad, it transferred around 30 T-90As to the Syrian Arab Army, as well as upgraded T-62Ms and T-72s. The Syrian military desperately needed this armoured reinforcement, as it had lost over 2,000 armoured vehicles in the preceding years, especially after Syrian rebels began receiving American TOW-2A missiles in 2014. The T-90As again were export models and less capable than the T-90M.

The Russian T-90M Breakthrough main battle tank – beside the T-14 Armata, the most advanced Russian tank; however, it has suffered defeats in Ukraine, including being famously engaged by an M2A2 Bradley IFV. (Photographer: Andrey Rudakov/Bloomberg via Getty Images)

RIGHT A Syrian Arab Army T-72A pictured in 2013. As the war in Syria progressed, so too did enhancements to vehicles; this T-72 is fairly clean, with only track links added to the lower hull, a technique widely used in World War II. (Photo by STR/AFP via Getty Images)

BELOW The evolution of Syrian Arab Army T-72s with generous fitting of Kontakt-1 ERA and workshop-produced slat armour on the MBT to the left. (STRINGER/AFP via Getty Images)

The upgraded armour package on the T-90M, the much heralded so-called 'Breakthrough' tank, takes the form of Relikt reactive armour and counter-RPG nets covering vulnerable areas of the tank. Both the T-90A and T-90M feature the Shtora-1 APS platform, which combines an infrared jammer and a laser detector that sets off the APS suite when the tank is 'painted' by a laser, such as that used to guide an ATGM to its target. The Shtora-1 is distinctive in featuring a pair of ominous 'red eyes' mounted to either side of the turret that are designed to jam the incoming missile by scrambling its guidance.

Ukrainian ATGM operators have, however, quickly learned not to 'paint' the target directly but to fire at a slight off-set before guiding the missile onto the tank during the last moments of its flight to negate the effectiveness of the Shtora-1. This vulnerability was widely known to Western armies, with even the Modern War Institute at West Point advising that gunners should be 'targeting a patch of ground three vehicle lengths away. This will allow the gunner to avoid being detected by Shtora.'[6]

The T-90A is by far the most common variant. A number have seen action in Syria and Ukraine with mixed results. T-90As in Ukraine have been filmed fitted with what Western analysts have dubbed 'cope cages' – field-expedient cages that are mounted to the top of the tank's turret as a countermeasure against top-attack munitions.

These cope cages have been roundly unsuccessful, with no appreciable impact on the devastation caused by a Javelin striking the top of the turret; however, they may have been primarily designed not to protect against Javelin but to assist against drone-delivered ordnance, a learning from the Nagorno-Karabakh War of 2020. There is, however, no data on their effectiveness, or otherwise, against small-calibre munitions (for instance, light mortar bombs, 40mm or RGD-5 grenades) dropped from commercial drones by Ukrainian forces.

As with the successful strikes by FPV and dropped ordnance drones, we don't know for sure how effective the cages are or aren't. Certainly, against Javelin they won't have any effect. But as a screen against grenades and similar small munitions dropped from a quadcopter, they likely have value. In fact, footage from Gaza in late 2023 showed Merkava Mk 4 tanks fitted with a similar screen as a counter-FPV measure.

At least one T-90M has been visually confirmed as being destroyed by an 84mm Carl Gustav M2 recoilless rifle donated by Canada. The M2 would not have triggered the Shtora, as it operates without laser or infrared guidance – and the fact that the T-90M can be penetrated by an 84mm round (roughly analogous to the RPG) is another indicator that the T-90M isn't as evolutionary as its makers have loudly proclaimed.

The elusive T-14 Armata allegedly features an improved smoothbore 125mm 2A82-1M main gun, also designed with the potential to be employed in the T-90 to up-gun its capabilities. Despite much muttering on Russian

NEXT PAGES Another evolution of Syrian Army T-72s – this with slat armour, ERA blocks and additional smoke dischargers. (LOUAI BESHARA/AFP via Getty Images)

RIGHT A Russian T-90M Breakthrough tank equipped with chains around the turret to disrupt RPGs and slat armour fitted to protect the rear flanks. Relikt ERA is fitted to the turret and hull, and the T-90M is issued with both Shtora-1 soft-kill APS and Arena-M hard-kill APS. (Photo by Tian Bing/ China News Service via Getty Images)

blogs, at the time of writing not a single T-14 has been visually confirmed to have been deployed to Ukraine (not surprising, since they apparently can't even manage a Red Square parade without breaking down).

Defence analyst Sergio Miller noted in an eye-opening piece for Wavell Room, a UK defence forum: 'The root problem with the engine means… the tank moves satisfactorily only under the cover of a group of technicians and engineers. Only one experimental company was ever formed anyway in Central Military District (CVO) and the chances it will appear on a frontline, except for propaganda purposes, are small.'[7]

Today tanks are seen as a warfighting capability rather than something one deploys to a counterinsurgency campaign to win over a population. They tend to be loud, threatening by their very nature, and their tracks chew up tarmacked roads and farmers' fields.

BELOW Excellent example of ad hoc field modifications to a Ukrainian T-64 to improve protection against FPV loitering munitions/attack drones. Note the 'cope cage' with additional chains and a homemade cage fitted around the turret. (Photo by Jose Colon/Anadolu via Getty Images)

Although Operation *Enduring Freedom* (OEF) in Afghanistan was initially largely an SOF-led campaign, as the campaign expanded under NATO into an effort to combat a resurgent Taliban and shore up the fledgling Afghan security forces (so thus a classic counterinsurgency campaign), main battle tanks made their first appearance. Several national contingents employed MBTs – notably the Canadians, the Dutch and the US Marine Corps.

MBTs proved useful primarily because of their sensors; their optics allowed for excellent surveillance of named areas of interest as suspect locations were known. They also allowed PIDing, or positive identification of individuals, again at extended range. With their thermal imaging, both activities were reliably conducted in the pitch dark of the Afghan night.

Tanks were also useful as a force multiplier. They were on occasion employed in offensive operations where their main guns proved useful in engaging defensive positions. In Afghanistan, most IEDs and mines were anti-personnel rather than anti-tank, and thus tanks, particularly when fitted with engineering dozer blades, were useful in safely clearing lanes for dismounted infantry.

Unlike OEF, Operation *Iraqi Freedom* (OIF) was a much more conventional campaign, at least during its invasion phase in May 2003. The invasion cemented the reputation of the M1A1 Abrams as the king of the battlefield, engaging Iraqi T-72 and T-55 main battle tanks and myriad armoured vehicles, including the standard Russian IFV, the BMP-1. All were predictably outclassed.

A number of Abrams suffered multiple strikes from RPGs without incident, although one M1A1 was famously disabled by a recoilless rifle round into its flank. The round, likely from a Russian-designed SPG-9, penetrated the rear of the engine deck and started a chemical fire that the crew could not extinguish. Another Abrams further disabled the immobilized Abrams with main gun rounds before it was later destroyed by a US airstrike.

Israeli Merkava IVMs fitted with manufactured cope cages to counter Hamas drone-dropped ordnance. Ukrainian M1A1 SA-UKRs (local/social media designation) began to feature cope cages in mid-2024 following installation of ARAT ERA earlier that year. This second set of modifications included additional Russian Kontakt-1 ERA on the frontal glacis and an extensive set of bar armour including the cope cage (unlike Russian models, however, the design does not block the smoke grenade launchers nor the hatches, allowing crew to escape). The bar armour also protects the turret blow-out panels which have been a weak point targeted by FPVs (some unverified reports claim that the majority of Abrams knocked out in 2024 were due to FPV strikes to this area). (Photo by Amir Levy/Getty Images)

WHAT IS ERA?

ERA stands for explosive reactive armour, a form of add-on armour that increases the protection of an MBT or other armoured fighting vehicle. Not surprisingly, the Israelis were the first to employ ERA in combat – in 1982, during Operation *Peace for Galilee* in Lebanon.

Since then, ERA has become widely employed, particularly as a method of up-armouring older model tanks. The Ukrainians employ ERA widely; their T-64BM Bulat is liberally slathered in ERA blocks, for instance, and the Russians have added ERA to everything with tracks (including on the turret top in an attempt to counter FPV attack drones).

It can also be used to address specific threats; US Army Abrams tanks deployed to Europe have been fitted with ARAT, or Abrams Reactive Armor Tile, as have the Abrams that have been donated to Ukraine to counter the proliferation of Russian ATGMs.

ERA works by destroying or degrading the projectile as it strikes the ERA block. It is generally successful against RPGs, recoilless rifles and earlier-generation ATGMs.

It is distinct from an active protection system (APS), which detects and attacks the incoming projectile, and applique up-armouring kits, which are additional layers of armour fitted to address specific threats in specific theatres.

Tandem charge warheads – such as those available for the RPG-29 – are designed specifically to counter ERA, with the initial charge detonating the ERA block and the second acting as the explosive penetrator.

What no known current ERA can defeat is the depleted uranium APFSDS fired by the Abrams; the depleted uranium rod cuts through the explosive with little to no degradation of penetration potential.

A superb close-up of a Ukrainian T-64B fitted with ERA blocks featuring the unique Ukrainian digital style camouflage. (Ministry of Defence of Ukraine)

The Russian next-generation MBT, the T-14 Armata, seen here, rather embarrassingly, being towed after a breakdown at a Victory Day parade. According to the UK MoD, the T-14 has entered service but will not be deployed in the foreseeable future to Ukraine, as Russia decides on the more economical T-90 family. The reputational damage of a T-14 being lost (and the technological intelligence bounty for NATO if one was recovered by Ukrainian forces) is believed to be simply too high. (Photo by Sasha Mordovets/Getty Images)

Vehicles that have been immobilized, known as a mobility kill, are routinely destroyed by their owners in an effort to deny the platform to the enemy. This process ranges from the crew dropping thermite grenades into the vehicle to an airstrike.

The Abrams excelled again during the Thunder Runs into Baghdad itself towards the end of the invasion phase. These Thunder Runs were officially armoured reconnaissance efforts to ascertain the displacement of Iraqi defences in the city but also served to smash the fighting spirit of said defenders when they saw US armour in downtown Baghdad.

One important lesson from the Thunder Runs was the criticality and vulnerability of the fuel required to keep the Abrams as well as the Bradley IFV in the fight. AFVs drink fuel at a glutinous rate and require a logistics chain that can shadow their advance, coming forward regularly to top up the gas tanks of the AFVs.

One refuelling operation was caught in an ambush, with several fuel tankers destroyed and the crews forced to defend themselves using small arms and the .50cal heavy machine guns mounted on accompanying M113s. They also received accurate and effective enemy mortar fire while pinned down.

A British Army WMIK (Weapons Mounted Installation Kit) Land Rover seen in Musa Qala, Helmand Province, 2007. Note the Javelins carried among the stowage. (Photo by SHAH MARAI/AFP via Getty Images)

TANKS IN THE URBAN JUNGLE

Urban terrain is a challenge for armour. Traditionally, tankers have tried to stay out of the cities, as they were viewed as death-traps of anti-armour ambushes while mitigating the advantages of the tank. Following Russia's disastrous experiences during the First Chechen War, there has been a reappraisal of how to fight tanks in cities.

Infantry/armour coordination is key, and the use of armour in urban terrain will succeed or fail based on how well this is conducted. Infantry need to act as the armour's eyes and ears, spotting and engaging anti-tank teams and providing a protective umbrella against RPGs.

Infantry are at risk from the very tanks they are working with too; ERA panels can wound or kill infantry who are too close to the tank when it detonates, and infantry should stay well clear of tank main guns when firing (or at least invest in robust hearing and eye protection).

MBTs are also force multipliers in this environment. RUSI noted that in 2023 Russian forces in Ukraine:

> … pushed armour in a supporting fire role for infantry in other urban battles. Here, tanks have proven critical for both suppression of urban structures and rapid breaching of buildings to avoid entering through choke points and known avenues of advance. The use of older tanks as assault guns in this role appears to be preferred as the urban environment does not give more modern Russian tanks with advanced optics and multispectral concealment a sufficient tactical advantage to justify their loss.[8]

A Russian T-80, likely a BVM variant, in Ukraine with extensive invasion markings. A dangerous spot for infantry to sit if the ERA is triggered. (Photo by Maximilian Clarke/SOPA Images/LightRocket via Getty Images)

American logistics vehicles are now armoured and equipped with a self-defence weapon. If at all possible, logistics or sustainment convoys should be escorted by infantry and/or armour. Logistics convoys in Afghanistan also suffered regular ambushes, leading to similarly robust force protection measures with gun-trucks and accompanying infantry.

The Russians developed the BMPT Terminator, a tank support AFV designed to operate alongside armour in cities, with twin 30mm cannon and a range of ATGMs and automatic grenade launchers. The BMPT was intended to negate the Grozny effect by engaging enemy firing points at all elevations. Deployed to Syria as a combat trial, the BMPT has also been seen in Ukraine, although in low numbers, which has impacted any evaluation of its performance.

One fascinating outlier during the Iraq invasion was the close-in knife fight in Baghdad between the Abrams and a number of Iraqi T-72s that had concealed themselves in the urban terrain. The fight occurred in Mahmudiyah, a southern suburb of the capital:

> 'Cobra Six, this is White One. We got tanks!' 'What do you mean you have tanks?' I asked, incredulous that we suddenly found ourselves fighting tanks in these tight quarters.
>
> The infantry often refers to urban combat as a knife fight in a phone booth. For us, it was more like a gunfight in a phone booth.
>
> I thought he was mistaken and saw BMPs or something else.
>
> 'I've got T-72s in the street!' he shot back.

The Russian BMPT Terminator tank support vehicle was designed in response to urban combat challenges in Chechnya; originally, a BMPT was supposed to accompany each MBT platoon. It is equipped with two 30mm autocannons, a pair of 30mm automatic grenade launchers, and four Ataka ATGMs. Small numbers have been deployed to Ukraine with little perceived impact and have proven susceptible to drone attacks. The vehicle behind the BMPT is the Derivatsiya-PVO anti-aircraft platform that mounts a 57mm cannon. (Photo by Andrey Rudakov/ Bloomberg via Getty Images)

The sound of a main gun round was enough to convince me that he was right.

Stewart's first shot hit the back slope of the T-72 sitting on the right side of the street. The extra fuel drums on back exploded, sending flames and black smoke shooting high into the late afternoon sky. The tank's turret popped off and the engine was knocked to the other side of the street.[9]

This vivid description comes from the book *Heavy Metal: A Tank Company's Battle to Baghdad*, written by US Army Captains Jason Conroy and Ron Martz, which comes highly recommended. Not surprisingly, the Iraqi T-72s lost the battle with no losses to the US tankers.

Later during the insurgency, however, and in common with more thinly skinned vehicles, tanks suffered from IED strikes. Due to their armour, the impact of the IED was nowhere near as significant, but an imported type of IED did cause issues for the tanks. In 2008, a British Challenger 2 was immobilized and the driver wounded by an Iranian-supplied EFP.

A British Army Challenger 2 TES (Theatre Entry Standard) pictured in Basra, Iraq, in late 2007. The TES upgrades included slat armour covering known vulnerabilities, Enforcer remote weapon station, and a suite of electronic counter-IED measures. (PA Images/ Alamy Stock Photo)

IEDS

As the insurgency in Iraq increased in ferocity during the 2004 to 2005 period, the insurgents began to rely on improvised explosive devices or IEDs. IEDs were an asymmetrical answer to the firepower and technological advantages of Coalition Forces. Instead of being outgunned in a firefight, insurgent groups instead turned to IEDs to ambush, harass and channel Coalition patrols.

Initial IEDs were unsophisticated and often victim initiated. As the insurgency gained pace and grew in experience and sophistication, so too did the IEDs. Sunni insurgents and al-Qaeda in Iraq began to use battery packs that were initiated by a cell phone. This reduced the chance of capture or death for an insurgent using a physical command wire, but they were relatively easily disrupted by jammers that soon became a standard feature on all Coalition vehicles. Backpack jammers also began to be issued.

These jammers caused unintended consequences, most notably sometimes interfering with Coalition radio signals and jamming all cell phone transmissions on a wide spectrum, causing inconvenience to the civilian population.

Iranian Quds Force advisers provided training and material allowing Shia insurgents to deploy the devastating EFP or explosively formed projectile, which shot a super-heated copper slug through even the heaviest armour. These were typically triggered by a vehicle breaking an infrared beam from a commercial remote control hidden by the side of the road.

Coalition Forces responded with a range of measures, including devices that were lowered in front of the vehicle to prematurely trigger the IED. The insurgents responded by angling the IED to avoid these countermeasures, and a game of cat and mouse developed as each side attempted to outwit the other.

An example from the journal Military Review highlights this: 'When insurgents employed cell phones and radios to remotely detonate IEDs, the coalition developed sophisticated methods of electronic jamming. When the coalition employed mine rollers to detonate pressure-plate IEDs in front of the vehicles, insurgents began to offset the charge from the triggering device (or to delay detonation) to ensure that the detonation would still damage vehicles.'[10]

The UK Ministry of Defence (MoD) were surprisingly nonchalant: 'This was not in any way new technology – the device involved was the same type of shaped charge that we have seen used very regularly. No one has ever said Challenger tanks are impenetrable. We have always said a big enough bomb will defeat any armour and any vehicle.'[11]

The insurgency used the anti-tank IED primarily to halt columns of vehicles, to allow the insurgents to conduct a quick ambush with RPGs and small arms before melting away to avoid a protracted gunfight that they would inevitably lose against US or British forces.

One such ambush occurred on 24 June 2004 in Baqubah:

That morning, dozens of insurgents ambushed Lieutenant Neil Prakash's four-tank platoon that was part of 2d Battalion, 63d Armored Regiment, 1st Infantry Division. An after-battle report stated that 23 IEDs and 20–25 RPG teams were located within the 1-kilometer stretch of road.

A Turkish Leopard 2A4 MBT in service in Syria in 2018. To the right is the domestically produced MRAP, the Otokar Cobra. The 2A4 fared badly, mainly due to poor tactics, and a number were destroyed or immobilized by ATGMs, suicide car bombs and IEDs. Two were even seemingly captured by Islamic State. The MBT is now being upgraded with an additional protection package known as TİYK 2A4. (Photo by OMAR HAJ KADOUR/ AFP via Getty Images)

Despite a disabled turret, Prakash kept his tank in the lead and engaged the insurgents by moving the vehicle to the left and right to align its guns on enemy targets. By the end of the fight, his tank had destroyed eight enemy strongpoints while surviving multiple IED blasts and at least seven hits by RPG rounds. The platoon was credited with 25 confirmed insurgent kills plus an estimated 50–60 additional destroyed enemy fighters.[12]

A decade later, during the initial lightning campaign by Islamic State in Iraq, the terrorists managed to capture a handful of export model M1A1s that had been provided to the Iraqi Army by the US. As far as can be ascertained, these were energetically pursued by Coalition aircraft and destroyed from the air as priority targets before they could see any real action.

As with any other technologically advanced weapons systems, supply of such systems to partners or proxy forces must be well considered to minimize the inevitable 'leakage' to non-state actors such as Islamic State. Other Iraqi Army Abrams appear to have been lost to fratricide incidents.

Next door to Iraq, in Syria, Turkey deployed MBTs into the country on a number of occasions, including the preposterously named Operation *Olive Branch*, which aimed to force Kurdish People's Defense Units (YPG) from border areas such as Afrin and Manbji. During 2016's Operation *Euphrates Shield*, unconfirmed reports indicate that Turkey lost at least nine Leopard 2A4s: five from ATGMs, two from IEDs/mines, and one to indirect fire. The ninth was the suspected victim of a suicide car-bomber, or SVBIED (suicide vehicle-borne IED).

Turkish Army tanks, a mix of upgraded American M60s and the aforementioned Leopards, were deployed with seemingly little regard for the terrain or the capabilities of the opposition. Videos of Turkish tanks show them sky-lighting themselves on ridges, remaining static when under fire, and highlighting a discernable lack of even rudimentary armoured tactics.

Core armoured skills such as overwatch and bounding movement, along with emplacement of vehicles to facilitate force protection (i.e., making sure threats from 360 degrees were covered by their guns), and even basic tank-infantry coordination would have saved some of those losses.

Suicide bombers versus tanks was a phenomenon witnessed during the Iraq insurgency, but SVBIEDs were elevated to a new level in Syria in the hands of Islamic State and related terrorist and insurgent groups. It's worth Googling some of the more hair-raising videos taken by Free Syrian Army (FSA) and Kurdish YPG forces when confronted by SVBIEDs – often armoured variants which shrug off small-arms fire as they close the distance towards friendly forces.

Along with targeting tanks and BMPs, Kurdish and Coalition ATGMs were employed against a new type of target: the suicide vehicle bomb. ATGMs proved useful, particularly when engaging the up-armoured car bombs favoured by Islamic State. Islamic State and the Salafist jihadist group al-Nusra Front used a range of AFVs modified as heavily armoured suicide bomb vehicles, with the BMP proving the most popular.

The SVBIED concept is a terrifying one. Drivers were strapped into their seat and equipped with a dead-man's-hand style device that ensured detonation even if the driver was killed by defensive fire. Many also suspected that the SVBIEDs were fitted with secondary detonators triggered by cell phone, out of the al-Qaeda in Iraq playbook, to assuage against any last-minute second thoughts by the driver.

All of the state and non-state actors in Syria employed tanks to varying degrees. All performed sub-optimally, even in contacts with non-state actors with zero training in the employment of the MBT (note previous comments on the Turkish experience). A wide range of reasons contributed to this uniformly poor performance. A lack of quality training is chief among them.

Videos produced by crews (often from Go-Pro sports cameras mounted on the turret) showed MBTs operating within urban environments with zero infantry support and often in static or semi-static positions, allowing ATGM and RPG teams to actively stalk the vehicles. As we've noted, tanks simply cannot survive without integrated infantry support. The infantry act as a security screen for the tanks, forcing tank-hunting teams to work harder and from increased range to attack the tanks.

The Abrams also saw action during the Yemeni civil war following intervention by a coalition of Arab nations organized by Saudi Arabia against the Iranian-backed Houthi rebels. The Saudi military have deployed US-supplied M1A2s against the Houthi to very mixed results. The Abrams sold to the Saudis is an export model like the Iraqi Army M1A1s, lacking many of the defensive and protective measures of US versions such as depleted uranium armour. Saudi AMX 30 and M60 MBTs have fared equally badly.

Again, the main culprit seems to have been how the Abrams was employed by Saudi forces. Like the Syrian Arab Army in Syria and Russian forces in Ukraine, there has been a very noticeable lack of that essential infantry/tank integration, with Saudi tanks often filmed seemingly deployed by themselves with no infantry (or sometimes with no nearby buddy tanks able to overwatch, inviting Houthi RPG teams to encircle them).

Incredibly, at least nine M1A2s were lost during operations, although total losses could have been far higher (the US agreed a deal to supply the Saudis with further M1A2s in 2016, including 20 'battle damage replacements'). Videos from the region also indicate at least one Abrams was captured relatively intact by Houthi forces; however, it appears it was later burnt out by its captors rather than being turned against its former owners.

The United Arab Emirates (UAE) deployed their French-made Leclerc main battle tank to Yemen but upgraded the design with a mixture of both

A Yemeni loyalist forces' French-made Leclerc in Yemen, 2017. The UAE-supplied Leclerc here features add-on CLARA ERA. (Photo by SALEH AL-OBEIDI/AFP via Getty Images)

Dynamit Nobel CLARA fibre-plate ERA and a smaller number of the Nexter AZUR – an urban operations kit of composite armour skirts and slat/bar armour to improve protection principally against RPGs.

The UAE AZUR versions used in Yemen only employed the slat/bar armour and additional armoured plates to protect the engine grills rather than the full kit which more closely resembles the US Army's TUSK.

The up-armoured Leclercs appear to have been far more successful than the Saudi M1A2s, at least in terms of combat losses. Four known incidents occurred where Leclercs were damaged but not destroyed: 'two incidents involved IEDs, a third involved a rocket-propelled grenade that deflected off the target tank's Azure slat armor and the fourth involved an anti-tank missile'.[13]

One Leclerc was damaged by a Houthi ATGM, likely the AT5 or AT5B Konkurs/Konkurs M, killing the driver and wounding the tank commander, while another was struck but survived a similar hit.

An additional Leclerc may have been damaged by a Tochka ballistic missile strike. Interestingly, UAE Leclercs were constantly subject to electronic attack by Houthi jammers, which affected their battlefield communications.

There were no confirmed tank battles during the height of the Yemeni civil war, although a number of curious AFVs were pictured in service with the Houthis, including former Yemeni Army T34/85 tanks and an SU-100 tank destroyer dating from World War II. ATGMs, RPGs and IEDs were the principal threats, typical of any modern asymmetric conflict.

During the 2006 campaign against Hezbollah, the Israelis lost a surprising number of tanks. The think tank RAND reported:

> Forty-five per cent of the Israel Defence Force's (IDF's) MBTs [main battle tanks] hit by Hizbullah ATGMs during the fighting were penetrated. Out of 50 IDF Merkava Mk 2, 3 and 4 MBTs hit, 21 were penetrated. Eleven of the incidents resulted in no fatalities while 10 incidents resulted in 23 crew casualties. During the fighting, the IDF encountered a wide variety of Russian- and Iranian-made ATGMs…[14]

David E. Johnson in *War on the Rocks* argued that the knee-jerk impact of the experiences of the IDF in the 2006 Lebanon War mirrored those from Ukraine in 2022:

> Almost immediately, the end of the tank was proclaimed, but this time at the hands of even sub-state actors. Cheap weapons were once again the nemesis of expensive main battle tanks. Nevertheless, the Israeli military realized that only the tank had the potential to survive on the battlefield, even against hybrid adversaries like Hezbollah. If tanks were vulnerable, then dismounted infantry were meat.
>
> Part of the solution for the Israeli military was to realize that Hezbollah was a competent adversary armed with very capable standoff weapons and demanded combined arms tactics. Tank crews had to again be trained in battle drills for high-intensity combat and air-ground integration and artillery suppression again came to the fore as capability requirements.
>
> Adversary weapons had to be suppressed to enable armored formations to get infantry into the close battle – the last 100-meter fight. Nevertheless, the Kornet, given its range and guidance system, needed a technical solution as well as a doctrinal/tactical approach. Even one ATGM surviving to engage meant the likely loss of an expensive system and casualties.[15]

One location where MBTs have been used extensively in their traditional role has been Ukraine. Much has been written about the confusing menagerie of Western tank types donated to Ukraine. Various marks of Leopard, the British Challenger 2, American M1A1s, and upgraded 'Westernized' T72s have joined an even wider array of lighter AFVs including Stryker ICVs (infantry carrier vehicles), Bradley and Marder IFVs, Cougar and Bushmaster MRAPs and others, in what must amount to a logistical nightmare.

Despite this, these Western AFVs have provided a significant psychological boost for Ukrainian forces. In a comparatively rare scenario of tank-on-tank engagements, though, the Western tanks provide a capability boost against any and all Russian armour.

In what was, at the time of writing, the largest tank battle of the war, approximately 130 Russian tanks and AFVs were destroyed during a Russian offensive near Vuhledar in the Donetsk during January 2023. The Russian advance repeated past mistakes by deploying armour without sufficient close infantry cover and preparatory artillery, allowing Ukrainian infantry to pick off Russian vehicles with ATGM ambushes and engage with MBTs from concealed and covered positions.

RUSI noted:

> Tank-on-tank engagements have become relatively rare, but when they occur they usually take place within 1,000m. Engagement speed has been the determining factor in these clashes. Ukrainian tankers note that one-shot kills are possible if the point between the turret and glacis is hit. Russian explosive reactive armour (ERA), however, has proven highly effective, preventing most anti-tank systems from defeating the tank's armour.
>
> Some operators have reported hitting tanks multiple times with barrel-launched ATGMs without knocking them out. Significantly, Ukrainian tankers report that mobility kills against the vehicle's tracks are also an effective means of removing Russian armour from the field because they usually cause the crew to abandon the vehicle.[16]

Indeed, the Russo-Ukrainian War has attracted much media comment about the alleged demise of the tank. Similar entirely predictable commentary has appeared in the mainstream media several times over the years as new weapons systems – typically some sort of guided missile – are heralded as the king-slayer of the MBT.

The employment of the AT-3 Sagger (its NATO reporting name; in Russian parlance, the 9M14 Malyutka) anti-tank guided missile during the October 1973 Yom Kippur War was perhaps the most infamous of these pronouncements. The Sagger, deployed via a suitcase that was carried into battle by its crew, could be fired somewhat remotely by the operator (although tethered by control wire) before a rapid re-deployment to another firing point could be made.

The missile itself was revolutionary at the time – light enough for non-mechanized crews, a range of some 3,000 metres, and a warhead that could threaten all Israeli MBTs then in service. It also had disadvantages: the operator could only retreat around 15 metres from the missile due to the short length of that control wire between the joystick and the missile; the missile itself was slow in flight, which allowed well-trained armour crews to react with countermeasures; and the design itself was MCLOS, or manual command line of sight.

MCLOS ATGMs require the operator to manually guide the missile onto the target using a command wire system attached to the missile to make course corrections. As can be imagined, MCLOS systems allow an alert target

ATGM GUIDANCE SYSTEMS

The oldest style of guidance is MCLOS, or manual command to line of sight. This denotes a weapon that requires constant input from the gunner from launch until impact, keeping the missile on target using a joystick or similar controller.

It is the easiest platform to counter, as spotting the backblast of launch and then suppressing the general area of the launch site with gunfire tends to cause the gunner to concentrate on self-preservation rather than guiding the missile to the target. Sagger is the classic MCLOS system.

The next generation of guidance was SACLOS, or semi-automatic command to line of sight. SACLOS improved on MCLOS, as the gunner only has to keep the target in the ATGM's sight rather than manually control the flight of the missile. Kornet and TOW are common examples.

The third generation was termed 'fire and forget': missiles could be 'locked onto' a target, the missile launched, and the gunner could then vacate the area to avoid retaliatory fire. Fire and forget missiles use either a laser or electro-optical seeker or a radar seeker. Javelin is the best example of a fire and forget system.

Fourth-generation ATGMs improved on the fire and forget model by using dual seeker systems that improved accuracy and reduced the risk of interference by countermeasures (on the principle of jam one, the other still works). The Israeli Spike LR demonstrates all elements of a fourth-generation ATGM.

But it is worth noting that radar guided systems are susceptible to jammers and laser/electro-optical can be knocked off course with laser countermeasure systems. Generally speaking, the more technologically advanced the seeker, the greater the chance that it can be affected by electronic countermeasures.

to attempt to disrupt the accuracy of the missile. Rapidly developed Israeli standard operating procedures (SOPs), for instance, included engaging the launch site to suppress the Sagger crew; launching turret-mounted smoke grenades to obscure the target; and, in an echo of World War II tactics against anti-tank guns, reversing quickly out of position to break line of sight. Unlike many modern ATGM platforms, MCLOS requires line of sight to be maintained from launch until the warhead strikes its target.

The AT-3 Sagger nonetheless managed to inflict heavy losses on Israeli MBTs during the Yom Kippur War, but the IDF was quick to implement these countermeasures against the Sagger and similar MCLOS ATGMs. NATO learned from the Israeli experience and altered its own countermeasure drills in an attempt to neuter the Sagger in any potential 'Cold War Gone Hot' scenario in Europe.

Incidentally, MCLOS has never fully been eclipsed as an operating system. The Sagger-D, an improved version of the 1960s vintage model that the Israelis faced, still soldiers on around the world. The 9M14-2M variant, which offers a tandem warhead to assist with defeating explosive reactive armour, saw significant use during the Syrian Civil War, although most of the press attention focused on the more modern AT-5 Spandrel (Russian name: the 9M113 Konkurs) and the American TOW-2.

In fact, the use of the American-supplied TOW-2 in Syria heralded an unlikely social media star in the form of 'Abu TOW', an FSA (Free Syrian Army) fighter with a claimed kill count of around 140 vehicles of the Syrian Army, al-Nusra Front and Islamic State. His favoured implement of tank destruction was, of course, the venerable TOW.

The 2020 Nagorno-Karabakh War was also replete with often-times hyperbolic pronouncements of the death of the MBT. Instead of the ATGM, the culprit this time was the drone. Nagorno-Karabakh was the public's introduction to the Turkish-manufactured Bayraktar TB2, which would become justifiably famous in the hands of the Ukrainian military during the Russo-Ukrainian War.

The TB2 was employed by the Azerbaijan military to great effect, striking both fixed and mobile positions, including Armenian armour. We discuss the TB2 and the employment of drones during the Nagorno-Karabakh War in some detail in Chapter 5.

Many column inches were devoted to the death of the tank and that the mighty drone would now rule supreme. Of course, armed (and unarmed) uncrewed aerial systems (US military speak for drones) will be a vitally important factor in any future war, but their impact during the Nagorno-Karabakh War was perhaps somewhat exaggerated. Azerbaijani drones were instrumental in destroying Armenian armour, but the Armenian armour performed poorly when faced by this new aerial threat.

Armenian armour was often engaged in the open, with little effort made by the crews to mask their visual signature. There was also a notable lack of close-in air defence platforms supporting the Armenian AFVs (a similar criticism was levelled at Ukrainian forces during the 2023 counteroffensive).

Counter-UAS has become the hot new offering in defence industry circles, and for good reason. AFVs need counter-UAS capabilities themselves or dedicated air defence platforms that can keep up with the armour and engage all manner of aerial threats (enemy close air support, attack helicopters and drones).

The US military have added another acronym to the lexicon: SHORAD, meaning Short Range Air Defense (again, see Chapter 3). A number of programmes are active under this definition, with a range of countermeasure types, although the first to see service will most likely be the Stryker-based M-SHORAD (Maneuver – Short Range Air Defense) variant equipped with both Stinger air defence and Longbow Hellfire anti-tank missiles, along with a 30mm XM914 cannon. The cannon will be able to fire proximity airburst rounds designed to detonate in the vicinity of the targeted threat.

This is only the first generation of M-SHORAD, with the eventual aim being fielding of a laser-based air defence platform, again mounted on the Stryker platform. Currently known as the DE-MSHORAD, a 50-kilowatt laser (or 'directed energy' weapon, to use the terminology) will be employed to disable aerial threats. It is also designed to intercept and engage enemy artillery, rockets and missiles (C-RAM or counter-rocket, artillery, mortar). If all goes according to plan, the first examples of both the M-SHORAD and the DE-MSHORAD will be in service by the time this book is published.

Returning to the supposed death of the tank, the effect of the TB2 drone and the oversized impact of Javelin and similar current-generation ATGMs, such as the next-generation light anti-armour weapons (NLAW) supplied to Ukraine, led to clickbait headlines that fail to consider the wider picture. As we have discussed elsewhere in this book, Russian TTPs (tactics, techniques and procedures) have been uniformly poor in Ukraine.

Retired Lieutenant Colonel Brendan B. McBreen commented in his insightful *Ukraine: Lessons for Leaders – What should Marines learn from this modern war?*:

A single tank is the most lethal weapon on any battlefield. We need tanks – for infantry support in close terrain. Reports: UKR has killed 1,000 RUS tanks, but who killed them – ATGM, UAS, UKR tanks, or indirect fires – and in what percentages is not known.

Infantry ATGM success is exaggerated. UKR has received 150 Javelins, 1,200 missiles, and 2,000 British next-generation light anti-armor weapons (NLAW), but how many ATGM gunners survived their encounters? In the early days of the war, RUS tanks were exposed, not protected by combined arms suppression or infantry escorts.

The tank is not dead, as many have predicted. UKR, whose units must withdraw when faced with even one RUS tank, wants more tanks. Between 2014 to 2018, UKR received 500 new tanks and built a force of 30 tank battalions. By the time of the invasion, February 2022, UKR fielded 900 tanks.

RUS tanks are generally employed three ways. First, as indirect fire platforms. Second, to raid – attack by fire – and then withdraw. And third, most importantly, to support infantry assaults. In this support by fire role, the tank is better than an infantry fighting vehicle – in firepower, protection, optics, and standoff range against ATGM. The tank is still essential in urban warfare.[17]

Combined-arms warfare whereupon tanks, infantry fighting vehicles, infantry, artillery, drones, attack helicopters and strike aircraft work together to complement each other, off-setting individual capability gaps, has been largely absent.

This appears to be the result of:

- widespread training deficiencies within Russian forces;
- corruption in the procurement system;
- fatally flawed intelligence assessment;
- recruitment problems (which have led to a noticeable shortage of infantry in motor rifle units, for example);
- lack of Western-style 'mission command' which relies upon an effective junior NCO corps (historically not an element of Russian military structure with its traditionalist structure).

Russian armour in Ukraine has been employed without infantry cover and with little use of bounding overwatch (a technique of one tank moving whilst another tank provides a look-out, ready to engage threats), allowing Ukrainian ATGM teams to have a field day. The late David Johnson summarized Russian armour and infantry performance during the early stages of the invasion:

> The Russian Army has shown that it is not competent in combined arms fire and maneuver. Where is the accompanying infantry with the tank formations, who are supposed to bust the ambushes executed by Ukrainian forces? Where are the suppressive mortar, artillery, and close air support fires? If the Russian Army was tactically skilled, then the Javelin and other ATGMs would be suppressed by artillery or air support and their surviving crews would be swept up by Russian infantry. Thus far, these key competencies seem to be lacking and Russian soldiers are paying a high price for their unpreparedness.[18]

Likewise, the dismal performance of the Russian Air Force in conducting the SEAD mission (suppression of enemy air defences – knocking out enemy surface-to-air defence platforms and their associated radars, sensors, and command and control). Along with their inability to control the air during the first month of the war, this allowed the TB2, Ukrainian attack helicopters and ground attack aircraft to decisively engage Russian armour.

The lack of effective SEAD and similar deficiencies in electronic warfare and counter-UAS during the first months of the conflict allowed all manner of Ukrainian drones to continue to assist with the reconnaissance, strike and counter-battery missions.

So, what does the future look like for the tank? Perhaps not surprisingly, it will include uncrewed innovation. As in the air, teaming has become the buzzword for uncrewed and optionally crewed AFVs, including tanks. Teaming, as we discuss in Chapter 5, involves a mothership vehicle controlling another vehicle or group of vehicles.

The ground variants of the 'Loyal Wingman' concept will likely be the first combat-deployed example of an uncrewed AFV operating alongside crewed platforms. At this point, the robot tank will have finally arrived – albeit one that will be under the direct control of a crewed armoured platform.

The benefits of uncrewed teaming in a ground war are plentiful. Uncrewed ground vehicles (UGVs) will be able to conduct reconnaissance and surveillance within the direct fire zone, which would be too risky for crewed reconnaissance vehicles or infantry teams. Protecting the flanks during an advance will also fall to UGVs; the uncrewed vehicles will act as mobile trip wires, giving the crewed platforms vital extra seconds to respond to enemy contact.

UGVs will also prove indispensable in providing armoured resupply to forward units – note the advances with artillery ammunition resupply vehicles that currently can conduct their resupply without a human soldier having to leave the safety of the armoured cab. Such duties will be soon undertaken by uncrewed equivalents. The same concept will be applied for resupplying tanks, which will pull back from the forward edge of the battle area to resupply with ammunition and fuel (and potentially water and food, if those tanks are crewed by humans, and at some point soon, they won't be).

One can envisage a day in the very near future, certainly by 2040 if not sooner, that uncrewed reconnaissance vehicles will contact and fight against an opponent's uncrewed platforms – the first true 'robotic tank fight'. In fact, in March 2024, two Russian UGVs were engaged and immobilized by a Ukrainian FPV drone in an eerie foreshadowing of that robotic future war.

All militaries are, however, conservative by nature, and this conservatism will likely see the teaming concept of crewed and uncrewed platforms as the first concrete step towards embracing autonomous and semi-autonomous platforms in the near future. Certainly, within the next decade, teaming concepts will transform into fielded combat-ready examples. The degree of autonomy allowed of uncrewed platforms will increase, although in the near term the teaming will likely more resemble remote control with some limited autonomy.

Western militaries will continue to mandate a person-in-the-loop when employing autonomous or semi-autonomous tanks; moralities require a human to make the decision to kill another human rather than an algorithm. Fully autonomous MBTs and AFVs will be fielded by Russia and China first – both militaries who place little importance on morality.

In the longer term, will uncrewed tanks even need to look like tanks? Do they need all that heavy armour and active protection systems if they are uncrewed? Instead, do manufacturers focus on lightly armouring to protect against threats that might result in a mobility kill but embrace the disposable reality and design more for speed and stealth than survivability?

Aerial drones will become far more disposable and will likely fall into a massed array of reconnaissance, electronic warfare and offensive models collected in a swarm, or larger more multi-role platforms that combine a number of functions. Some of these will be launched from tanks. Indeed, small reconnaissance drones and loitering munitions are already capable of being launched from small racks fitted to armoured vehicles and many manufacturers are offering this capability at trade shows around the world.

Despite the advent of the drone and its integration with armour, militaries will still be buying traditional MBTs and AFVs. Near-future AFV purchases in the West will focus on four broad types: the MBT, tracked IFVs, wheeled ICVs/APCs and wheeled light armour/MRAPs. Ukraine has shown the advantage of the tracked IFV when dealing with muddy and rough ground (for example, previously chewed up by artillery), while the wheeled ICV or APC offers a cheaper and faster ride for motorized infantry.

The US Army's Next Generation Combat Vehicle programme is researching platforms for the successors to the M1A2 Abrams along with vehicles to plug capability gaps within the Army's future force structure. An identified need has been for a direct fire support platform for Infantry Brigade Combat Teams – a latter-day assault gun capable of neutralizing 'enemy prepared positions and bunkers and defeating heavy machine guns and armored vehicle threats during offensive operations or when conducting defensive operations against attacking enemies'.[19]

The requirement for the MPF (Mobile Protected Firepower) platform called for a lightweight, air-transportable (note, not air-droppable, i.e., by parachute), tracked armoured vehicle that could be integrated into Army light infantry, air assault and airborne divisions that currently do not have a similar protected firepower capability.

The US Army's Stryker Brigade Combat Teams up until 2022 were equipped with the M1128 MGS (Mobile Gun System) that carried an M68A2 105mm gun and served a similar purpose to the MPF: 'For over 15 years, the Stryker MGS has enabled Stryker brigade combat teams to provide direct supporting fires to assault infantry by destroying or suppressing

A Ukrainian T-64BV displaying the distinctive Ukrainian flag painted ERA bricks. The T-64 has been the mainstay of Ukrainian tank forces and has more than held its own against Russian T-80s and T-90s. (Photo by ARIS MESSINIS/ AFP via Getty Images)

hardened enemy bunkers, machine guns and sniper positions in urban, restricted and open-rolling terrain.'[20]

The MGS was not designed as an anti-armour platform, but the Army noted its 105mm gun was 'designed to be effective against a range of threats up to T-62 tanks'.[21] Problems with integrating reactive armour packages to improve survivability, along with the fact that the MGS was built on older hulls not upgraded to DVH (double-V hull) standard, meant that the vehicle was susceptible to both IEDs and RPGs. Its gun pod, the main armament, was also considered too lightly protected and could have been knocked out by artillery during any near-peer conflict, let alone RPGs.

The Army has selected the General Dynamics Griffin for the MPF requirement, type-classified as the M10 Booker, with a total of 42 MPFs planned to be assigned to each battalion at the time of writing – a very significant enhancement to capabilities.

The Booker's rifled 105mm main gun will destroy all known Russian and Chinese APCs and IFVs while also offering a more than sporting chance against enemy MBTs. An M393A3 high-explosive plastic (HEP) round, useful for bunker-busting, is also being produced.

For US Army airborne units, their last tracked armoured platform was the M551 Sheridan, an air-droppable light tank equipped with a 152mm hybrid gun/missile launcher. Soviet-era designs often incorporated a missile-launching ability with their tank main guns, but the Sheridan was the first such design in US service.

Unfortunately, the recoil of the 152mm was reported to cause issues with the electronics on-board the MGM-51 Shillelagh ATGMs, and the problems were never fully rectified before the M551 was retired from service in the 1990s. The gun-fired Shillelagh itself also never lived up to expectations, particularly in terms of range.

The concept was to allow the Sheridan to engage enemy armour out to 2,000 metres, a similar idea to the TOWs now mounted on Bradley IFVs. Instead, problems with the missile's infrared sensor meant that the missile was limited to a range of roughly 800 metres.

Despite seeing action in Vietnam and Panama (the latter featuring the only occurrence of an operational airdrop of light tanks post-war), the Sheridan's Shillelagh ATGM killed only one tank in its years of service – an Iraqi Type 59 – during the initial stages of Operation *Desert Storm* in 1991. The gun/missile combination was phased out by the US as was the concept of a light tank.

In Russia, the gun/missile concept soldiers on, with the 9K112 Kobra/ AT-8 Songster fired from the standard 125m main gun of the T-72, T-80 and T-90 series. In Ukraine, they appear to have been rarely employed, if at all (only the BMD-3 has been visually documented firing its low-velocity 100mm cannon employing 9M117 Bastion/AT-10 Stabber missiles).

RIGHT A close-up view of the M153 series Common Remotely Operated Weapon Station – Low Profile (CROWS-LP) equipped with an M2 .50cal heavy machine gun on an M1A2 Abrams. Remote weapons stations allow the crew to engage targets with externally mounted weapons without putting themselves at risk. (Photo by Artur Widak/ NurPhoto via Getty Images)

BELOW The US Army M10 Booker light tank/assault gun. A procurement of 504 vehicles to provide organic fire support for infantry units is planned. Its 105mm M35 main gun can destroy most older Russian MBTs from the frontal arc and all known Russian IFVs and APCs. (Photo by US Army)

So, what will that future tank look like? The South Korean Hyundai Rotem Next Generation Main Battle Tank unveiled in 2022 may be the clearest indication of a near-future MBT, although only scale models of a prototype are currently available for reference. Certainly, the design spec is a shopping list for near-future AFVs.

The next-generation MBT is envisioned to mount a 130mm smoothbore main gun with secondary armament to include a laser platform and ATGMs; both the laser (intended for use as a counter-UAV weapon) and the ATGM launcher will be carried internally to reduce the profile of the vehicle and erected only for employment. Common to most next-generation designs, the next-generation MBT will be developed for both crewed and uncrewed operation.

Full 360-degree APS is planned, including defence against top-attack missiles, along with an integrated counter-IED system. The smoothbore Rheinmetall 130mm Future Gun System (featured on the KF51 Panther) will be paired with the Israeli HERO 120 loitering munition (an optional enhancement offering four on-board HERO 120s), along with a .50 coaxial

heavy machine gun and integration options for remote weapons stations that could mount directed energy or similar counter-UAV systems.

Intriguingly, there is mention of 'on and off-platform sensors coupled with active, reactive and passive protection and a dedicated top attack protection system'.[22] The top-attack system is known as the Rheinmetall TAPS (Top Attack Protection System). The off-platform comment could indicate teaming with other platforms or inputs from its own UAVs or UGVs, or perhaps both.

The 130mm main gun will drastically increase engagement range and, according to its adherents, dramatically improve lethality. French company Nexter are developing an even bigger gun – the smoothbore 140mm ASCALAON concept (Autoloaded and SCALable Outperforming guN) for the MCGS (Main Ground Combat System, a joint venture between Germany and France to develop a next-generation MBT). The 140mm will employ Nexter's telescoped ammunition concept, allowing use of its next-generation long-rod penetrators.

According to Nexter, the ASCALAON will offer 'a wide choice of terminal effects: the enlarged calibre enriches the range of ammunition for an optimal effect on the target thanks to rods of unparalleled length. It also makes it possible to foresee intelligent ammunition for firing beyond direct sight (BLOS/NLOS), which will provide new capacities while reducing the vulnerability of the tank.'[23]

As we have noted, by its recent use by Ukrainian tank crews, indirect fire by tank main guns has long been trained for but is rarely employed on the battlefield. BLOS/NLOS, perhaps informed by an on-board UAS system or feeding data from battlefield management software marking enemy targets, could see such tanks engaging 'over the horizon'.

Perhaps more importantly, the ASCALAON will also feature 'an innovative muzzle brake, adjusted external pressure fields and an optimised firing impulse will strongly limit the blast effect of the shot. ASCALAON will thus allow the presence of infantrymen in the vicinity of the tank for joint combat, particularly in urban areas.'[24]

Finally, integration of the ASCALAON 140mm will also be possible on lighter weight class vehicles. According to the manufacturer, the gun system will be 'compatible with mobile and projectable platforms weighing less than 50 tonnes, while preserving the vehicle's layout capabilities'.[25] This is potentially evolutionary news for light tanks, such as the US Griffin MPF and future IFV designs. Of course, it remains to be seen if the ASCALAON will deliver on all of its promises.

The Russians are also looking at 'up-gunning'. Uralvagonzavod have announced a 2A83 152mm cannon that could be integrated into the T-14 Armata platform (an unsuccessful programme had earlier tried to mate a 152mm with the T-80BV tank); however, with the T-14 resembling vapourware, the gun's future is in doubt.

The M1150 Assault Breacher Vehicle (ABV) as employed by the US Army and Marine Corps. Armoured breaching platforms like the ABV will be increasingly critical in future conventional wars (as evidenced by Ukrainian attempts to breach Russian fortifications) and in IED-rich urban operations. (US Marine Corps photo by Lance Corporal Rhita Daniel)

As a curious aside, the latest Russian tank at the time of writing is a T-72 based variant variously termed the 'Turtle'. This appears to be a T-72 encased in a welded steel structure and equipped with counter-UAV jammers and a mine plough. The truly unusual design is likely intended as an armoured breaching vehicle, particularly since the up-armouring to protect the tank against artillery and FPV drones means that the turret cannot be traversed. An unusual footnote in the annals of AFV history and the war in Ukraine.

The German KF51 Panther, the Franco-German MGCS and the South Korean NG MBT are all intended to incorporate C5ISR: Command, Control, Communications, Computers, Cyber, Intelligence, Surveillance and Reconnaissance systems. These will be the first tanks built as a digital platform from the ground up.

All future MBT platforms will face the challenge of weight. Mark Cazalet, writing for *European Security & Defence*, states:

> Compared to legacy vehicles, common contemporary vehicle requirements include more and better passive armour protection, larger weapons, more capable sensors in greater quantities, active protection systems (APSs), sophisticated networked radios, and various other functionality-adding subsystems. These have in turn necessitated more powerful engines to maintain mobility with the increased weight of the armour and mission systems and to meet their power supply demands.[26]

Cazalet again notes:

> More powerful engines often consume more fuel and thus necessitate the addition of auxiliary power units (APUs) or batteries to provide adequate power to the mission systems without relying on the engine alone. Additionally, modern AFV diesel engines and transmissions have become about as small as they can realistically be with present-day engine technology, thus eking more power out of the same weight and volume of engine has become very difficult. All of this means that unless a radical new powerpack design arrives on the scene, it will become more and more difficult to make AFVs heavier while maintaining existing dimensions and mobility characteristics.[27]

The possible answers to the challenges of increasing the weight of AFVs are varied, with only a few showing true promise. Chief among these is the uncrewed turret, which reduces weight by eliminating both the human crew (General Dynamics' Abrams X technology demonstrator features an uncrewed turret) and a likely consummate reduction in armour around the turret (as there are no humans to keep alive).

According to Tristan Sauer, land domain analyst at GlobalData, 'The integration of an AI-enabled unmanned turret with an autoloader streamlines operations by reducing the vehicle crew down from four to three while reducing platform weight and providing more room for additional subsystems.'[28]

Another potential answer is the entirely uncrewed tank. In October 2020, the first three concept designs for a proposed optionally manned tank (OMT) were unveiled by the US Army's Ground Vehicle Systems Center at Detroit Arsenal. One version appeared to dwarf even the M1A2 and was likely envisaged to mount the new Rheinmetall 130mm main gun.

Concept images were blurred in the few images released from the event as were 1/35 models produced of the three concepts, which were displayed alongside models of latest-generation vehicles such as the T-14 Armata.

A more prosaic answer to reduce at least some weight lies in the replacement of steel tracks with composite rubber tracks (CRTs). CRTs work best on vehicles under 55 tonnes and offer an average weight saving of around 5 percent. They do, however, potentially increase the vehicle's thermal signature, particularly if the vehicle has been driven for longer periods.

So, in closing, near future MBTs will likely feature a range of these technologies: advanced ERA, an APS system that can counter FPV drones and top-attack munitions, integral UAV/UGV launcher, teaming technology to control robot tanks, a dedicated counter-UAS system likely using both EW and kinetic technologies; and will be optionally crewed with their turrets likely uncrewed to improve survivability.

A glimpse into this future likely lies with the Israeli Carmel programme:

In this future AFV programme, Israeli design efforts have coalesced around the working model of two crewmembers supplemented by sophisticated automated subsystems, sometimes referred to as 'virtual crew-members'. Under the Carmel model, the two human crew effectively function as tactical decision-makers and the 'human in the loop' and/or manual override safeguards, while lower-level functions such as driving, navigation, and portions of the engagement cycle are automated.

This model even envisages fire control as being almost entirely automated, with the machine performing automatic target detection, tracking, ranging, gun-laying, and even recommending a particular weapon or ammunition suited to the target type, then presenting this to the crew for approval to engage.

The crew are then free to modify these choices, for instance selecting a different weapon/ammunition for the engagement, but once the crew have given final approval to conduct the engagement, the machine carries out the rest of the attack autonomously. The Carmel model addresses many concerns with full automation and doesn't suffer from many of the previously-discussed downsides associated with remotely-operated vehicles [as it is an 'assisted' model rather than opting for completely uncrewed].[29]

We'll leave the last word, however, to the group of influential American tankers who co-authored *The Tank is Dead… Long Live the Tank – The Persistent Value of Armored Combined Arms Teams in the 21st Century*:

… UAS, loitcring munitions, and the ability to detect force concentrations via their electromagnetic signature and attack them with precision munitions necessitate adaptation rather than outright removal [of the tank] from the battlefield.

Such adjustment includes understanding how friendly forces look from an enemy perspective, enhancing masking and camouflage, greater dispersal, and faster dissemination of orders and the related convergence of combat power at decisive points in time and space. These actions, combined with a judicious application of new technologies into armored organizations [will] ensure their continued effectiveness.[30]

CHAPTER TWO
ARMOURED FIGHTING VEHICLES

'In short, while seventy percent of the M113s and YPR-765s that get hit end up as a total loss, only about thirty percent of the hit Bradleys are being assessed as total losses – and the Bradleys are, arguably, engaged in a far tougher fight.

Craig Hooper,
Forbes Business, 18 June 2023[1]

The Canadian Army during World War II was perhaps the first to recognize the advantage of a heavily armoured tracked vehicle that could protect its infantry passengers during an assault against enemy positions. The Kangaroo was a modified Priest self-propelled gun, with its gun removed to allow transportation of infantry in relative safely (being open-topped, it was still susceptible to airburst and artillery fragments).

The success of the Kangaroo led to the post-war development of a new class of armoured vehicle – the armoured personnel carrier. The Soviets developed both wheeled and tracked APCs, such as the BTR 152 and the BTR 50. The Americans designed the M113 as their principal tracked APC, while the British developed the FV432 series, both of which are still soldiering on in some form some 60 years later.

ABOVE An M2A2 Bradley IFV in Ukrainian service. Note the Bradley Reactive Armor Tiles (BRAT) and elements from the Bradley Urban Survival Kit (BUSK). The Bradley has been very well received and is popular with crews. Its 25mm Bushmaster is particularly valued as is its survivability – particularly in comparison with Russian IFV designs. (Photo by Marek M. Berezowski/Anadolu via Getty Images)

RIGHT A donated Dutch YPR-765 PRI.50 armoured personnel carrier operated by Ukraine. Note the incoming round impacts on the frontal glacis. The YPR-765 employs a spaced steel laminate armour design that protects against small arms and artillery fragmentation but is outdated against larger threats. Despite this, the YPR-765 has proven popular due to its reliability and speed. It is also considered far more survivable than the BMP series according to Ukrainian users. (Photo by GENYA SAVILOV/AFP via Getty Images)

BELOW RIGHT An RAF Regiment FV430 Bulldog Mk3 in Iraq, 2009. Bulldogs are upgraded FV432 armoured personnel carriers fitted with either a manned turret or remote weapons station and equipped with WRAP-2 applique armour. Areas not covered by the WRAP-2 are fitted with slat armour. (Photo by Matt Cardy/Getty Images)

LEFT A British Army Warrior of the Queen's Royal Hussars in Basra, Iraq, 2006. Note the addition of slat armour to increase protection against RPGs and recoilless rifles. The slat armour was replaced a year later with the WRAP-2 applique armour package. (Photo by ESSAM AL-SUDANI/AFP via Getty Images)

BELOW LEFT A British Army Warrior fitted with slat armour and WRAP-2 applique armour – its ridged appearance helps negate the effect of shaped-charge projectiles. (PA Images/ Alamy Stock Photo)

While widely implementing the APC concept in the immediate post-war period, the Soviet Union was also developing what would become the first true infantry fighting vehicle – the BMP-1.

As well as acting as an armoured personnel carrier, capable of carrying a motor rifle squad of dismounts, the BMP also carried its own integral offensive armament. A turreted 73mm low-velocity cannon was paired with an AT-3 Sagger anti-tank guided missile. At the time of its debut, the BMP was genuinely revolutionary: there was no Western equivalent, and the BMP caught NATO by surprise. It was an evolution of the APC to which there was no clear peer.

NATO and the West would struggle for decades to develop a platform that could match the BMP's simple utility and firepower. By the early 1970s, the West Germans would begin to field the Marder infantry fighting vehicle, an armoured troop carrier with a turreted 20mm cannon and Milan anti-tank missile. The mid- to late 1980s would finally see the US and UK catching up, with the introduction of the Bradley and Warrior IFVs, respectively.

DO NOT STAND

A close-up of the WRAP-2 armour of a British Army Warrior, pictured in Basra, Iraq, 2009, as the UK commitment in Iraq was wound down. (PA Images/ Alamy Stock Photo)

The concept of the IFV differed from that of the APC both in design and intended application. While the APC was merely a battle taxi to transport infantry towards the edge of the direct fire zone, the IFV was designed as an integral element of the infantry squad. The IFV could provide organic, intimate fire support for the dismounted squad. It could also engage enemy soft skins, APCs, other IFVs and even opposing tanks in extremis.

As analyst William F. Owen has opined:

> The roles of IFVs and APCs differ in one essential way. The IFV is designed to fight; that is, to engage in direct-fire combat with the enemy: either with the infantry section or fire team mounted, or in support of a dismounted section. Some designs even allow for the infantry to fire their weapons from within the vehicle, or via roof hatches. In contrast, the APC is and was designed to deliver the infantry to a point where they dismount and fight on foot. The APCs then withdraw until required to perform support tasks (such as re-supplying ammunition, bringing up reinforcements, evacuating casualties), after which they might transport the infantry for subsequent tasks.[2]

So, although both the APC and the IFV can protect their passengers from artillery shrapnel, the offensive capability of the IFV sets it apart. Soviet (and later Russian Army) doctrine called for the BMP to follow a tank advance against enemy positions, suppressing with its 73mm cannon until it reached a theoretical 300 metres from the enemy, when the motor rifle squad would dismount.

The infantry would then advance in a skirmish line, engaging targets with small-arms fire. The BMPs would maintain direct fire support as the infantry closed on the enemy. The infantry could also fire enclosed within the BMP, as it featured firing ports for this purpose. In practice, this proved to be wildly inaccurate.

The BMP-1's first combat deployment was during the 1973 Yom Kippur War. It was an inauspicious start. Egyptian and Syrian crews largely employed the vehicle as an APC rather than enabling their infantry to close on Israeli positions. The vehicle was not used doctrinally, and subsequent criticism of the low-velocity cannon was based on ill-advised attempts to engage Israeli tanks.

The BMP would become a depressingly familiar sight on the world's battlefields throughout the Cold War and beyond. It served in both the Iran–Iraq War and in the Iraqi Army against Coalition Forces in Operation *Desert Storm* and *Iraqi Freedom*. When directly facing its Western equivalents such as the Bradley, the BMP typically fared badly, although one US Bradley was successfully engaged by an Iraqi BMP-1 during the famous tank battle of 73 Easting in 1991.

A BMP-1 infantry fighting vehicle pictured in Aleppo, Syria, 2016, seemingly operated by Islamic State or an allied jihadist group. (Photo by OMAR HAJ KADOUR/AFP via Getty Images)

In the first decades of the new century, the BMP family would see action in both the Middle East and Europe. The BMP-1 was largely superseded by the BMP-2 in Russian service, which replaced the 73mm gun with a more effective 30mm cannon in a larger, two-man turret and swapped out the ageing AT-3 Sagger ATGM for the more modern AT-4 Spigot and AT-5 Spandrel but also reduced the troop-carrying capacity to seven in the process.

This reduction in the number of dismounts an IFV could carry also plagued Western designs, causing changes to mechanized infantry tactics and a conundrum for platoon leaders who had to fit their infantry and supporting enablers into their vehicles. Surprisingly, most IFV designs currently in service do not allow a full squad to be transported under armour.

This is primarily caused by the inclusion of a manned turret, which takes up space and requires additional power. Designs that feature remote weapons stations – essentially remote-controlled gun mounts that are controlled by an operator inside the hull of the vehicle using a screen and a joystick-style control interface – do better in terms of room for dismounts.

Wheeled designs also tend to fare better in this regard. In the 1990s, the US developed the eight-wheel Stryker infantry carrier vehicle. The Stryker largely replaced the M113 in mechanized infantry formations. They were eventually developed into their own Stryker Brigade Combat Teams whose role 'fills the operational gaps between the Army's light forces and the heavy forces still fielded with Abrams tanks and Bradley Fighting Vehicles'.[3]

In Iraq, the Stryker was popular due to its speed and relative quietness, at least compared with a Bradley. It suffered due to its size, particularly when fitted with cage/bar armour, in urban streets and was vulnerable to bottom-attack IEDs. Despite this, the platform was adopted by the US Army's Ranger Regiment which, operating as part of a larger SOF task force, required a light armoured vehicle to transport its raid teams to and from an objective.

A Stryker M1134 Anti-Tank Guided Missile Vehicles equipped with TOW 2 (at rear), with a Stryker M1126 Infantry Carrier Vehicle in the middle and an M1127 Reconnaissance variant in the lead, seen in Najaf, Iraq, in 2004. Note the slat armour added to counter RPG and recoilless rifle rounds. The M1134 has since been upgraded with the double-V hull and is known as the M1253. (Photo by Scott Nelson/Getty Images)

Its vulnerability to bottom-attack IEDs was largely addressed by a widescale programme to modify Strykers to a new double-V hull (DVH) standard, which channelled the blast away from the vehicle.

As we previously noted, the Stryker MGS or Mobile Gun System, formally the M1128, was an effort to provide Stryker units with an assault gun capability (three per Stryker company). An M68A2 105mm cannon was mounted in a 'gun pod' with a coaxially mounted 7.62mm machine gun: 'The Stryker Brigade Combat Team uses the MGS to create openings in walls, destroy bunkers and machine gun nests, and defeat sniper positions and light armor threats. The primary weapon systems are designed to be effective against a range of threats up to T-62 tanks.'[4]

The MGS was popular with its crews, and its sensors provided a capability leap for accompanied infantry. As Sergeant Justin Parrot, an MGS gunner who served in Iraq on the vehicles, recalled, 'We use thermals to find insurgents. We report everything we see to the dismounted troops.' Sergeant 1st Class Scott Collum added, 'I have used thermals to find freshly dug holes, recently driven cars, insurgents placing IEDs. I have also used thermals to tell if a weapon has been fired recently.'[5]

Unfortunately, although proving promising during operations in both Iraq and Afghanistan, the MGS programme was discontinued and the MGS was withdrawn from service. A press release issued in 2021 explained, 'It was the first Army system fielded with an autoloader, but over time it has become costly to maintain. In addition, the lethality capabilities provided by the Stryker MGS were based on the flat-bottom chassis, and the system was never upgraded against more modern threats such as improvised explosive devices or anti-tank mines.'[6]

TOP LEFT A fascinating shot of an M1126 Stryker in Iraq in 2010. Note the extra armour protecting the wheels and lower half of the vehicle and the multitude of counter-IED technologies on display, including the Rhino Passive Infrared Defeat System, which is a fold-out boom with a heat source to prematurely denote angled EFP IEDs triggered by passive infrared devices and the AN/VLQ-12 CREW DUKE jammer. (Photo by PV2 Deangelo Wells, DVIDS)

Wheeled platforms were also by nature much lighter and could be delivered to conflict zones by air. All of this comes with a trade-off in protection and offensive capability: wheeled IFVs, ICVs and APCs tend to be less armoured than their tracked counterparts, but their speed, lighter weight and generally larger troop-carrying capacity makes them a good choice for expeditionary forces.

The Stryker design was relatively successful in Iraq, where its speed and relative stealth were prized, but less so in Afghanistan, where roll-overs were common. As noted, the common use of RPGs saw the Stryker fitted with additional cage or bar/slat armour, which worked well as a countermeasure to specifically defeat RPG warheads but significantly added to the weight and reduced the manoeuvrability of the platform, particularly in urban areas.

The concept harks back to Soviet field expedient 'bedspring armour' fitted to their T34/85 tanks in 1944/45 as an additional defence measure against the Panzerfaust handheld rocket. The modern version employed on the Stryker relies upon 'trapping the RPG round between a pair of bars far enough away that the initial shaped charge cannot damage the armor, while short circuiting the piezoelectric precursor to either prevent the HEAT charge from detonating or at least denying the charge's molten jet a route into the tank's interior'.[7]

TOP RIGHT The now retired M1128 Stryker Mobile Gun System (MGS), which mounted a 105mm rifled main gun. Despite its general popularity with crews and its usefulness in urban combat (particularly for breaching walls of target buildings), it was retired due to the maintenance requirements for its autoloader. The capability has now been partly resurrected with the M10 Booker assault gun. (US Army photo by Private 1st Class Alicia C. Torbush)

LEFT A useful profile shot of the M1128 Mobile Gun System (MGS) serving with the US Army's 1/38 Infantry Regiment in Baqaba, Iraq, 2007. (Photo by ALEXANDER NEMENOV/ AFP via Getty Images)

DO V-SHAPED HULLS HELP AGAINST IEDS AND MINES?

Yes, V-shaped hulls are very effective in deflecting the blast of a mine or IED from under a vehicle. They do this by channelling the blast away to the sides, reducing the blast wave, which travels upward into the vehicle. Significantly, the smaller the angle of the V-shaped hull, the greater the deflection but greater the chance of the vehicle overturning.

V-shaped hulls can also affect the stability of an armoured vehicle traversing over uneven ground, also increasing the risk of a roll-over. The design of MRAPs developed to withstand IED and mine blasts also factors into this. The US Army noted when discussing their MaxxPro MRAP: 'To withstand the greatest underbody threat, the highest amount of distance from the bottom of the vehicle to the ground is required. However, maximizing this distance raises the vehicle's center of gravity and reduces stability, giving MRAP vehicles like the MaxxPro a higher propensity to roll over.'[8]

V-shaped hulls also do not address mines and IEDs that launch a projectile or penetrator. Iranian-designed EFPs (explosively formed projectiles) encountered by the British Army in southern Iraq were capable of punching through even the heaviest armour, including at least one Challenger II main battle tank. To combat EFPs, extra armour plating was fitted to the undersides of some vehicles along with employing varying methods to force the EFP to detonate prematurely ahead of the vehicle.

During the cage armour's first year of deployment in Iraq, '91 RPG strikes were recorded against the Stryker with no loss of life – all but two RPGs were defeated by Stryker's slat armor. During a six-month period, one Stryker, C21, had been hit by a suicide car bomb, nine improvised explosive devices, and eight RPG direct hits, but had not lost one crew member.'[9]

Cage armour offers zero protection against other threats such as tank main gun rounds and ATGMs. In terms of protection against RPGs, it provides 'statistical protection; that is, while the system doesn't offer a complete defense against RPGs, it does lower the probability that a tandem charge shot will be successful by 50 to 70 percent, depending on where and how the RPG connects'.[10]

As noted earlier, the preponderance of improvised explosive devices in both theatres led to a redesign of the Stryker to feature the double-V hull, a design incorporated from MRAP trucks. The V-shaped hull channels the blast away from the body of the vehicle, often losing wheels but reducing the chance of serious injury to occupants inside.

The Stryker DVH modification also saw the addition of 'enhanced armor, a new suspension and blast-attenuating seats. This rapid engineering effort went from conception to production in less than one year and debuted in Afghanistan in early summer 2011'.[11]

Remembering former UK Prime Minster Boris Johnson's dramatically ill-timed statement, 'We have to recognise that the old concepts of fighting big tank battles on the European land mass are over',[12] wheeled and tracked IFVs, ICVs and APCs are being modernized to increase survivability and lethality on future battlefields to be able to operate alongside tanks on that same 'European land mass'.

ABOVE A close-up of slat or bar armour applied to the M1126 Stryker in Mosul, Iraq, in 2005. The addition of the armour added weight, increasing the rollover hazard, and made the vehicle less manoeuvrable in often tight urban laneways and alleys (which, ironically, is one of the key benefits of the Stryker platform). (Photo by US Army, DVIDS)

LEFT A US Army Stryker mounting the Javelin-equipped CROWS-J remote weapons station. Most Stryker ICVs are planned to be fitted with CROWS-J or the Dragoon turret with 30mm cannon. (Photo by Michael Ciaglo/ Getty Images)

The Stryker Dragoon M1296 is the latest variant of the Stryker and was designed to engage Russian IFVs, such as the BMD-3 and BTR-82A. The Dragoon uses the highly effective 30mm Mk44 Bushmaster II autocannon firing both incendiary HE and sabot. (US Army photo by Sergeant Sara Stalvey)

DID THAT BRADLEY REALLY KILL A T-90M?

In January 2024, now famous drone footage emerged of a close-range gunfight between a Ukrainian-operated M2A3 Bradley IFV and a Russian T-90M 'Breakthrough' main battle tank. The footage was released by the 47th Separate Mechanized Brigade who were defending the village of Stepove in eastern Donetsk.

It shows a Bradley engaging a T-90M with highly accurate 25mm HEIT (high-explosive incendiary tracer) rounds as the T-90M attempts to acquire the Bradley, reversing backwards and forwards in apparent confusion as a fire ignites on the tank from the incendiary rounds. Moments later, a large explosion occurs, likely the tank's Relikt ERA cooking off. A second video shows the tank striking a tree and being hit by a Ukrainian FPV drone before the crew finally bail out.

So did the Bradley, an IFV not a tank, kill the T-90M, the most advanced MBT in service with Russian forces? The short answer is no. The onslaught of 25mm rounds may have destroyed the optics and sensors on the T-90M, accounting for its erratic performance. Additionally, the on-board fire and the relentless strikes of cannon rounds would have contributed to a morale failure on the part of the Russian tankers. Certainly, if the FPV hadn't finally caused a mobility kill, the T-90M would have more than likely retreated to lick its wounds after the punishment dished out by the Bradley.

Could the Bradley have killed the T-90M? Yes, but not with its Bushmaster cannon. The Bradley mounts a twin TOW 2 ATGM which could have destroyed the T-90M at ranges out to almost 4km. Why the Bradley chose to engage in a relatively close-range gunfight with the tank is likely a question of terrain. From the video, it appears the IFV was involved in the mobile defence of a village, so lines of sight would have been short, blocking any long-range ATGM shots.

A US Army M2A2 Bradley infantry fighting vehicle deployed to north-eastern Syria fires a TOW-2 anti-tank guided missile. Along with its 25mm Bushmaster autocannon, the Bradley carries a pair of TOW-2 missiles in an external mount. (Photo by DELIL SOULEIMAN/AFP via Getty Images)

The M1126 Stryker, the basic troop carrier normally protected by a heavy machine gun or automatic grenade launcher in a remote-controlled mount, is now being upgraded with CROWS-J (Common Remote Operated Weapon System – Javelin), a remote weapons station that combines the machine gun with a pair of Javelin ATGMs. Each Stryker will now have the capability to engage and destroy enemy MBTs and lesser armoured threats.

Other DVH Strykers are being modernized as the M1296 Dragoon, featuring an unmanned turret mounting a 30mm cannon and coaxial 7.62mm machine gun. The 30mm is effective against all enemy IFV types and, as seen in Ukraine with the similar Russian 30mm, can cause problems for MBTs. With programmable airburst rounds, it can effectively engage drones and dug-in infantry.

The Bradley with its 25mm Bushmaster chain gun has also proven highly effective in Ukraine, with one famous incident seeing a Bradley engage and suppress a Russian T-90M 'Breakthrough' tank. The close-range gunfight between the T-90M and the Bradley was filmed by a drone, and the footage is suitably terrifying as the Bradley methodically engages the T-90M with its cannon (according to the Ukrainian gunner, they had a problem with their API or armour-piercing incendiary feed and had to resort to HEI or high-explosive incendiary).

An M2A2 Bradley IFV fitted with the BRAT (Bradley Reactive Armour Tiles) system in Syria in 2021. M2A2s supplied to Ukraine have also been fitted with BRAT, which has been praised by Ukrainian tankers. (US Army photo by Sergeant Torrance Saunders)

Some nations have decided upon an upgraded APC rather than an IFV. One such country is Israel, which deploys the Namer series of heavily armoured APCs. This decision was based on direct combat experience and the loss of multiple infantry in single engagements, in which a Zelda M113-based APC was destroyed. Up-armouring makes sense for the Israelis, who operate predominantly in an urban or semi-urban environment.

Again, from William F. Owen writing in *Military Operations* in 2012:

> The Israeli experience of the Lebanon War of 2006 confirmed their opinion (from 1973) that an APC with MBT-like levels of protection offered the best fit to combined arms tactics. That is not to say that MBT levels of protection are required, but there must be a judgement as to what is adequate. Tactics tell us how to employ the APC, because its role is to deliver the infantry to fight. From a technical standpoint, its mobility and protection must merely be equal to that task.[13]

The Israelis have also adopted the Eitan, an eight-wheel APC, which premiered during operations in Gaza in November 2023. The V-shaped-hull Eitan can carry nine dismounts and is fitted with the Iron Fist active protection system – one of the only wheeled APCs in the world to successfully employ an APS (they are heavy and a drain on the vehicle's power; note that the US Army has had significant issues deploying an APS to Stryker).

The provision of an APS, however, reduces the need for heavy conventional armouring of the base vehicle, meaning that it only has to protect against small arms, heavy machine guns and artillery fragmentation. The Eitan was designed with a remote weapon station (RWS) mounting a .50cal heavy machine gun, but plans were unveiled in 2023, following Ukrainian experiences, to add a turret fitted with a 30mm cannon. The 30mm will be employed to engage not only light armour like BMPs but UAVs with airburst ammunition.

The US Army began replacing their legacy M113-based platforms in 2023 with the M1283 Armored Multi-Purpose Vehicle (AMPV) family – another platform that acts as an APC but with IFV-level armour. Indeed, the AMPV uses the hull of the Bradley IFV and is designed in five current variants: General Purpose, Mortar Carrier, Mission Command, Medical Treatment and Medical Evacuation. A Counter-Unmanned Aircraft System (CUAS) prototype was unveiled in late 2023.

The AMPV can keep pace with Bradley and Abrams and presumably the future OMFV/XM30 Mechanized Infantry Combat Vehicle (MICV). It provides far greater armour protection than the M113 and can integrate counter-IED and emerging CUAS systems and sensors along with the capacity for mounting an APS. While not designed to operate consistently in the direct fire zone, the AMPV can provide protected mobility against most peer direct fire threats short of main tank guns and ATGMs.

OPPOSITE TOP An Iraqi M113 armoured personnel carrier seen in 2014. Note the workshop-produced turret cupola housing an M2 .50cal heavy machine gun. (HAIDAR MOHAMMED ALI/AFP via Getty Images)

OPPOSITE BOTTOM An Israeli Namer infantry fighting vehicle seen in 2024, with an Israeli-designed cope cage to counter grenades or RPG rounds dropped by Hamas drones. (Photo by Amir Levy/ Getty Images)

The Bradley itself is slated to eventually be replaced with the result of a programme called the Optionally Manned Fighting Vehicle (OMFV). The OMFV is now designated the XM30 MICV. We know that it will be armed with the XM913 50mm cannon in an unmanned turret and ATGMs along with APS optimized to counter the loitering munition threat. It is envisaged the MICV will be crewed by two soldiers with a 'virtual' third crew member likely managing systems. It will be able to carry six infantrymen. The first XM30 is expected to be fielded in 2029; however, delays are endemic in defence procurement.

The Russian Army also employs the BMD series for its VDV or airborne troops. The BMD is a lighter and more compact IFV designed to be air-dropped (stories abound of VDV BMDs being parachute-dropped with the crew inside!). The most recent versions are the BMD-3 and 4, armed with a 30mm cannon and a combination of 30mm cannon and 100mm main gun (in common with the BMP-3). Both mount the AT-5 Spandrel (Konkurs) ATGM. The West has no direct equivalent to the BMD series and the capability they bring – namely being able to quickly support paratroopers on an objective with light armour.

Although the US fielded the M551 Sheridan air-droppable light tank from the 1960s, it was retired in the 1990s. The closest the US has to the BMD is likely the Stryker, but that must be transported in a cargo aircraft and doesn't provide the immediate intimate support to an airborne or airmobile operation. The General Dynamics MPF light tank – the M10 Booker – is not air-droppable but is designed to be flown in on C-5s and similar.

Intriguingly, the US Army's storied 82nd Airborne Division procured a company's worth of former USMC LAV-25A2 light armoured vehicles in 2018 to provide the capability 'to suppress the enemy as they come up with vehicles that are larger than ours by providing a support by fire element'.[14] The LAV-25 has previously been evaluated and cleared for airdrop. The acquisition by the 82nd is considered only a stop-gap measure until the MPF is issued; however, its lack of air-drop capability will be both a tactical and strategic quandary for airborne units.

Along with air-portable platforms, amphibious designs must be considered. The USMC has been attempting to divest itself of its ageing AAVTP7 'Tuna Shark' Amphibious Assault Vehicle (AAV) for decades. The AAV is an exceptionally large vehicle that presents a massive target both in and out of the water and is difficult to manoeuvre in urban environments. It was deployed during the invasion phase of Operation *Iraqi Freedom*, with the Marines advancing from the south, but its size, land speed and poor armour proved less than ideal. The USMC is finally replacing the AAV with the Amphibious Combat Vehicle – Personnel (ACV-P), an eight-wheeled amphibious carrier equipped with a remote weapons station and able to carry a full 13-person squad of dismounts. The Marines term the vehicle a 'ship-to-objective amphibian platform', as it was designed to ferry Marines from landing ships to shore.

OPPOSITE TOP A Ukrainian-operated, Russian-produced BMP-2 infantry fighting vehicle with workshop slat or bar armour added. Despite an infusion of Western models, the BMP-2 is still the most commonly encountered IFV on both sides of the conflict. (ANATOLII STEPANOV/AFP via Getty Images)

OPPOSITE BOTTOM A Russian BMP-3 IFV pictured in Mariupol. New production BMP-3s are being fitted with Kaktus ERA and slat armour, the former to combat Ukrainian 25mm and 30mm autocannons that tend to slice through all Russian IFVs, the latter to protect against handheld anti-tank weapons. (Photo by Maximilian Clarke/SOPA Images/LightRocket via Getty Images)

NEXT PAGES Red Square Parade showing a good profile view of the BMP-2M Berezhok, an upgraded BMP-2 that features a new engine, new optics, improved applique armour, an AGS-17 automatic grenade launcher and a pair of Kornet-M ATGMs. (Photo by Nina Zotina – Host Photo Agency via Getty Images)

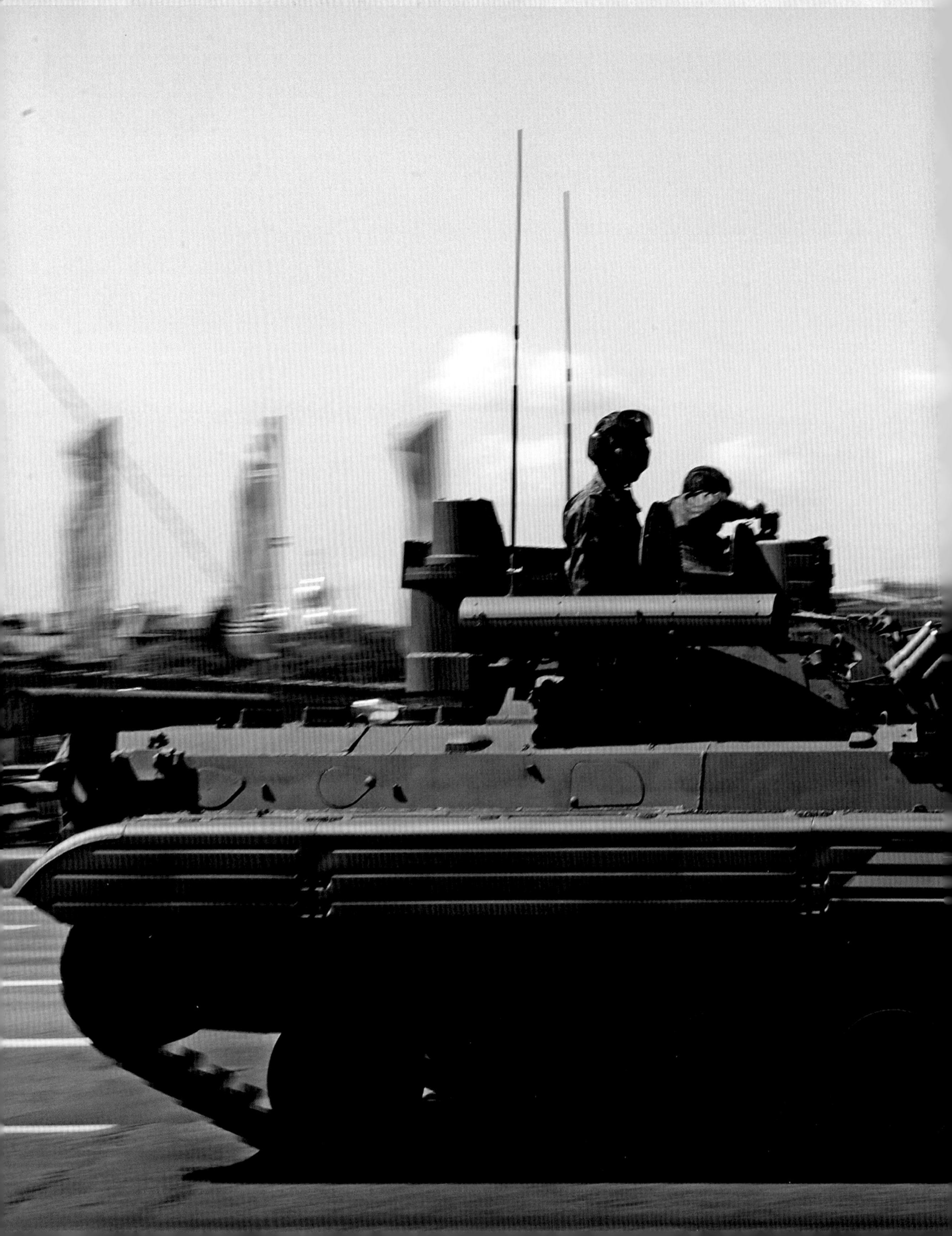

The Ukrainian BTR-4 Bucehalus infantry fighting vehicle in the distinctive AFU digital camouflage pattern. BTR-4s were later fitted with slat armour to improve protection against RPGs. (Photo by Pavlo Palamarchuk/SOPA Images/Light Rocket via Getty Images)

A version equipped with a Kongsberg remote turret fitted with a 30mm cannon is also slated to enter production. It is unclear how this version (the ACV-C, for cannon) will be incorporated within units fielding the ACV-P, although one imagines 30mm airburst will be on the shopping list for counter-UAV.

The Russians have also continued to develop new models of their venerable BMP, with the BMP-3 in production. The BMP-3 is heavily armed with both a 100mm rifled gun that can launch the 9M117 Bastion ATGM, and a 30mm autocannon. It has also been equipped with ERA and cage armour to improve its survivability.

A version featuring a remote-controlled turret-mounted 57mm cannon has also been produced but is intended as a local air defence platform to accompany BMP-equipped units. BMP-3s have also been supplemented by the BMP-2M, with the new Berezhok turret with twin ATGM launchers alongside the 30mm. Even the BMP-1 has received an update thanks to Ukraine: the BMP-1AM dispenses with its turret and instead features a remotely operated 30mm cannon.

Ukraine has also been operating its own family of wheeled IFVs – the 8x8 BTR-4 Bucephalus series are often confused with the BTR-70/80 but are wholly different vehicles only bearing a passing resemblance. The BTR-4E has served well during operations against Russian forces, with the 30mm cannon being particularly prized. The vehicle also mounts two ATGMs and has been seen equipped with anti-RPG cage armour. Another version mounts the GROM turret with four ATGMs.

TOP LEFT The supposed next-gen heavy infantry fighting vehicle of the Russian Army, the T-15. Based on the T-14 Armata, the T-15 is modified, with the engine placed in the front of the hull to allow a troop compartment in the rear. The T-15 is armed with an uncrewed remote weapon station mounting a 30mm autocannon and a pair of twin Kornet-M ATGM launchers. At the time of writing, the T-15 has not entered service with no announced procurement timeline. (Photo by NurPhoto via Getty Images)

CENTRE LEFT The Russian Kurganets-25 amphibious heavy IFV is the likely eventual replacement for the BMP series. Armed with a 30mm autocannon and four Kornet-Ms in a similar fashion to the T-15, an APC version armed with a 12.7mm heavy machine gun also exists. (Photo by Andrey Rudakov/ Bloomberg via Getty Images)

BOTTOM LEFT Russian Kurganets-25 heavy tracked armoured personnel carriers when first unveiled to the public in 2015. The APC version uses a remote weapons station fitted with a 12.7mm heavy machine gun and can carry a squad of infantry. (AFP via Getty Images)

ABOVE Chinese PLA ZTL-11 wheeled assault vehicle equipped with a rifled 105mm main gun that can also fire ATGMs. The ZTL-11 is designed to provide organic infantry fire support in a similar manner to the retired Stryker MGS and now M10 Booker. (Photo by Costfoto/NurPhoto via Getty Images)

RIGHT The fully amphibious Chinese PLA ZSL-92A (WZ-551B) armoured personnel carrier with turret-mounted 12.7mm heavy machine gun. It can carry a full infantry squad of up to 11 personnel. (Photo by China Photos/Getty Images)

Ukraine has also resurrected the age-old argument of whether wheels or tracks are the better option for IFVs and APCs. Both have their critics and adherents, with the Czech Army noting in 2022:

> It should also be noted that the Ukrainian terrain is ideal for [tracked] IFVs. The same was the case during World War II, when the most extensive battles characterised by large-scale deployment of armoured vehicles took place in Ukraine.
>
> The experience in Ukraine is therefore quite different from the conflict between Armenia and Azerbaijan, where the fighting was fought in mountainous, very difficult and impenetrable terrain. Western IFVs would probably have fared much better in this situation, not only due to significantly stronger armour, but also due to more advanced sensor equipment capable of detecting an adversary in time.
>
> Another problem for both the Ukrainian and Russian armies is the lack of deployment of modern tracked IFVs, which is somewhat paradoxical given that the arms industries of these countries have already managed to develop such vehicles as the BMPV-64 in the case of Ukraine or the Kurganets-25 in the case of Russia, the development of which has not yet been completed.[15]

Jane's Defence analyst Sam Cranny-Evans spelled out the schools of thought in a January 2023 article in *European Security & Defence*:

> The arguments are broadly divided between those who advocate for wheeled vehicles based upon their supposed reduced logistics burden and cost when compared with their tracked counterparts, those who argue that the better mobility of tracked vehicles makes them a more optimal choice, and those who support the use of both but recognise the maintenance burden this imposes.[16]

The likely operating environment plays a massive factor in the selection of wheeled or tracked vehicles:

> For example, countries that are predominantly covered in sandy terrain with urban settlements, might find wheeled vehicles as effective a purchase as tracked vehicles. This is because wheeled platforms can approach the mobility characteristics of tracked vehicles on sand and will exceed them on roads. However, a European country would likely have to contend with wet soils that at times are very weak, which severely limits the off-road mobility of wheeled vehicles.[17]

RIGHT The Russian BTR-82A APC with slat armour fitted. The BTR-82A is armed with a 30mm dual-feed cannon, which has performed well in Ukraine although the thin armour of the vehicle makes it susceptible to attack drones. (Photo by Pavel Pavlov/Anadolu Agency via Getty Images)

BELOW RIGHT The Russian VPK-7829 Bumerang K-17 variant mounting a 30mm autocannon and Kornet-M ATGMs (in a similar fashion to the T-15); another APC variant – the K-16 – is armed with a 12.7mm heavy machine gun. The Bumerang has yet to enter service at the time of writing but is understood to be the replacement for the BTR-80/82 series. (Photo by Pavel Pavlov/Anadolu Agency via Getty Images)

For nations such as the United States and to a lesser degree China and Russia, however, they must be prepared to fight in any and all environments. Having said that, the strategic alignment of the US Army (to Europe and the Middle East) and the USMC (to the Indo-Pacific) gives some indication of what types of environments will need to be faced; note the USMC's divestment of MBTs and focus on light wheeled and amphibious vehicles.

The US Army is an equally intriguing case study in this regard. Possessing both light wheeled armour (the Stryker family) and medium tracked IFVs (the Bradley), in many ways the Army is hedging its bets, with the Strykers seen as the immediate reaction force to stem or slow a breakthrough while the Bradleys are transported into theatre by sea and air lift or brought forward from European bases by rail.

Cranny-Evans has weighed the problem in some detail, particularly in light of the lessons of Ukraine:

> The question of mobility is compounded by the roles that wheeled vehicles are required to perform. They are increasingly procured to operate as infantry fighting vehicles (IFV), which requires them to carry additional armour, infantry, and weaponry commensurate with that role. They are typically unable to carry as much armour as tracked alternatives because the size of the tyres cannot be increased to meet the additional weight. That said, modern designs such as Piranha 5 and Boxer are designed to be fitted with extensive armour suites protecting them from 30mm rounds across the frontal arc. This limits their mobility characteristics further, which can impact the utility of the vehicles in the IFV role, where they are required to move off-road to support the infantry in dismounted combat.
>
> ... An IFV must fight onto an objective with the infantry it carries. Assuming that the formation is supported by artillery, the effects of a typical fire mission would last about 60 seconds, following which the vehicle has to get within 30 seconds of the objective to deploy its infantry with maximum impact. If it is stuck in mud and unable to close this gap, the infantry will be exposed and vulnerable, or require longer artillery bombardments closer to them as they attack – neither outcome is optimal.
>
> It could be argued that the extreme protection requirements are another Western reflection, however. The BTR-3, BTR-4, and BTR-80 vehicles used by Russia and Ukraine are only armoured to protect against 12.7mm rounds across the frontal arc and armour piercing small arms from the side. Despite this, they have proven themselves to be very effective during the war in Ukraine, especially in their application of firepower using the 30mm 2A72 and ZTM-1 cannons they carry as a main armament. There is evidence that these vehicles have encountered the limits of their mobility, with some images showing BTR-4s stuck in agricultural fields having left hardened roads, but their lethality and mobility in urban environments has featured prominently throughout the war. Therefore, perhaps there is a case to be made for lighter 8×8 and 6×6 vehicles, but with a greater acceptance of the risk that comes with reduced levels of armour.[18]

Jack Watling and Nick Reynolds from RUSI interviewed Ukrainian forces and found the following:

Ukrainian troops note that Western-provided platforms are vastly superior to their Soviet-legacy protected mobility platforms for one fundamental reason: crew survivability. Whereas for a Soviet mechanised section, its BMP was its primary weapons system, and so Soviet planners treated as synonymous the loss of the BMP with the loss of the section, Western armies treat mechanisation as an addition to basic infanteering.

Protected mobility is aimed at delivering infantry to their objective, which the infantry then assault. This difference in mindset, combined with a different approach to losses, means that there is a heavy emphasis in Western platforms on the survivability of dismounts even if the vehicle is mission killed. By contrast with Soviet-legacy platforms, the compromise of the vehicle's armour is also usually catastrophic for those inside it. Life support systems are a secondary consideration.[19]

One type of armoured platform that has largely been divested from US and UK armies is the MRAP. Some, including the US MaxxPro, have been donated to Ukraine, but most have been sold (and in the US some have been gifted to local police tactical teams) or otherwise disposed of.

The MRAP was a class of vehicle designed from the ground up to do one thing – ensure the survivability of the crew and passengers from IED and mine strikes. Some innovations, such as high-wheelbase V-shaped hulls to direct the blast to the sides and away from the hull, caused their own challenges, increasing the risk of rollover, for example. Most were designed with Iraq in mind, and in Afghanistan, particularly in the mountainous regions to the east, the vehicles were ill-suited for the narrow (and often crumbling) paths.

The MRAP concept was a success from a tactical standpoint; it certainly saved lives and limbs. The unfortunate downside was that patrolling was reduced to mounted operations in hulking metal trucks with little to no opportunity to interact with local civilians – an irony for a measure that was introduced during a counterinsurgency campaign.

Saudi and the United Arab Emirates (UAE) operated US MRAPs in Yemen, the UAE-designed NISR MRAP, alongside Emeriti BMP-3s and Leclerc MBTs. Alwiyat al Amalqam, a Yemeni Salafist militia group now supported by UAE, has been seen operating MaxxPro and Caimen MRAPs that were originally supplied to UAE by the US. Several MRAPs were also captured and turned against their former owners by Islamic State in 2015 as Iraqi forces retreated.

The UK still operates the Foxhound, officially a protected patrol vehicle but an MRAP design nonetheless. Many of the UK MRAP fleet were rushed into service as part of Urgent Operational Requirements for service in Afghanistan, and a whole gaggle of vehicles were purchased with abbreviated

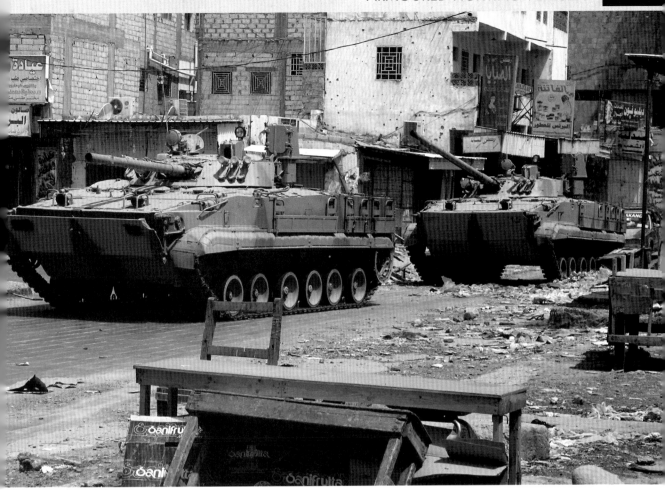

ABOVE Pro-government Russian-manufactured but UAE-supplied BMP-3 IFVs seen in Yemen's southern Lahj governorate in 2015. One hopes they aren't anywhere near hostilities judging by the lack of accompanying infantry cover. (Photo by SALEH AL-OBEIDI/AFP via Getty Images)

LEFT A Yemeni Qutaish-2 infantry mobility vehicle based on a Land Cruiser but capable of carrying eight soldiers under armour. Chains have been added over the front and back of the wheels, presumably as an up-armouring measure against RPGs. (Photo by Abdulnasser Alseddik/ Anadolu Agency/Getty Images)

A Yemeni Houthi technical, pictured in 2024, mounting an aged Soviet-era 57mm S-60 anti-aircraft cannon. (Photo by Mohammed Hamoud/Getty Images)

timelines to get them into theatre as quickly as possible. A range of these – Wolfhounds, Huskies and Mastiffs – are in service now with Ukraine.

Most armies also operate some form of lightly armoured or soft-skin (unarmoured) vehicles for reconnaissance or patrolling. The UK again is a good example, with the Supacat family of Jackal, Jackal 2 and now Jackal 3. A cross-country platform designed with no roof to improve situational awareness and with very little armour beyond hull armouring to counter mines and IEDs, the Jackal is a contentious vehicle. In its latest iteration, the Jackal 3 features armour and a windshield (surprisingly not a previous feature).

The Jackal family serves as a reconnaissance vehicle in the British Army, but critics argue that experience from Ukraine, namely the high proportion of casualties caused by indirect fire and drones, brings into question the wisdom of a vehicle without at least an armoured cabin. The Jackal and similar vehicles are not meant to operate in the direct fire zone – that's what tanks and MBTs are for – and the Jackal's speed and manoeuvrability is meant to keep them alive, but the range and responsiveness of modern artillery and UAVs might mean the end for such vehicles.

In less kinetic environments, such as counterterrorist or counterinsurgency operations, with likely a far reduced threat from indirect fire, the Jackal and similar vehicles can be upgraded with counter-IED and counter-UAV technologies and employed very effectively as patrol or reconnaissance platforms. British Jackals deployed with the Light Dragoons to Mali under Operation *Newcombe* and proved successful in conducting long-range reconnaissance operations.

ABOVE A British Army AJAX Ground Based Surveillance Reconnaissance and Strike Platform seen in 2017. The AJAX, a replacement for the Scimitar and Scorpion, was the cornerstone of the Army's Strike Brigade concept; however, the vehicle has had a lengthy and problematic development. (Photo by Finnbarr Webster/Getty Images)

LEFT Immobilized and abandoned Russian GAZ Tigr-M reconnaissance vehicles (note the prominent 'Z' invasion marking) after encountering stern Ukrainian resistance near Kharkiv in February 2022. (Photo by SERGEY BOBOK/AFP via Getty Images)

The US has adopted a light all-terrain-style platform called the infantry squad vehicle (ISV), which can transport a full nine-person infantry squad and is light enough to be carried under a Blackhawk or inside a Chinook. It features no armour or weapons, but its role is purely one of transport. The ISV gets the soldiers to where they are needed faster than their feet can carry them, and then the ISV is left behind – more a battle pushbike than a battle taxi. The USMC have found success with their Polaris Utility Task Vehicle and are replacing with a similar platform known as the Ultra-light Tactical Vehicle.

The Russians too deploy a light armoured vehicle – the GAZ Tigr, which has seen extensive use in Ukraine. The Tigr is more akin to the now retired Humvee – lightly armoured and mounting a machine gun or automatic grenade launcher. Russian forces use it to transport infantry forward and as a reconnaissance vehicle. Despite this, it has been pressed into service as an assault vehicle against Ukrainian positions to poor results.

The Ukrainians have employed US-donated Humvees in a similar role but to some notable success – the speed and mobility of the vehicle give it a tactical advantage in some circumstances, including what would otherwise be near-suicidal direct mounted assaults against Russian-held villages.

Insurgents have also increasingly employed their own form of light, armed transport – the technical. While the use of armed pickup trucks dates back decades (to include the famous 'Great Toyota War' in Chad in the 1980s), the phenomenon really came to prominence with the use of these so-called technicals by the Afghan Taliban and, later, Islamic State.

While the Taliban largely used unarmed pickups as troop transporters, they also mounted captured Soviet 14.5mm and 23mm anti-aircraft guns to the beds to provide organic fire support. The origin of the name 'technical' is debated although likely related to the 'technical' support payments provided by media and NGO teams to Somali militias to provide protection.

Islamic State's terrifying advance through Iraq in 2014 saw the insurgents mounted in long columns of often armed pickup trucks, festooned with Islamic State flags. Technicals served with Islamic State and many other insurgent groups in Syria with a bewildering array of heavy weapons mounted upon them, from 12.7mm heavy machine guns to rocket pods scavenged from Hind attack helicopters and even turrets recovered from destroyed BMP infantry fighting vehicles.

The insurgents also utilized a particularly terrifying variant of the technical – the VBIED, or vehicle-borne improvised explosive device. These were trucks (and occasionally armoured vehicles) modified to carry a large amount of explosive and to be driven into their target. Many featured homemade armour plating to defend against small arms. These VBIEDs, or more precisely SVBIEDs, with the 'S' prefix denoting 'suicide', were triggered by the driver or by remote control, which macabrely functioned as an insurance policy against the driver losing his zeal at the last minute.

An internet search will turn up numerous videos of Islamic State SVBIEDs being employed in Iraq and Syria; Coalition and Kurdish forces found that engaging them with Javelin and similar ATGMs proved most effective in non-urban environments. Consequently, the insurgents would try to move the SVBIEDs as close as possible to their target using a covered avenue of approach, negating line-of-sight weapons. In the tightly packed streets and alleyways of Mosul, for instance, SVBIEDs would appear with little warning (often with the driver directed on his route by a small commercial UAV flown overhead).

The Washington Institute, in their insightful study of Islamic State tactics, *Soldiers of End-Times*, noted, 'Coalition Forces cratered roads to block IS vehicles. These efforts reduced the effectiveness of SVBIEDs, though IS sometimes managed to penetrate barriers with its own up-armored bulldozers to make way for car bombs. Anticipating ISF advances, the jihadist group also concealed SVBIEDs in garages and launched them during clearing operations.'[20]

Hugo Kaaman, an analyst who has long studied VBIEDs and SVBIEDs, saw significant adaption by Islamic State to disguise their vehicle bombs:

> During the battle of Mosul, IS began using what I like to call 'camouflaged' SVBIEDs. The mounted armour on these overhauled vehicles would be painted in the same colour as the shell vehicle, and a later upgrade would see fake windshields, grilles and wheels painted in black added on top of the already painted armour. This was an attempt at emulating the characteristics of civilian vehicles while at the same time maintaining a considerable degree of armour on the vehicle.
>
> In turn, this was supposed to increase the reaction time of the Iraqi forces advancing in the city when they were met with the use of SVBIEDs, potentially allowing for the defending IS contingent to increase the success rate of such defensive attacks. (It should be noted that 'camouflaged' SVBIEDs were not the first environment specific SVBIED designs. Desert-coloured up-armoured SVBIEDs had already been used for some time in the open plains and desert areas of Northern Iraq.)[21]

Conventional forces are also looking at technicals, with the PLA and Russia both adopting domestic pickup designs. Western conventional forces are also examining integrating pickup trucks, particularly as a means of providing light, air transportable transport for infantry and airborne units. A number of Western analysts have called for the widespread adoption of the technical, complete with a number of RWS weapon options, and their use as ISR platforms carrying battlefield radars and sensor packages.

Ukraine has also seen the use of technicals in conventional warfighting. The technical has again emerged as a direct fire support platform used by both sides, and to facilitate Ukrainian anti-armour ambushes by providing a speedy and agile means to stalk Russian armour.

SOF increasingly employed their own technicals, particularly in Afghanistan and later in Africa, from the early 2000s. The primary reasons for their preference for the commercial trucks rather than Humvees was one of maintenance and profile. In terms of maintaining vehicles in remote conflict zones, operators stand a far greater chance of finding Toyota parts (or knockoffs) than they do of being able to access Humvee parts, which are often at the end of a long and complicated supply line.

Close-up of an Iraqi workshop up-armoured Humvee turret with a 12.7mm heavy machine gun and 7.62mm PK-type medium machine gun. (Photo by Feriq Ferec/Anadolu Agency/Getty Images)

The other big advantage of the technical is its profile. Blending in with local vehicles (and vehicle types used by the enemy) reduces the profile of the foreign operators. This assists from a counterinsurgency perspective (people are more likely to approach a Hilux than a hulking M-ATV or similar wheeled MRAP or armoured vehicle) and from a tactical perspective – a Hilux or Land Cruiser will raise much less suspicion as operators approach a target, for instance.

US special operations are sourcing the PB-NSCV, or Purpose Built Non-Standard Commercial Vehicle. The idea is to provide special operators with a vehicle that can be disguised as a common commercial type, such as the Toyota Hilux or Land Cruiser, by using a bolt-on kit. The PB-NSCV also offers the capability to mount a heavy weapon or RWS in the tray.

And what of the iconic Humvee? The HMMWV, or Humvee, proved entirely inadequate in terms of protection in Iraq, with non-armoured versions susceptible to even small-arms fire (notwithstanding a comparatively small number of M1114 armoured Humvees, which were rated against small arms and fragmentation).

In their insightful history of the history of the development of the MRAP, 'Of IEDs and MRAPs: Force Protection in Complex Irregular Operations', authors Andrew F. Krepinevich and Dakota L. Wood note: 'The first Humvee up-armoring kits arrived in Iraq on 27 October [2003]. They were designed to defeat RPGs and snipers, not IEDs.' By early 2007, 'there were 21,319 up-armored Humvees and even more add-on armor kits…'.[22] They add:

The only resistance to the up-armoring program from among troops came from their belief that speed itself might be effective protection and that every additional pound that lowered speed was dangerous. Unfortunately, they were largely wrong.

Additionally, the Humvee chassis and suspension and transmission could take only so much additional weight. Some of the additions made the vehicles top-heavy, and sometimes they rolled over when a roadside bomb exploded. As the Humvees became heavier, roll-overs became a worsening problem. This was not generally a matter of stability: roads often gave way because they could not take the weight of a vehicle.

That was particularly unfortunate when a stream or a drainage ditch bordered the side of a road, because when the edge of the road gave way, it could throw a vehicle into the water. Sometimes, the roll-over would damage the vehicle, preventing the doors from opening. Gunners needed restraints so that they would not simply be blown or thrown out.[23]

It was the impact of the IED (and to a lesser extent the RPG) that led directly to the development of the MRAP to largely replace the Humvee as a combat vehicle:

The enemy responded to Humvee and other up-armoring with two new types of IED, under-body mines (which attacked the unprotected underbody of a vehicle) and EFPs. Both completely overmatched existing add-on side protection. A belly mine destroyed a vehicle with an underbody blast.

It was relatively easy to fashion, and MRAP vehicles were initially designed specifically to defeat this threat. Anything larger or different from a first-generation IED (such as an under-body IED) required far more effort on the enemy's part. The larger the mine required, the more difficult to assemble, transport, and emplace it – the greater the vulnerability associated with using IEDs.

A workshop up-armoured Humvee operated by Iraqi aligned forces outside Mosul in 2017. (Photo by AHMAD AL-RUBAYE/AFP via Getty Images)

An American Oshkosh M-ATV MRAP serving with the USMC in Afghanistan in 2011. Note the litter (stretcher) on the hood and counter-IED AN/VLQ-12 CREW DUKE jammers. (ADEK BERRY/AFP via Getty Images)

For that reason, the enemy was careful to use just enough to kill those in a vehicle, for example, a Humvee. Simply replacing Humvees with first-generation MRAP vehicles increased the required explosive by a factor of ten, and that was just to damage the vehicle. The two new threats were concentrated in different places.

EFPs proved more a threat to the Army in Baghdad (mainly in Sadr City) and to the British in Basra than to the Marines in Anbar province. That was because they had to be emplaced in built-up areas and also because bottom-attack IEDs and mines were more difficult to emplace in paved streets. Conversely, the under-bottom IEDs were initially concentrated in Anbar province where there were few paved roads. The MRAP program grew out of the Marines' experience of under-body IEDs in Anbar, and later expanded to deal with the threat that the Army initially faced.[24]

The countermeasures used against EFPs were ingenious. To counter the EFP threat, a specific add-on armour package was developed and fielded, in May 2009 – the MRAP Expedient Armor Protection, or MEAP, comprising a classified substance nicknamed 'peanut butter':

EFP protection required a mass of 'peanut butter': it took about 8,000 to 12,000 pounds of armor to provide a reasonable level of protection. Protection was typically in the form of 'effector boxes' – hollow boxes filled with material that absorbed the EFP blast.

They were hung 6-to-12 inches outboard of the truck, the thickness depending on the 'recipe' inside the hollow boxes. These effector boxes were proven to be quite effective against the threat, but the extra weight imposed a requirement to 'beef up' other truck components, such as the power train, transmission, and suspension.[25]

The Humvee has been at least partly retired, at least from frontline service with the US Army and Marine Corps. Many still serve as transport vehicles for non-combat arms, but the Humvee was largely superseded by the MRAP, and later the JLTV, for duties anywhere near the battlespace. The JLTV has greater cross-country ability and is more heavily armoured; it can also be equipped with a wide range of weapons systems, including Javelin mounts and counter-UAV systems.

What will the future hold for armoured vehicles? We'll see the age-old wheels-versus-tracks argument continue apace but with a realization that terrain means everything. There will be an integration of drones and perhaps even uncrewed ground vehicles along with the almost mandatory counter-UAV systems – likely a jammer on every vehicle, although 30–35mm cannon will also be widely adopted.

Some form of top-cover protection against UAV-dropped munitions and artillery fragments will likely become more common for previously open-top vehicles (see the Russian Typhoon armoured truck as a potential example of how to cheaply move troops up to the forward edge of battle). And even the lowliest 'combat golf cart' will be digitized and interconnected with battle management systems.

The Ukrainian Kozak (Cossack) 2 MRAP pictured in 2022. The Kozak is a domestically produced platform by PJSC RPA 'Practika' that can carry five soldiers and is typically armed, as here, with a 12.7mm NSV heavy machine gun. Note the strategically placed body armour plate carrier draped across one of the ballistic glass windows, perhaps to reinforce the glass. (Photo by MIGUEL MEDINA/AFP via Getty Images)

CHAPTER THREE

GROUND-BASED AIR DEFENCE AND CLOSE AIR SUPPORT

'Air defense isn't going to win the war for you, but the lack of it could lose it pretty quick.'

Tom Karako,
Center for Strategic and International Studies,
2023 Stimson Center streaming seminar,
'Ukraine and the Future of Air Warfare[1]'

Since the dawn of aviation, aircraft have been used in warfare, and from the first instances of aircraft attempting to bomb or strafe ground targets, their opponents have attempted to shoot them down. In this chapter, we will consider these two intimately interlinked topics – both air defence in the broader context of modern land warfare, and close air support (CAS) attack aircraft being employed to support troops on the ground in contact with the enemy or in preplanned attacks on enemy elements or defences.

ABOVE Ukrainian gunners fire a 23mm ZU-23-2 twin-barrel cannon at Russian aerial targets. The ZU-23-2 has been mounted on an MT-LB tracked carrier. (Photo by ANATOLII STEPANOV/ AFP via Getty Images)

AIR DEFENCE

World War II saw the invention of what the wartime German Army called the Flakpanzer and what post-war armies would term, with possibly the most unwieldy acronym ever coined, the SPAAG, or self-propelled anti-aircraft gun – essentially a mobile anti-aircraft gun for shooting down enemy aircraft.

These SPAAGs (or 'flak wagons', as sometimes colloquially known) mounted cannon, and often multiple cannon, on the tracked chassis of various AFVs. Thus, they could maintain speed alongside advancing mechanized units while providing a mobile air defence umbrella guarding against enemy airstrikes (the nature of the weapon system also meant they could be decidedly useful against enemy infantry, particularly those caught in the open; see, for instance, the quad .50 calibre used by the US Army).

The development of the surface-to-air missile (SAM) supplemented and then largely replaced the SPAAG in most NATO armies, including the US and UK. Russia and China, along with then West Germany and a scattering of European nations, were the outliers and persevered with the SPAAG concept, employing both mobile tracked and wheeled SAMs and SPAAGs for the majority of the Cold War. As we will learn when analysing recent events in Ukraine, these armies made the right call with their mix of guns and missiles.

A Russian Buk (Viking) M2 (SA-17 Grizzly) medium-range surface-to-air missile platform. Ukrainian Buks, after engineering changes, are now able to fire the Raytheon RIM-7 Sea Sparrow missiles provided by the US (the Sea Sparrow is normally used by maritime SAM systems on warships). (Photo by Andrey Rudakov/ Bloomberg via Getty Images)

The iconic Russian ZSU-23-4 Shilka anti-aircraft platform, seen here in Iraqi service in 1991. The Shilka demonstrated Russia's early commitment to a SHORAD platform (it replaced the twin-barrelled ZSU-57-2 SPAAG). (Photo © CORBIS via Getty Images)

The two weapon systems provided an integrated capability, the SAMs providing a much longer-ranged response to intercept enemy air activity while the SPAAGs were tasked with dealing with closer-ranged threats, such as pesky enemy attack helicopters popping up unexpectedly from behind a nearby tree line.

Following the Russian lead, most Middle Eastern armies also deployed a mix of gun and missile systems (the majority being Russian client states to a greater or lesser degree) as did the Israelis. The tracked SA-6 Gainful (2K12 Kub) SAM launcher employed by both Egypt and Syria proved to be a success against Israeli aircraft during the 1973 Yom Kippur War, as did the now venerable ZSU-23-4 Shilka and the older ZSU-57-2 flak wagons. Israeli pilots would adopt low-flying tactics to avoid the SA-6, only to be engaged by the Shilka and its radar-slewed quad 23mm cannon or the formidable 57mm guns of the ZSU-57-2.

Today's armies are very rapidly returning to a mixture of gun and missile systems, with some platforms incorporating both. As we shall see, much of the renewed interest in air defence has been driven by unmanned aerial vehicles (UAVs) and their use in recent conflicts in Europe and the Caucasus.

While we will primarily concern ourselves here with the air defence platforms encountered at the tip of the spear in land warfare (those that provide air defence cover for frontline forces), it is useful to understand that air defence involves much more than just the SAMs and flak wagons throwing up the protective umbrella over armoured or infantry units.

Air defence is actually composed of two separate but interrelated disciplines: active air defence and passive air defence. Active is the identification, targeting and interdiction of enemy aerial threats (including not just aircraft but cruise and ballistic missiles) by a range of means, including interception by aircraft and unmanned aerial systems; by electronic and cyber warfare; and by ground-based air defence.

Passive air defence is anything that reduces the likelihood and effectiveness of enemy air activity. This includes:

- traditional physical camouflage of ground targets;
- deception (employing fake vehicles – for instance, the famous inflatable Sherman tanks used during the D-Day build-up or the fake radars built by the Armed Forces of Ukraine);
- mobility (making targets harder to strike by keeping them moving);
- ensuring dispersion of likely targets (to reduce the potential impact of a successful strike);
- and, increasingly, the minimization of the electronic signature of friendly units (which can be tracked and used to develop a target for an airstrike or cruise missile attack).

The Center for Strategic and Budgetary Assessments, in their 'Integrated Air and Missile Defense: Early Lessons From The Russia-Ukraine War' report, identified passive measures as a key learning from the Russo-Ukrainian conflict. Indeed, 'Protection of IAMD assets (e.g., S-300s, PAC-3s, THAADs) should include passive defenses measures, such as hardened shelters and Camouflage, Concealment and Deception (CCD); active defenses, including counter-UAS and cruise missile defense; left of launch counter-offensive capabilities; and retaliatory strike capabilities against enemy launchers.'[2]

Active and passive measures come together in what is generally termed an integrated air defence network (IADN), one that brings together battlefield sensors and radars, air defence weapons systems, and both fire control and command and control nodes. Modern integrated air defence networks target not only enemy aircraft and UAVs but all aerial threats, including indirect fire, be that mortars, rockets or conventional artillery.

NATO's Integrated Air and Missile Defence (IAMD), for instance, notes the following as taskings: 'air defence; ballistic missile defence; cruise missile defence; counter rockets, mortar and artillery; or counter unmanned aircraft systems'.[3]

Within such an integrated air defence network, a range of kinetic (the buzzword for engaging the enemy with direct or indirect fires) air defence systems will be employed with specific but often overlapping responsibilities. Traditionally, these were defined as area defence, point defence and self-defence.

NEXT PAGES The FIM-92 Stinger man-portable air-defence system (MANPADS) in Ukrainian hands. The Stinger provided much of the SHORAD capability until Gepards entered service. The Stinger is infrared homing and reports indicate that Russian aircraft using flares as countermeasures have defeated the missile in some instances. (Photo by Pierre Crom/Getty Images)

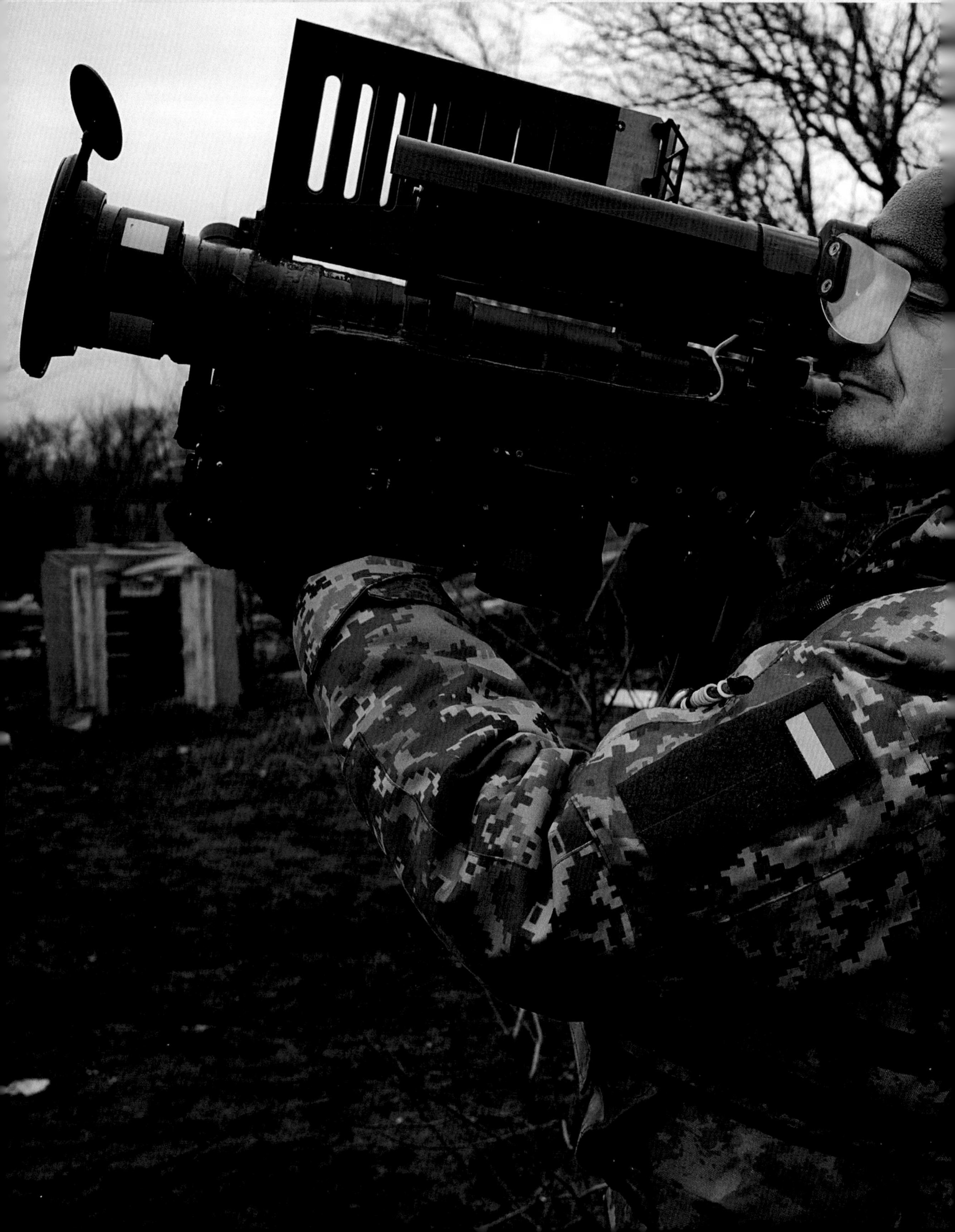

The C-RAM stationed at Joint Base Balad, Iraq, in 2010. The C-RAM provides point defence against indirect fire, missiles and drones, firing a 20mm HEIT-SD (High Explosive Incendiary Tracer, Self-Destruct) projectile at a cyclic rate of up to 4,500 rounds per minute. (US Air Force photo by Senior Airman Brittany Bateman, DVIDS)

Area defence is, as the name implies, a system typically composed of medium to high-altitude SAMs, with their attendant radars and fire control, that provides umbrella coverage over a larger area. Area defence is designed to intercept enemy airstrikes, ISR platforms, including larger surveillance UAVs, and cruise or ballistic missiles.

Point defence, conversely, is the direct protection of units or facilities and is typically relatively short ranged in comparison to area defence systems. Point defence AD (Air Defence) includes mobile short-range air defence (SHORAD) tracked or wheeled vehicles, and man-portable air-defence systems (MANPADS), such as the famous Stinger deployed by specialist air defence units.

Point defence also encompasses fixed or semi-fixed capabilities installed at forward operating locations, such as the counter-rocket, artillery, mortar (C-RAM) Phalanx system (the R2D2-like turret features the fearsome M61A1 20mm Gatling gun, which has been deployed to protect US sites in Iraq and Syria against indirect fire attacks by Islamic State and Iranian-backed militias).

Self-defence AD denotes those systems that are organic to a unit, which may be employed against enemy air threats; these may include mounted machine guns, MANPADS carried by an infantry unit, and increasingly more high-tech capabilities including counter-UAV attack UAVs and Ghostbuster-like electronic guns designed to down UAVs by jamming their signals.

As an example of this integrated, tiered approach, the US employs the Forward Area Air Defense Command, Control, Communications and Intelligence (FAAD C3I) system, a mouthful of an acronym that brings together a wide range of sensor data to form an air defence picture that, in theory, should allow for the identification of all enemy aerial threats before cueing ground-based air defence platforms to engage these threats.

FAAD C3I integrates the Patriot PAC-3 short- to medium-range SAM with a range of some 40km, the Terminal High Altitude Area Defense (THAAD) SAM with a classified but estimated range of 200km, and SHORAD gun and missile platforms. Both the PAC-3 and the THAAD are so-called 'kinetic kill' missiles, meaning they directly impact the incoming aerial threat (the earlier PAC-2 Patriot was equipped with a proximity fuse that exploded the SAM in the general vicinity of the target; this sometimes resulted in only knocking the incoming missile off-course rather than destroying it).

The more recent THAAD is designed for medium- to long-range engagements and is optimized to interdict ballistic missiles. The US military says THAAD provides it 'with a globally-transportable, rapidly-deployable capability to intercept and destroy ballistic missiles inside or outside the atmosphere during their final, or terminal, phase of flight.'[4]

The iconic PAC-3 Patriot surface-to-air missile, the latest version of which – the Missile Segment Enhancement – has a 35km engagement range and can strike targets up to an altitude of 40km. (Photo by Jaap Arriens/NurPhoto via Getty Images)

ABOVE The notorious S-400 Triumf (Triumph) (SA-21 Growler) is a Russian long-range (400km), high-altitude (48km) surface-to-air missile system that has been effective in Ukraine in downing aircraft and missiles but has itself been successfully targeted by Neptune anti-ship missiles modified for land use, ATACMS, and loitering munitions. (Photo by ANDREY SMIRNOV/AFP via Getty Images)

ABOVE RIGHT Gunners from Ukraine's 93rd Brigade firing a 9K35 Strela-10 (SA-13 Gopher) SAM against a Russian drone. The Strela-10 is yet another MT-LB based platform – the workhorse of Russia and Russian client states. (Photo by Ed Ram for *The Washington Post* via Getty Images)

Other NATO systems compete with Patriot; the most well known, and now combat proven in Ukraine, is the National Advanced Surface-to-Air Missile System or NASAMS. NASAMS uniquely employs conventional air-to-air missiles typically found on NATO combat aircraft rather than a dedicated SAM warhead, vastly simplifying the supply chain. These missiles include the advanced medium-range air-to-air missile (AMRAAM), the advanced medium-range air-to-air missile extended range (AMRAAM-ER), and the venerable AIM-9X Sidewinder.

Russia splits responsibility for ground-based air defence across its Space Forces (for intercontinental ballistic missile defence), Aerospace Forces (VKS) (for homeland defence), and Land Forces Air Defence (for defence of deployed ground forces, for instance in Syria or Ukraine). Land Forces Air Defence focuses on the 'defeat of enemy aviation, missiles and unmanned aerial vehicles... to deny enemy air reconnaissance, deter enemy air strikes and prevent or interdict enemy air assaults'.[5]

Long-range SAM capability is provided by S-300, S-350E, S-400 and S-500 high-altitude SAMs. The short- to medium-range band is managed by the Tor-M2E and SA-13 Gopher/Strela-10 tracked SAM systems.

Unlike the US and most NATO nations, however, as previously noted Russia never gave up on gun-based SPAAGs. Instead, the Russians today field three primary types: the legacy ZSU-23-4 Shilka 23mm SPAAG, the 2S6 Tunguska self-propelled anti-aircraft gun and missile (SPAAGM) (the Tunguska is rumoured to be due for replacement by a new vehicle equipped with a 57mm cannon), and the wheeled, truck-based, Pantsir S-1 (SA-22 Greyhound) SPAAGM. Local tactical ground-based air defence (GBAD) is provided by SA-24 and SA-25 Igla and Verba handheld MANPADS.

The Russian Pantsir-S-1 (aka SA-22 Greyhound) anti-aircraft vehicle mounts a pair of radar-controlled dual 30mm autocannon and carries two six-pack SAM launchers. (Photo by Andrey Rudakov/Bloomberg via Getty Images)

In many ways, Russian GBAD is superior to NATO, if not in terms of absolute technical sophistication then certainly in numbers and density. Unlike the West, GBAD has always been seen as an essential component of Russian manoeuvre warfare doctrine. While initially assessed as less than optimal in the early months of the Russo-Ukrainian War, Russian GBAD has improved over the course of the war.

GBAD systems were linked into a network of air defence fire control radars, creating an integrated air defence capability that has successfully engaged all manner of aerial threats, including Ukrainian Guided Multiple Launch Rocket System (GMLRS) rockets and HARMs (High-speed Anti-Radiation Missiles) launched by Ukrainian aircraft against Russian radars.

Indeed, General James Hecke, commander of the United States Air Force in Europe, commented on the efficiencies of both Ukrainian and Russian IAMDs: 'The problem is both of the Russian as well as the Ukrainian success in integrated air and missile defense have made much of those aircraft worthless. They're not doing a whole lot because they can't go over and do close air support.'[6]

The Russian 2S6 Tunguska replaced the ZSU-23-4 Shilka in Russian service and has had some export success. Ukraine also operates a small number. This is a destroyed Tunguska in Russian service. Note the 'Z' invasion markings. (Photo by SERGEY BOBOK/AFP via Getty Images)

Conversely, Russian supplied systems – including the S-300 and S-400 – have seemingly had little to no impact on Israeli Air Force strikes on Syrian targets. This is likely due to Israeli Air Force strikes being conducted under a heavy and effective electronic warfare umbrella, jamming their radars and fire control systems.

Syrian air defence has since been promised an upgrade in the form of Iranian Khordad-15 air defence systems, although whether this will result in any marked improvement remains to be seen. The Israeli Air Force is a good example of the capabilities of a modern Tier One air force against a Tier Two air defence network: the Israelis can conduct successful strikes against ground targets in Syria, even in heavy air defence environments, with relative impunity.

From the strategic to the tactical, we return to frontline GBAD and specifically SHORAD. To provide an air defence umbrella over often fast-moving ground units has always proved challenging. Such mobile GBAD platforms need to be able to reliably keep up with the speed of AFVs (some of which can barrel along at 50 kilometres per hour) to maintain the umbrella while also proving resilient enough to provide a reasonable level of crew protection.

As we have seen during the Russo-Ukrainian War, GBAD vehicles accompanying advancing forces need to be at least armoured enough to survive hits from small arms and fragmentation from enemy mortars and artillery. The threat of mines can also not be discounted (note the debilitating effect of Russian minefields on Ukraine's 2023 counteroffensive).

Ukrainian forces have been faced with the dilemma of ensuring local air defence cover while attempting to husband and protect their precious few air defence platforms. By accompanying advancing forces, the GBAD is put at significant risk, but to not do so leaves friendly units with limited or no air defence umbrella, allowing an opponent the opportunity to utilize fast or rotary air attack assets.

The answer to this dilemma is a robust SHORAD platform that can engage the most likely enemy aerial threats while manoeuvring, under armour, alongside friendly mechanized forces. Like all armoured vehicles, compromises must be made; for example, armour that is too heavy slows the vehicle; too light and the vehicle can be easily immobilized.

The US military's post-war history of attempting to develop a credible SHORAD system that could accompany mechanized units has been a tale of false starts and institutional apathy. A tracked SPAAG called the Sergeant York was built in the 1970s but failed to be adopted after exhibiting embarrassingly poor accuracy, a radar that often failed to differentiate between ground clutter and aerial targets, and an aversion to water that infamously affected its electronics. After massive cost overruns (another depressingly common factor in US Army procurements), Sergeant York was cancelled in 1985.

NEXT PAGES An AN/TWQ-1 Avenger Air Defense System donated by the US to Ukraine. The Avenger offers a .50cal heavy machine gun and a multi-launch Stinger system. Despite its lack of armour, the Avenger has been effective at protecting key points against Shahed and similar attack drones. (Photo by Kostya Liberov/Libkos/Getty Images)

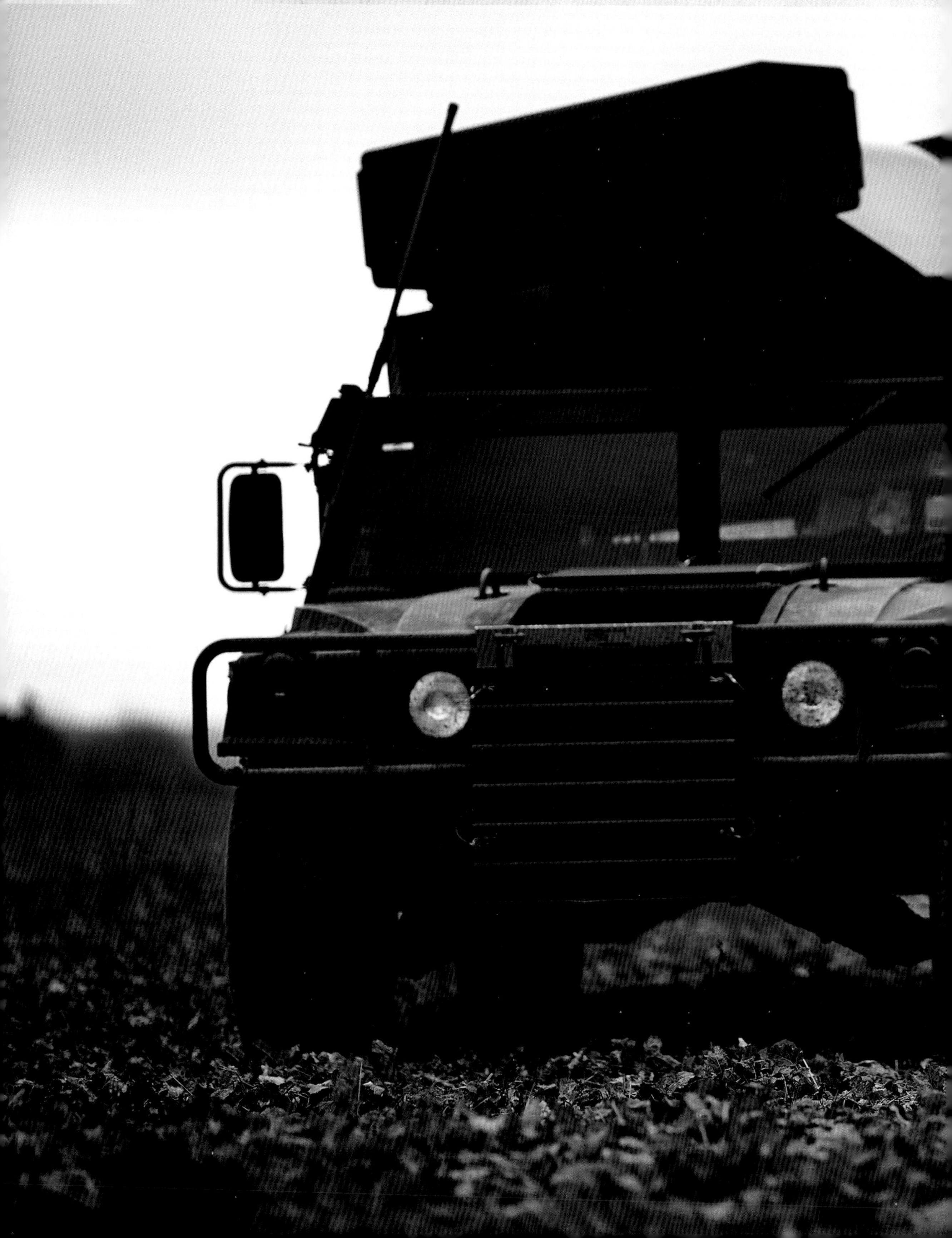

A number of largely ad hoc SHORAD platforms were developed to fill the gap left by the failed Sergeant York programme. Until the early 1990s, the Army relied upon the legacy M113-based M163, which bolted a six-barrel 20mm Vulcan cannon and radar to the top of the venerable APC.

As we have noted elsewhere, the Israelis effectively employed the M163 against Syrian helicopters and aircraft and proved useful in engaging militia RPG teams hiding in multi-floor buildings during the urban fighting of Operation *Peace for Galilee*. In fact, the IDF still employs an upgraded version of the M163, which is now paired with an integrated Stinger launcher.

The US Army also created the Avenger – a Humvee-based design that incorporated a brace of Stingers in two four-shot pods and a .50cal machine gun slaved to a AN/MPQ-64 Sentinel radar. The Avenger was first deployed operationally in Operation *Desert Storm* and later in Afghanistan and Iraq, although the Avenger was employed as a force protection platform, escorting logistics convoys due to the lack of an aerial threat (a number of Avengers were modified for service in Iraq by the removal of one of the Stinger pods to allow the .50cal to be fired over the cab of the Avenger).

A third platform, the M6 Linebacker, was a conversion to the Bradley IFV (infantry fighting vehicle), replacing the TOW 2 ATGMs (anti-tank guided missiles) with Stingers. FAAD C3I provided the targeting data to slew the Linebacker onto aerial targets. The vehicle was again short-lived, however, and the M6s were converted back to regular Bradleys during the Iraq War.

The Modern War Institute noted the malaise around GBAD platforms as the Army focused on counterinsurgency and counterterrorism efforts following 9/11: 'Stinger procurement dwindled to 139 units delivered by 2005 and no contracts awarded after. Army SHORAD by 2014 was, for all intents and purposes, extinct.'[7] Indeed, during much of the first two decades of the 2000s, GBAD was ignored by the US Army, with the Avengers relegated to National Guard units and little mention of SHORAD in the relevant field manuals.

It was not until the general organizational realignment towards Great Power Competition – the return to a state of a Cold War between the major powers marked by proxy warfare and economic and political coercion – late in the 2010s that the Army began to identify GBAD and by extension SHORAD as a key capability in a peer/near-peer fight with China or Russia. Following the invasion of Ukraine, the US shipped Avenger to Ukrainian forces to improve their GBAD capabilities.

The downside to the provision of Avenger to Ukraine was its relative fragility. The US Army notes, 'Avenger systems should not be integrated into the maneuver force when contact is expected because it is a lightweight vehicle and is extremely vulnerable to direct fire, small arms and indirect fire.'[8] In Ukraine, the Avenger is obviously particularly susceptible to Russian artillery fires.

The US Army has commenced an aggressive programme to fill this capability gap with the M-SHORAD Stryker-based platform already in service with Stryker Battalion Combat Teams in Europe.

The Army has also introduced a 20-kW-class laser system mounted on the ISV – an all-terrain-vehicle-based design intended to provide rapid movement for non-mechanized infantry units, with the Army declaring, 'The primary mission will be defending tactical army units from UAS and manned helicopters, as well as incorporating a counter rocket, artillery and mortar (C-RAM) capability.'[9]

The latest platform being introduced into service, again with European-based US Army units, is the Directed Energy Maneuver Short-Range Air Defense (DE M-SHORAD), another Stryker-based platform mounting a far more powerful HEL (high-energy laser) 50-kW-class laser intended to target all UAV types along with incoming rockets, artillery and even mortar rounds.

The US Army has noted, 'The unique design of the DE M-SHORAD leverages the Stryker's gas-powered engine to energize its batteries, cooling system, and laser. The self-contained system has enough electricity to address multiple threats at a time before needing a period to recharge…'[10]

A US Army M-SHORAD Stryker equipped with Stinger surface-to-air missiles and a 30mm cannon. The M-SHORAD has replaced the Humvee-based Avenger. (US Army photo by Specialist Andrew Simeri)

An early developmental platform using the Mobile Expeditionary High Energy Laser (MEHEL) Directed Energy SHORAD mounted on a Stryker. (Photo by Monica K. Guthrie, DVIDS)

M-SHORAD will be eventually deployed in three batteries of a dozen M-SHORADs each. These batteries can then be chopped out and attached to the Armored Brigade Combat Teams, while the divisional artillery will have their own integral M-SHORADs and counter-UAV battery. They will also have an organic Indirect Fire Protection Capability (IFPC) battery using an as yet unknown system, such as the Israeli Iron Dome, which has been adopted by the US Army as the interim platform.

A number of fixed and semi-fixed base defence systems are also on the books, including both laser and microwave-based systems. The Indirect Fire Protection Capability – High Energy Laser (IFPC-HEL) is a 300-kW laser intended to be mounted on an 8x8 truck such as the US Army's HEMMT; the likely range of the IFPC-HEL remains classified, but it appears to be designed to provide a protective umbrella over a battalion or similar grouping.

According to the US Army, the Indirect Fire Protection Capability – High Power Microwave (IFPC-HPM) will provide 'much needed protection against adversarial UAV swarms capable of targeting and overwhelming U.S. and allied air defense systems.'[11] The microwave attacks UAVs in a wide arc by frying their electronics and will be deployed in concert with lasers, with the HPM employed against swarms and the HEL taking out individual command and control or ISR UAVs.

A further system, the Directed Energy Counter-small Unmanned Aircraft System (DE C-sUAV) Palletized High Energy Laser (P-HEL) will be tested with both 10- and 20-kW lasers and will offer a palletized, 'straight off the C-130' rapid deployment base defence capability against Group 1 and 2 UAVs.

These systems seem squarely aimed at countering future Russian tactics. In 2023, Russia employed the tactic of deploying large numbers of relatively inexpensive UAVs to deplete the reserves of Ukrainian GBAD missiles and ammunition. The *Washington Post* has reported that 'Ukrainian officials have said one Russian strategy is to attempt to exhaust air defense systems by saturating the sky with targets, some of which are decoys meant to confuse the interceptor, allowing the real missile to slip through.'[12]

Industry journal *European Security & Defence* expanded on these tactics and considered the possible impact on a future peer war involving the US:

> High-end air- and missile-defence systems such as Patriot are capable of intercepting UAVs. However, except for neutralizing large, high-altitude or very fast unmanned aircraft, they are rarely the optimal choice.
>
> Small, low- and slow-flying drones are difficult for high-end systems to locate and impact. As for medium-sized UAVs, there is a significant risk that an adversary would saturate the airspace with comparatively cheap drones in hopes that US forces would expend their stock of expensive air-defence missiles, leaving batteries depleted and ill-equipped to combat follow-on waves of cruise missiles or manned tactical aircraft.[13]

This is where SPAAG platforms come into their own; the German Flakpanzer Gepard with its twin 35mm cannon has proven an unlikely star in the conflict against the drones. Retired by the German Army in 2010, the Gepard was designed to counter Russian SU-25 strike aircraft and Hind attack helicopters in a Cold War Gone Hot scenario that never happened.

Instead, the ageing SPAAG has found a new lease of life engaging Russian UAVs. The advantages of the Gepard are its respectable detection range (its radars can track targets out to more than 14km distant) and its devastating 35mm twin cannon, along with its cost effectiveness (it is far, far cheaper in dollar terms to destroy a UAV with a 35mm cannon than a Patriot). It has proven particularly deadly against the Iranian-produced and supplied Shahed-136 UAVs and Russian domestically produced copies.

The problem of countering UAVs has become a constant source of discussion and lively debate by military think-tanks and defence contractors, with both the Russo-Ukrainian War and the Nagorno-Karabakh War bringing the problem into increasingly sharp focus.

An analyst with industry website *Real Clear Defense* placed the near-future UAV threat into perspective (and consider this was written before the Ukraine invasion!):

One prominent Washington think tank described the challenge facing the U.S. military as that of 'a drone saturated future'. More than 30 nations have either fielded armed drones or are developing them. Armed UAS, including so-called suicide drones, have figured prominently in Libya, Syria, the Caucasus, and Yemen. Non-state actors, such as the Islamic State, Boko Haram, Hezbollah, and the Palestinian Islamic Jihad, have employed various UAS to collect intelligence and attack soft targets. In 2018 defectors from the Venezuelan military even attempted to assassinate the country's authoritarian president, Nicolás Maduro, with explosive-laden, Chinese-made, commercially available drones.[14]

A number of venerable institutions have opined on the current and emerging threat posed by UAVs and the difficulties countering them. The Modern War Institute reported:

Small and micro-UAVs are a different challenge. These give too little of a reflective cross section to be easily picked up at a distance by tactical air defense radars and are too small and cool to be easily targeted by MANPADS. Their signature is so small that even modern dual-detector heat/ultraviolet-tracking seekers specifically designed for low-profile aircraft have difficulty tracking them.[15]

The DroneGun Tactical by Australian firm DroneShield in use in Ukraine. A directional handheld counter-UAV device, it jams the connection between drone pilot and drone, either sending the drone back to its base station or crashing it. (Photo by Ukrinform/NurPhoto via Getty Images)

RUSI agreed:

> Low-flying targets, particularly UAVs, are a challenge for air defenses for a number of reasons. They typically have low cross sections, are difficult for radar to distinguish from stationary clutter, and can travel on a number of

To counteract this explosion in UAVs, and along with dedicated SHORAD platforms, several mobile counter-UAV platforms are in operational use, with many companies rushing to develop their own offerings. L3Harris for instance offers the VAMPIRE, which has been adopted by the US Army. It 'consists of a four-cell 70mm rocket launcher and the WESCAM MX-10 stabilised infrared sighting system. The firm plans to further upgrade the weapon system by adding a radar'.[17]

The 70mm launcher uses the APKWS (Advanced Precision Kill Weapon System). The VAMPIRE can be mounted on virtually any light vehicle, making it ideal for motorized infantry or special operations. It has been deployed operationally in Syria with US SOF.

The US Army has also adopted the LIDS (Low, Slow, Small UAS Integrated Defeat System), which uses a radar-guided Coyote UAV (which operates in a similar way to a short-ranged SAM) to intercept the target. LIDS 'provides both kinetic and non-kinetic options to neutralise individual armed and reconnaissance drones up to Group 3 UAV as well as UAV swarms. The system's operational debut came in January 2023 when Coyotes downed two attack drones targeting a US outpost in south-eastern Syria.'[18]

A Syrian militia Land Cruiser technical engaging Syrian Air Force helicopters conducting barrel bombing. The weapon is the widely employed 14.5mm ZPU-2, which has proven effective in engaging drones like the Shahed 136 in Ukraine. (Photo by KARAM AL-MASRI/AFP via Getty Images)

In January 2022, the M-LIDS (Mobile – Low, Slow, Small UAS Integrated Defeat System) also entered operational service with the US Army, and illustrates the kind of rapidly developed and fielded counter-UAV platforms that will be increasingly commonplace. M-LIDS is a pair of JLTVs equipped with sensors, electronic warfare systems, the Coyote killer UAV, a 30mm cannon and an M134 minigun, which operate together to identify, track and engage UAVs.

One vehicle identifies and tracks the target, transmitting the data to the second vehicle, which engages the enemy UAV through either kinetic (gun) or non-kinetic (electronic warfare) means. The Army aims to incorporate both the sensors and the weapons onto a single vehicle platform, most likely a Stryker, as part of a phase three development of the M-LIDS programme.

US Army M-ATV mounted M-LIDS Kinetic Defeat Vehicle. The system uses two vehicles; this one is equipped with an XM914 30mm cannon and Coyote laser-guided rockets. Both vehicles are being integrated onto a single Stryker platform as of 2024. (Captain Austin May, US Army, DVIDS)

The other half of the M-LIDS equation – the Electronic Warfare Vehicle – which mounts radar and other sensors to slave the weapons of the Kinetic Defeat Vehicle against opposing drones. (US Army photo by Specialist Damian Mioduszewski)

As counter-UAV tactics and technologies mature, electronic warfare will continue to be the primary means of UAV defeat – scrambling, jamming, or causing enemy drones to crash or self-destruct. Following the experiences in Ukraine and Syria, counter-UAV will see a massive return to radar-controlled 30mm and larger autocannon loaded with proximity-fused rounds as the most economical and efficient way to engage swarms of lower-altitude UAVs.

Standalone UGV platforms dedicated purely to intercepting UAVs and attack helicopters would seem to be an obvious near-term solution to providing a protective umbrella for a combat unit. Dependent on what sensors are employed, these may also be able to provide protection against indirect fire from artillery, rockets and mortars (C-RAM).

What will also become common in the immediate term will be a proliferation of local counter-UAV systems on most tactical vehicles, along with technologies to allow infantry to intercept enemy UAVs, including Drone Buster guns or interceptor UAVs like the Coyote. In a similar fashion to the widespread adoption of tactical electronic countermeasures (ECM) to combat IEDs in Iraq and Afghanistan, counter-UAV electronics will become a common feature on everything from light vehicles to main battle tanks.

NATO armies will likely quickly adopt turrets, such as the Rheinmetall Skyranger, which mates either a 30mm or 35mm cannon, both capable of firing advanced airburst ammunition, with a suite of sensors that employs AI algorithms to classify and track aerial targets. Both turrets can be mounted on suitable IFVs or even 6x6 trucks. The latest variant, the Skyranger HEL, combines the cannon with both missiles and a laser.

CLOSE AIR SUPPORT

While UAVs garner most of the recent column inches by defence analysts, countering traditional aerial threats also remains a priority. The Russo-Ukrainian War has highlighted the challenges of employing attack helicopters and ground attack aircraft in a near-peer conflict, with large numbers of GBAD platforms making the airspace over Ukraine a very challenging environment for both manned and unmanned platforms.

Close air support (CAS) is doctrinally defined as 'air action by fixed-wing and rotary-wing aircraft against hostile targets that are in close proximity to friendly forces and requires detailed integration of each air mission with the fire and movement of those forces'.[19] This differs from a range of other air missions, including deep strikes against enemy facilities or troop concentrations, and ISR (intelligence, surveillance and reconnaissance).

This is an important distinction. CAS is the tactical application of air power to support ground units during a TiC, or troops in contact, event. Deep strike is similar to the artillery concept of deep fires – striking more strategic targets well to the enemy's rear. ISR is the 'eye in the sky' – manned or unmanned platforms (including satellites) that provide real-time intelligence.

CAS is also divided into two types: generically preplanned and on-demand. The former is tasked with supporting specific ground actions – breaking through an enemy line of defence, for example, or flying top cover for a convoy. On-demand is the classic TiC – ground forces are in contact with the enemy and require immediate and timely air support to win the fight or extricate from the contact.

To conduct any of these types of air missions, some level of control of the skies is required. This level of control is described by several terms on a sliding scale. Parity is the lowest, where the air environment is actively contested by both parties, giving neither side an advantage; in the doctrine it is 'a condition in which no forces has control of the air'.[20] Air operations can still be conducted under air parity but with an increased likelihood of losses. At the time of writing (2024), the Russo-Ukrainian War is a good example of air parity.

Air parity in the skies over Ukraine has been one of the key reasons that the counteroffensive started in June 2023 has been particularly challenging – in similar operations, the attacker can normally rely upon a massive level of air support, conducting both preplanned CAS against tactical targets and deep strikes to target command and control or artillery batteries.

Without air support, offensive operations against static defensive lines (called defence in depth because of the multiple lines of trenches and fields of mines and anti-tank obstacles) become very resource heavy, with attendant high casualties.

The next level up from air parity is air superiority, which may be localized or broad and denotes a situation where one side can conduct air operations 'without prohibitive interference'[21] by the enemy. Finally, there is air supremacy, which denotes a situation where the enemy is effectively negated from conducting effective air operations. An example of air supremacy would be Coalition operations in Afghanistan following the initial air campaign in October 2001– the Taliban air defences and air force were destroyed in place.

For many years, NATO and US planning has assumed air superiority if not supremacy thanks to the might of the US Air Force; however, in a future peer conflict against China or even a resurgent Russia, air superiority will be far from guaranteed. In a war over Taiwan, for instance, the People's Liberation Army Navy will make the skies a very unfriendly place indeed.

Thus, in any near-future peer or near-peer conflict, close air support for ground combat elements will be far from guaranteed. As mentioned, in Ukraine neither side has managed to achieve air superiority let alone air supremacy, and this should be the base line assumption for any future war.

General Charles Brown, Chief of Staff of the United States Air Force, noted in 2023:

> We cannot predict the future of what kind of environment we're going to fight in, for one, but I fully expect it'll be much more contested. The amount of close air support we will do will probably be less than we've done in the past, typically in the Middle East, because that environment was that we didn't have an air threat or a surface-to-air threat.[22]

Even in limited conflicts and COIN/CT (counterinsurgency/counterterrorism) campaigns, air support can be delayed or missions aborted by a number of factors, including but not limited to enemy GBAD, weather conditions (including dust storms), or aircraft being tasked to more pressing TiCs.

Professor Justin Bronk, Senior Research Fellow at RUSI, told the BBC in May 2023 that even with modern Western aircraft for CAS missions, 'Ukrainian pilots would still have to fly very low anywhere near the front lines because of Russia's ground-based threat and that would limit effective missile range. And it also means employing air power in the way the West did in wars like Iraq, Libya, Afghanistan, isn't possible in Ukraine.'[23]

Near-future ground combat units will not be able to rely on CAS as they have in Afghanistan, Iraq and Syria. In Ukraine in 2023, the air environment was characterized by a 'combination of threat from long-range ground-based anti-air capabilities, medium-altitude look-down radar, long-range air-to-air missiles, and effective point defence systems [making] the air combat environment extremely lethal.'[24]

CAS and strike tactics have had to adapt to meet these punishing conditions. Russian attack helicopters have suffered disproportionate losses, although with improper tactics being the primary cause: 'These losses are largely due to Russian pilots' failure to use terrain and appropriate flight techniques to mask and protect themselves. Those failures, coupled with the country's inability to gain air superiority, allow the Ukrainians to destroy Russian helicopters in the air and on the ground,'[25] *Defense Post* reported in March 2023.

Russian aviation faced similar challenges in the mid-1990s in Chechnya. The Russians responded with evolving techniques just as they are doing in Ukraine: 'Pilot tactics included flying at extremely low altitudes and at very high speeds to the targets, thereby limiting Chechen visual detection and response time; approaching targets from different directions; making hard maneuvers before the approach to the target; departing at low altitudes; providing mutual covering fire; and using EW equipment (as well as decoy flares and other devices).'[26]

Even irregular and insurgent forces, without sophisticated gun and missile systems, can cause challenges to aviation. Again, in Chechnya in the 1990s, Russian pilots were forced to adapt and adapt quickly to insurgent air defence tactics:

> At the start of the conflict, Russian pilots had only a poor understanding of Chechen tactics, which included controlling mobile air defense weapons via radio and changing these systems' positions constantly. The Chechens also tried to integrate and synchronize the employment of these weapons, attempting to engage targets with the full set of weapons in the inventory: small arms, heavy-caliber machine guns, cannons, and grenade launchers. The Chechens made wide use of ambushes, trying to pin down a helicopter once it entered a zone of effective fire by massing fire from several points.[27]

As something of an indictment on the institutional learning of the organizations involved, the US would encounter similar 'low-tech' tactics in Iraq and Afghanistan years later (and many of these air defence techniques had their genus in Vietnam).

NATO and the Warsaw Pact developed both armoured attack helicopters (the Apache and the Hind respectively) and specialist ground attack aircraft (the A10A and the SU-25) during the Cold War, with the aim of maximizing the survivability of the airframes in a conventional peer conflict in Western Europe.

Despite this, attack helicopters like the Apache are still fragile, as evidenced by the disastrous March 2003 raid against the Iraqi Republican Guard Medina Division. Thirty-two AH-64 Apaches from the 11th Aviation Regiment were launched on a nighttime operation into the Karbala Gap. Planners declined to employ preparatory artillery against the planned route due to collateral damage concerns.

In a coordinated air defence ambush, Iraqi anti-aircraft gunners opened fire. One of the Apaches was shot down and the rest retreated, many with damage from the anti-aircraft fire. Similarly, an air assault mission in Afghanistan in February 2002 saw multiple Apaches damaged by small arms, machine-gun and RPG fire.

Despite their sophisticated sensors, Apaches were successfully ambushed by a relatively technologically inferior force on at least two occasions; if the Afghans or Iraqis had had access to MANPADS in either scenario, the result would have been even more sobering (there are unconfirmed reports that Coalition aircraft were engaged by SA-7 MANPADS during *Anaconda*, although evidently no aircraft were shot down by missiles).

To provide effective close air support in land warfare, friendly aircraft obviously have to be able to close within striking distance of the enemy target. To do that, they must be able to negotiate both enemy GBAD and enemy fighter aircraft sent to intercept them.

A Ukrainian pilot interviewed by the BBC claimed, 'Our biggest enemy is Russian Su-35 fighter jets. We know positions of [Russian] air defence, we know their ranges. It's quite predictable, so we can calculate how long we can stay [inside their zone]. But in the case of fighter jets, they are mobile. They have a good air picture and they know when we're flying to the front lines.'[28]

A staged photograph of Iraqis celebrating on a downed US Army AH-64D Apache attack helicopter near Karbala in March 2003 – the result of a successful anti-air ambush in the Karbala Gap. (Photo by KARIM SAHIB/AFP via Getty Images)

The fearsome Russian Kamov Ka-52 Alligator attack helicopter. Large numbers have been downed in Ukraine; however, Russia has altered tactics and is working to increase the engagement range of the helicopter's sensors to allow it greater stand-off. Its Vitebsk 25 EW system has also been enhanced against the MANPAD threat. (Photo by Russian Defence Ministry/Handout/Anadolu via Getty Images)

Other challenges for the Russian VKS in Ukraine have been caused by the type of guidance used by Russian ATGMs. The Kamov KA-52 ('Alligator') attack helicopter, for instance, employs the 9A1472 Vikhr-1 (AT-16 Scallion) ATGM. Despite it offering excellent penetration against enemy armour, the Vikhr suffers, as it must be guided by a laser designator. David Axe at *Forbes* reported:

> The missile is a 'beam-rider.' A gunship crew hovers a few hundred feet off the ground, shoots a laser beam at the target from as far as six miles away, then fires the missile, which follows the laser all the way to the target. The problem is the firing helicopter can't move until the missile hits. And that can take tens of seconds – an eternity when Ukrainian air-defenses are nearby.[29]

The big advantage of the Vikhr-1 is a substantial range increase over older ATGMs – this has been used to the advantage of Russian attack aviation during mid-2023 as Russian forces attempted to blunt the Ukrainian counteroffensive. KA-52s launched from the extreme limits of the ATGM's range (circa 8km), significantly reducing the impact of GBAD.

The laser-guided Ataka (NATO reporting name AT-9 Spiral-2) has a range of some 8km and features a tandem HEAT warhead for defeating ERA. The LMUR (*Legkaya Mnogotselevaya Upravlyayemaya Raketa* or light multi-purpose guided rocket) is a more recent design that has seen combat use in Syria and Ukraine, in the latter mounted on modernized Mi-28NM and Ka-52M helicopters.

Britain's Ministry of Defence noted in July 2023:

In recent months, Russia has highly likely augmented the force in the south with at least a small number of brand new, Ka-52M variants: a heavily modified aircraft, informed by lessons from Russia's experience in Syria.

Another key improvement to the Ka-52 fleet is the integration of a new anti-tank missile, the LMUR, which has a range of approximately 15km. Ka-52 crews have been quick to exploit opportunities to launch these weapons beyond the range of Ukrainian air defenses.[30]

It operates from an inertial satellite/thermal-imaging homing system that means the missile can be directed by GPS beyond line of sight before being guided onto its final target by the launch helicopter via the thermal-imaging camera in the missile's nose. Or it can be fired in the more traditional 'fire and forget' mode.

Armament of a Ka-52 Alligator (Hokum-B), consisting of unguided rocket pods and Ataka ATGMs. (Photo by Russian Defence Ministry/Handout/Anadolu via Getty Images)

ABOVE A Ukrainian Mi-8 HIP helicopter equipped with likely S-8 rocket pods. (Photo by Carl Court/Getty Images)

RIGHT Ukrainian Mi-24 mounting what appears to be S-8 pods. The US have since supplied M261 Hydra-70 rocket pods along with the APKWS laser-guided rocket. (Photo by MIGUEL MEDINA/ AFP via Getty Images)

During the counteroffensive, Ukraine failed to push SHORAD up with the breaching units, as we have noted earlier in this chapter – likely due to fear they would be immobilized by mines during the breach – and consequently left its forces open to attacks by Russian helicopters.

Ukrainian TB2s have reportedly been fitted with Sungur air-to-air missiles (AAMs) in an effort to counter the Shahed 136 and Arash-2 supplied to Russia by Iran as well as attack helicopters such as the Havoc and Hind. Critics argue that UAV-launched AAMs will not help blunt the swarming tactics increasingly employed by Russia to overwhelm Ukrainian air defences and would require a fleet of hundreds of TB2s flying a constant combat air patrol over Ukraine. An integrated SHORAD capability would be far more effective.

Apaches use the Hellfire, as the weapon is 'fire and forget' – the airframe can pop up from behind cover, having already registered and locked onto its target using its mast-mounted sensors, launch its Hellfires and then either descend behind cover again or rapidly depart the area.

Ukrainian pilots, forced to fly legacy platforms such as the Mi-8/17 Hip and Mi-24 Hind, instead rely on their piloting skill – typically flying 'low and fast', often no more than 5 metres off the ground. This does nothing to improve their accuracy with their rocket pods, which are typically lobbed at targets, but does improve their chances of surviving the sortie.

RUSI explained that the density and effectiveness of MANPADS led to the initial adoption of this technique by Russian crews:

> However, losses to MANPADS were heavy and so Russian tactics shifted during March [2022], with penetrating sorties becoming less and less common; they were replaced by rocket 'lofting' attacks from a safe distance.
>
> Since April [2022], Russian attack helicopters have been used extremely cautiously, with a heavy reliance on standoff rocket attacks rendering them little more than flying rocket artillery assets. Despite this cautious approach, they continue to be shot down regularly by Ukrainian frontline units using MANPADS, Javelin and, occasionally, ATGMs.[31]

RUSI's 'Meatgrinder: Russian Tactics in the Second Year of Its Invasion of Ukraine' report of May 2023 described this tactic of lofting strikes:

> … lofting S-8 unguided rockets from both fast air and aviation assets on a long arcing trajectory at distant targets… first seen soon after the invasion, has been the subject of significant curiosity due to its inefficiency and inaccuracy. However, when conducted at ranges of approximately 12km at area targets such as Ukrainian ground formations attempting to form up for attacks, the concentration of effect has proved sufficient to break up these formations and prevent attacks from taking place.

A Ukrainian Mi-8 lofting unguided rockets – a tactic adopted by both sides to reduce their exposure to air defence fire. (Photo by ANATOLII STEPANOV/AFP via Getty Images)

Interestingly, these lofting strikes appear to be the primary use of Russian attack aviation on the current battlefield. Although the technique is used across the front, its most pronounced effects are in areas where the Russians have a dearth of ground-based fires, as the responsiveness of this method of attack can increase the threat to Ukrainian troops with very little notice.[32]

Seemingly forgotten is evidence of earlier Russian use of such techniques. In *Air Operations in Low Intensity Conflict: The Case of Chechnya*, published by the US military's Foreign Military Studies Office, Timothy Thomas notes the following from the 1994 Russo-Chechen War: 'Some helicopter crews employed a new tactic, that of launching their S-24 unguided rockets with a pitch-up maneuver, increasing the range of the weapon by six to seven kilometers. This allowed pilots to fire without entering the kill zone of the air defense weapons of Dudayev's forces.'[33]

This very tactic used by Ukrainian crews exposes them to a Russian counter. The Russians adapted coordination of their AEW (Airborne Early Warning) aircraft with low-level fighter aircraft to counter Ukrainian helicopter attack missions. When the Ukrainians employ their attack helicopters and the helicopter flares up to fire rockets, the Russian fighter aircraft fires an air-to-air missile at the second helicopter.

The majority of the missile's flight path is passive, emitting no signals, and it activates its seeker only when approaching the designated area, searching for its target autonomously. In this situation, the helicopter pilot has only a few seconds to attempt evasive manoeuvres to avoid the incoming missile.

There have been instances where Armed Forces of Ukraine (AFU) helicopters were unable to carry out the attack and were forced to land without shutting down the engines, repeating this process up to three times in a row.

Additionally, unguided rockets have a large dispersion ellipse, making them primarily suitable for engaging area targets. The effectiveness of their application diminishes when only one helicopter is able to launch the rockets, significantly decreasing their overall effectiveness.

Employing attack helicopters primarily as aerial artillery platforms, launching unguided rockets from hover positions at maximum ranges from the security of Ukrainian-controlled territory, there is minimal interaction between helicopter crews and the low density and high demand forward aviation controllers.

The main focus of the helicopter crews is interacting with UAV operators who identify and transmit the enemy's location for helicopter strikes. The Ukrainians have very effectively integrated attack helicopters with UAVs for reconnaissance and target designation.

Indeed, despite adaptions in tactics, attack helicopters are likely to face a very uncertain future. The continued viability of such platforms in a peer conflict is open to question. Will they be supplemented or replaced by unmanned platforms?

Attack helicopters have been lost in large numbers in Ukraine. This is due to several factors. One is the relative sophistication of the Russian-designed airframes used by both sides, all of which are technically inferior to Western platforms such as the AH-64E Guardian.

The AH-64D and E both feature mast-mounted radar, enabling targets to be identified, tracked and firing solutions completed before the aircraft must expose itself from behind cover. The AH-64 series was designed from the outset to take advantage of terrain masking to improve its survivability in a hypothetical Cold War Gone Hot scenario.

In a contested airspace, attack helicopters require significant support to enhance their chances – electronic warfare to mask their presence and suppression and destruction of enemy air defence (SEAD/DEAD), which combines both EW and kinetic strikes by radar-seeking missiles to secure airspace.

Future attack helicopter platforms, and the current AH-64E Guardian, will be 'teaming enabled', meaning the aircrew will be able to control their own dedicated fleet of UAVs. These UAVs, such as Loyal Wingman and likely smaller, more inexpensive types, can be used in the SEAD/DEAD mission, becoming expendable targets to safeguard the passage of the attack helicopter itself. They will also greatly extend the range that ground targets can be tracked and targeted.

In early 2024, the US announced the cancellation of its Future Attack Reconnaissance Aircraft (FARA), its next generation armed reconnaissance helicopter to replace the OH-58 Kiowa, after what reports noted was a 'sober assessment of the modern battlefield'.

A US Air Force F-16C launching a GBU-31 2,000-pound Joint Direct Attack Munition (JDAM). Russia has manufactured a similar but more primitive JDAM kit to turn its dumb bombs into glide bombs, with some level of precision and increasing stand-off engagement range. (Photo by Michael Ammons/US Air Force/Getty Images)

'We are learning from the battlefield – especially in Ukraine – that aerial reconnaissance has fundamentally changed,' explained US Army Chief of Staff General Randy George. Instead of pursuing a next gen helicopter, the focus (and budget) would be on 'Army's unmanned aerial reconnaissance capability including Future Tactical Unmanned Aerial System and Launched Effects'.[34]

The close air support star of the COIN campaigns in Iraq and particularly Afghanistan was a fixed-wing aircraft designed for Cold War Gone Hot tank-busting: the venerable A10A Thunderbolt II, better known as the Warthog. Build around an immense 30mm seven-barrel cannon, the heavily armoured aircraft took on almost mythological status among troops on the ground.

The Warthog was supremely effective in both of these theatres, as the enemy lacked an appreciable level of GBAD. Once the Iraqi military had been toppled in 2003, the Warthog faced only heavy machine guns, the occasional light cannon such as the ZU-23, and the even rarer MANPADS. For the majority of its engagements, the A10A faced only small-arms fire during its gun-runs.

The US Air Force, however, has been attempting to retire the airframe for many years, arguing that its CAS role can be handled by multi-role aircraft – initially the F-16 Viper and more recently the F-35 Lightning II. In a peer or near-peer war, the contested air environment would see the Warthog struggle: it is slow and ponderous, it has no stealth characteristics to fool enemy air defence radars, and it's easily out-manoeuvred by enemy interceptor aircraft.

Can the vaunted F-35 really replace the A10A in its specialized CAS role? First, and most important, the F-35 has the technological advantages to operate in contested environments: its stealth characteristics will give it a better chance of evading surviving enemy GBAD and, in particular, SAM systems.

It mounts an effective 25mm cannon; however, this will likely see little use in a future peer or near-peer war – aircraft will not be able to get close enough to enemy ground targets to use their cannon before they are shot from the sky. Instead, the F-35 will use long-range air-to-ground precision munitions to strike.

Its speed and manoeuvrability will give it a greater chance of surviving in comparison to the A10A, and it can engage enemy interceptor aircraft sent to interdict it. It can also operate in a teaming relationship with UAVs, such as the Loyal Wingman concept. This will see UAVs acting as both scouts and decoys for an F-35 CAS mission.

Russia will continue to employ the SU-25 Frogfoot as its primary CAS platform, although the SU-34 Fullback has been employed in Ukraine in a tactical bombing role. Whatever platform is employed in the CAS role, along with contested environments, future wars will see an increased requirement for CAS missions over major urban areas.

Coordinating close air support above an urban environment is challenging, made even more so by the inclusion of friendly indirect fire assets (mortars, artillery, MLRS) and UAVs flown and controlled by disparate entities (conventional forces, special operations, and intelligence agencies, for example). CAS requires deconfliction with both the indirect fires and the UAVs to avoid potential collisions and fratricide.

This excerpt from the USMC's official narrative of Operation *Phantom Fury* in Fallujah, Iraq, in 2004 illustrates a crowded airspace requiring complex deconfliction:

> The high volume of indirect fire and unmanned aerial vehicles posed other challenges. Marine air planners developed a system called 'keyhole,' which involved vertically separating the different types of aircraft and projectiles over a five-mile circle over Fallujah and Ar-Ramadi.
>
> Rotary-wing attack aircraft would operate on the city's fringes below 1,500 feet. They would not be allowed over the city but would rather be posted at battle positions outside the city's boundaries and be available when specifically requested.
>
> Fixed-wing aircraft would stay above 9,000 feet and would not be allowed within the five-mile circle unless they were cleared by a regimental or battalion air officer – or were talking to a forward air controller – and were ready to immediately attack a target. Artillery, mortar fires, and a dense assortment of unmanned aerial vehicles would operate in between.

TOP A screen grab of a Russian Su-25 Grach (Frogfoot) launching what appears to be an S-25 unguided rocket at Ukrainian ground targets in 2024. (Photo by Russian Defence Ministry/Handout/Anadolu via Getty Images)

ABOVE A Ukrainian Air Force Su-25 pictured in 2006. For the first two years of the war, both sides in Ukraine have employed the same types of fighter and ground attack aircraft, increasing the risk of fratricide. (GENIA SAVILOV/ AFP via Getty Images)

Until they were cleared into the keyhole, fixed-wing aircraft were stacked at points north, east, south, and west, around Fallujah, outside the five-mile keyhole but within a 15-mile outer perimeter. They would be available at a moment's notice.

Only one aircraft would be allowed directly over the city at a time. Once in the keyhole, fixed-wing aircraft had free reign [sic] to maneuver in order to maximize their chances of hitting the assigned targets. However, they had to get ordnance on target quickly because other forward air controllers were waiting their turns.[35]

Even in the largely rural environments of Afghanistan, coordination for CAS missions was often challenging:

Coordination became a pick-up game, generally at the worst possible time. Once responding and arriving on station, aircrew would have to begin building awareness of the ground situation from zero to 'hopefully good enough.' Below them, helicopters routinely flew across the battlefield with limited communication and coordination below something appropriately called the coordination altitude.

Sometimes they were just transiting the area, while other times they were attack helicopters supporting the same ground unit but being controlled on a different frequency. Artillery was often used, but it was only de-conflicted, not integrated, with air support. Then aircrew had to account for where the friendlies were, how many there were, where they were going, and the intent of the ground commander.[36]

Consider such coordination and deconfliction challenges while in a heavy enemy GBAD scenario, and traditional CAS becomes virtually impossible, at least using the tactics and techniques employed during the long wars in Iraq and Afghanistan.

As noted above, CAS in urban areas poses its own unique set of challenges. A modern GBAD network would make such missions even more difficult, requiring the employment of stand-off munitions and UAVs rather than the traditional gun-run using cannon or rockets. Urban canyons provide ample opportunity for anti-aircraft ambushes.

In Iraq, helicopters were engaged by insurgents using 14.5mm or 23mm cannon mounted on technicals; in one famous case, an AH-6 Little Bird was downed by such a technical during a 2006 Delta Force raid, forcing the operators to defend the crash site until the pilots could be recovered. In the same incident, an F-16C pilot flying a CAS mission in support crashed while conducting gun-runs on the technicals.

Urban environments also often feature locations that are listed as 'no strike', meaning that for collateral damage reasons, certain locations are not meant to be targeted. In Iraq, various insurgent groups, including in Fallujah,

Specialist US CSAR aircrew, known by their iconic Pedro callsign in Afghanistan, seen here in their HH-60G Pavehawk helicopter preparing for a mission in Iraq, 2003. (Photo by Shane A. Cuomo/US Air Force/ Getty Images)

took advantage of this and used mosques and other culturally sensitive sites as staging or resupply points.

Even in a future conventional war, Western nations will attempt to limit collateral damage and aim to respect any such 'no strike' list. Their likely opponents, however, as evidenced by Russia striking clearly civilian targets in Ukraine, will display no such qualms.

US (and some NATO aircrew) in the late 20th and early 21st century could also rely upon CSAR, or combat search and rescue, assets to retrieve them should they be forced down. This was due to an air environment that was permissible to the introduction of helicopters to rescue downed aircrew. In Iraq and Afghanistan, CSAR missions could be launched with the knowledge that GBAD threats were typically limited to heavy machine guns, RPGs and the occasional rare MANPADS.

These weapons certainly provided a significant threat; however, the threat was deemed manageable by techniques and procedures to reduce that risk. Importantly, CSAR units were not facing any sophisticated GBAD threat. In a peer or near-peer conflict, CSAR will be operating in a far more hazardous environment, with a correspondingly far lesser chance of safely penetrating contested airspace to retrieve aircrews.

Stephen Losey of *Defense News* noted:

Combat search and rescue airmen in the next war will likely have to navigate a contested airspace with enemy surface-to-air missiles, radar and hostile aircraft. The missions could come days – perhaps even weeks – after the crash, as the rescuers wait for an opportunity to go in. And there could be much more rescuing of downed pilots from the open sea.[37]

The future of CAS, and indeed CSAR, looks distinctly unmanned, and that future is likely the UCAV (unmanned combat aerial vehicle). This is a recent classification of larger classes of UAV (think the Reaper or Predator) that conduct offensive air missions or armed reconnaissance. The Russians have employed their S-70 Okhotnik or Hunter UCAV over Ukraine, while the Reaper has long been a presence over Syrian battlefields.

UCAVs are typically designed with the capability of manned-unmanned teaming (MUM-T), allowing the unmanned platforms to be controlled by manned airframes; in the case of the S-70, it is designed for MUM-T with the Su-57 next gen fighter aircraft (the Su-57 can control up to four S-70s). The US and its allies are using the Loyal Wingman concept of MUM-T, which will see a single manned aircraft mated with and controlling multiple UCAVs in a similar fashion.

The UCAVs themselves may also be deployed with and control their own fleet of UAVs, including loitering munitions. One can envision a near future where manned aircraft lead air missions that are largely conducted by swarms of UAVs and UCAVs. In many scenarios, MUM-T will not be needed, and instead the UCAV will become the controller airframe leading and controlling the mission.

As the Joint Air Power Competence Centre (JAPCC) has noted, rapid developments in the UCAV space offer 'improved stealth features, enhanced countermeasures capabilities, and the ability to have buddy drones or small-sized UAS (such as Harpy) to execute Suppression of Enemy Air Defences (SEAD)',[38] all of which encourage their employment in contested air defence environments.

CSIS reported, 'AI-embedded swarming UAVs could be programmed to identify approaching, potentially hostile targets and observe, and engage, if ordered. UAV swarms could obscure vision, disrupt communications, and even cause physical damage. At a more advanced level, the swarm could learn how to prioritize targets or split to cover multiple targets.'[39]

The lack of a human crew has operational, moral and political dimensions. From a political point of view, the 'death' of an unmanned platform is obviously far more palatable than a human loss, although in a peer or near-peer conventional war, the large and ongoing numbers of casualties will likely numb the public's reaction to individual losses. Morally, committing human aircrew to near-suicidal CAS missions into heavy GBAD environments provokes its own quandary, although wartime commanders have been forced to make such calls since the dawn of warfare.

Operationally, unmanned CAS provides a capability that may not otherwise exist: launching CAS to support ground troops without risking aircrew in a fifth-generation airframe like the F-35. Both China and Russia will continue to deploy high-density GBAD with ever greater range and accuracy. With AI incorporated, they will also react faster. Employing UAVs as the primary CAS provider may be one of the 'least bad' solutions to a very difficult problem.

CAS and deep-strike missions could be tasked to semi-autonomous teaming groups of UAVs, with larger UCAVs carrying the precision munitions and support by UAVs dedicated to the EW and SEAD mission. Indeed, swarms of UAS acting as decoys to create false target returns for enemy air defence, striking air defence platforms and control nodes directly in loitering mode, and transmitting their own EW attacks on radars could support future CAS missions.

JAPCC further argues that 'Effective use of UAS swarms in contested airspace will be crucial in guaranteeing the airspace access requirement, which is vital for CAS, especially by permanently neutralizing local adversary AD capabilities or, at least, for a defined period of time.'[40]

As a recent early example of the UCAV in combat, the Modern War Institute at West Point positively compared the experience of employing MQ-9 Reaper UCAVs versus fixed wing or rotary platforms in CAS missions supporting Libyan militia 'partner forces' battling Islamic State in Sirte:

> Flying at high speeds with a much larger turn radius, fighters and bombers generally need to orbit around a city, rather than maintain a specific position. This subjects them to masking from buildings, towers, and trees – forcing them to rely on off-board targeting or to employ larger weapons.
>
> The MQ-9 can maintain a precise offset to see through an urban canyon, or simply hold directly over the target and look straight down. Attack helicopters, operating at much lower altitude, are even more subject to obscuration than fighters – while exposing their aircrews to a much higher threat. Additionally, neither fighters nor helicopters have real-time intelligence support to analyze what they see.[41]

The argument for UAVs and UCAVs in particular is persuasive. Near-future CAS will not be performed by the Warthog or Su-25; it will be unmanned platforms that are far more expendable in heavy air defence environments than human-piloted craft. They can operate for longer (aerial refuelling of UCAVs is already being developed) and in more dangerous skies (fleets of UCAVs may include specialist EW/ECM platforms for electronic attack, neutering enemy sensors before the arrival of their armed brethren carrying precision munitions).

CHAPTER FOUR
INDIRECT FIRE

'Even today, in Ukraine, Russia's use of traditional artillery coupled with UAV forward observation has created a lethal and efficient deep fire affect [sic] – if you can be found you can be killed.'

UK Defence Secretary Ben Wallace,
Royal United Services Institute, 2020[1]

Stalin termed artillery the 'god of war', and it is still the weapon that wins wars. During the February 2022 invasion of Ukraine, the weapon that stalled and eventually halted the Russian advance was artillery. Britain's RUSI thinktank declared in its examination of lessons learned in the first 12 months of the conflict, 'Despite the prominence of anti-tank guided weapons in the public narrative, Ukraine blunted Russia's attempt to seize Kyiv using massed fires from two artillery brigades.'[2]

Before we look at how artillery has been used in modern warfare and how it is likely to be used in the near future, let's examine what artillery, and more generally indirect fires, can accomplish and how it accomplishes it.

Modern field artillery is generally composed of four interconnected elements: the guns, mortars or MLRS that conduct the actual fire missions; the ISR or STA (surveillance and target acquisition) assets that identify, track and call in the fire missions; the fire control systems that develop the firing solutions and coordinate the guns; and finally, the transport and

ABOVE A Libyan National Transitional Council technical mounting an unguided rocket pod scavenged from a strike aircraft, pictured in 2011. (Photo by John Cantlie/Getty Images)

logistics assets that move, replenish and maintain the guns and rockets that do the shooting.

The Royal Australian Artillery Corps provides a succinct definition of the indirect fires process:

> The objective of all artillery systems is to get an artillery projectile close enough to the target to create the desired effect. The system is made up of an observer who identifies and locates the target, a command element that authorizes engagement, a fire control element that receives the observer's information and then calculates firing data and relays it to the delivery system (such as a howitzer), and a delivery system to fire on that data to create the effect.[3]

So artillery – whether guns (known as tubes or tube artillery), rockets or mortars – fire indirectly, meaning that they do not need to have a direct line of sight to their targets. Traditionally, indirect fire has been guided to target by forward observers, either on the ground with a pair of binoculars and a radio or in an orbiting aircraft.

In simple terms, the forward observer provides the coordinates of the target which the artillery battery translates into a fire mission using some fairly complicated mathematics, generating a firing solution. Once the first round is fired, the impact is registered by the forward observer, and adjustments are provided to the artillery battery to increase accuracy. Once the forward observer is happy with the location of the impacting rounds, the immortal call of 'fire for effect' is made.

Latest generation artillery offers MRSI, or multiple rounds simultaneous impact. This is a capability that allows a brace of rounds to be fired at slightly different trajectories, ensuring that all arrive near simultaneously on or above the target. In previous decades such techniques required several guns firing. With modern platforms offering computerized firing solutions, MRSI can be accomplished with a single gun.

Artillery guns are loaded by a crew or, increasingly, by automated loaders. Charge bags of propellent are used to increase range, and the number of charge bags required for a particular fire mission is itself part of the firing solution.

Precision artillery rounds are available and have largely replaced conventional 'dumb' artillery rounds in the West, the best known being the M982A1 Excalibur (a GPS-guided round that has a range of some 50km, striking within 2 metres of the GPS coordinate). Russia, however, still employs a majority of 'dumb' rounds, particularly post 2024, when the majority of its 152mm ammunition was being sourced from North Korea.

Along with precision and 'dumb' high-explosive rounds, artillery ammunition comes in many shapes and sizes. Chemical screening or irritant smoke, including white phosphorus, submunitions designed to deliver multiple smaller charges, mine-laying rounds, and even dedicated anti-tank penetrators are available. Even artillery-delivered UAVs are in the pipeline.

Whether conventional tube artillery, guided or unguided rockets, mortars or missiles, all indirect fire has four doctrinal missions:

1. Suppression fires intended to degrade the performance of an enemy unit or weapons systems (including counter-battery, which interdicts and restricts the enemy's ability to target friendly forces with their own artillery).
2. Destruction of high-value targets (these could be leadership, resupply or communication/EW nodes, for example). A moving or transitory high-value target is known as a 'time sensitive target'.
3. Interdicting enemy troop or vehicle concentrations (the classic fire mission for artillery) or terrain denial fires (for example, cratering roads to impede suicide vehicle bombs as conducted in Iraq and Syria).
4. Firing in tactical support of friendly units either as preplanned fires to support a specific operation or in reactionary support of 'troops in contact'.

In NATO terms, there are also four principal planned effects caused by artillery: harassment, suppression, neutralization and destruction.

The Polish Military University of Land Forces provides useful definitions:

Harassment is defined as repeated, deliberate and intimidating activities intended to discourage, impede and disrupt. Those fires are delivered on an irregular timeframe and location with a reduced amount of delivery platforms.

Suppression fires are fires on/or about a weapon system to degrade its performance below the level needed to fulfill its mission objectives. The effect of suppressive fires usually lasts only as long as the fires are continued. Suppression is used to prevent effective fire on friendly forces. It is typically used to support a specified movement of forces.

Neutralization fire is fire delivered to render the target temporarily ineffective or unusable. Neutralization fire results in adversary personnel or materiel incapable of interfering with a particular operation or the accomplishment of a particular course of action.

Destruction fire physically renders an adversary force combat-ineffective unless it is reconstituted, or so damaged that it cannot function as intended nor be restored to a usable condition without being entirely rebuilt.[4]

In Western armies, artillery is used to enable manoeuvre and to conduct deep strike (strategic targets well beyond the forward edge of the battle space).

Enabling manoeuvre means suppressing, fixing in place or destroying enemy forces or positions, screening advancing friendly forces with explosive or chemical smoke fires and generally integrating into the battleplan as an enabler. Russia views artillery very differently.

The European Army Interoperability Centre has noted:

> Traditionally, in Russian military doctrine, manoeuvring troops support the artillery rather than the reverse. The preferred role of massed artillery and rockets systems is to destroy enemy formations, whilst manoeuvring infantry and tank formations have the role to fix the enemy.
>
> This last point is in stark contrast with Western military thinking, where artillery is used to support manoeuvring troops. For this reason, it is widely recognised that the use of en masse indirect fire support at the tactical level is a signature characteristic of the Russian way of war.[5]

According to RUSI:

> During the initial invasion, between one and two batteries of howitzers were assigned to each BTG along with an MLRS battery. By summer 2022, the Russians had consolidated artillery into artillery tactical groups. Russia is currently utilising artillery brigades, which allocate batteries in support of axes, and hold a significant force under direct command for counterbattery fire and to support the sector's main effort. Russian fires continue to be the main shaping effect on the fighting.[6]

A Russian BM-27 Uragan (Hurricane) MLRS firing one of its 16 220mm rockets against Ukrainian positions in Donetsk, 2024. (Photo by Russian Defence Ministry/Handout/Anadolu via Getty Images)

The Russian 152mm self-propelled 2S19 Msta-SM2, which can fire up to ten rounds per minute with a range between 30km with conventional ammunition and 40km with rocket-assisted rounds. (Photo by Nikita Shvetsov/Anadolu Agency/ Getty Images)

Doctrinally, Russian and Russian-trained armies have five fire methods as detailed by the US Army's Asymmetric Warfare Group (a unit raised during the Iraq War to learn and disseminate lessons learned, and sadly, and shortsightedly, disbanded in 2021):

1. **Single Target Fire:** fires directed against self-acquired targets or direct fire.
2. **Concentrated Fire:** fires employed by more than one artillery system directed against the same target.
3. **Fixed Protective Curtain Fires:** a continuous fire barrage which is delivered on one of, or simultaneously on, several fronts of an attacking enemy.
4. **Moving Curtain Fires:** a continuous fire barrage created on one or multiple fronts along the axis of advance of the enemy's armored units, which can later be directed at follow on locations depending on the withdrawal of the enemy's advance.
5. **Accompanying Fires:** the concentration of fires on targets located in front of an advancing friendly force, their flanks, and can later be directed at the enemy's rear area targets.[7]

Russia also focuses on quantity over quality, particularly in terms of precision fires. Russian forces will mass as many batteries as possible on a single target – effective in the end but costly and wasteful. In defensive battles, Russian artillery is employed in a similar way to sustained-fire machine guns – to cover an allocated sector of the battlefield with pre-registered fires. In both cases, Western forces will likely use a much greater percentage of precision munitions to generate a similar outcome – quality over quantity.

Russian artillery does have access to precision or guided munitions but to a much lesser extent than the US (and now even more so as Russia fires thousands of rounds of artillery ammunition daily in Ukraine). For instance, the 2K25 Krasnopol-D laser-designated round is fired from the 2S19 MSTA self-propelled artillery gun. The round is used in conjunction with the Orlan-30 UAV, which carries a laser designator to mark the target.

In terms of effects on target, the West and Russia use very different metrics that illuminate the centrality of artillery to the Russian way of war. The US defines neutralization as at least 10 percent destruction, and destruction at 30 percent. In contrast, Russian artillery forces see 30 percent destruction of targets as simply suppression, with destruction (termed 'annihilation' by Russia) set at 70 to 90 percent.

The European Army Interoperability Centre also noted another major disparity:

> Unlike their Russian counterparts, the European and American militaries have, for the most part, overlooked the modernisation of their ground-based indirect fire support capabilities. This is a result of years of fighting low-intensity conflicts, where artillery has a minor role and most of the fire support to the troops on the ground is delivered by air.
>
> This is, in part, thanks to the Western air forces' ability to establish undisputed air supremacy over the various battlefields and provide around the clock quick-precision-strikes. Consequentially, most Western artillery forces now lag behind their Russia counterparts in terms of quantity and capabilities.[8]

In the Russo-Ukrainian War, the Russian Air Force's inability to gain air superiority has meant that its impact has been greatly reduced. The Russian Army, however, always plans for the domination of the battlefield by indirect fire without a reliance on air superiority. US and NATO armies have conversely always considered artillery to be one part of the combined-arms matrix, with air superiority, if not supremacy, considered an equally essential element of the mix.

As the US, UK and NATO allies have concentrated on COIN warfare since 2001, there has been a dangerous institutional malaise regarding the import of artillery and the capability of massed fires. Because such capabilities were largely not required in Afghanistan or Iraq, this malaise has seen artillery (and indirect fires of all types) pursue a path to precision (to reduce collateral damage, i.e., unintended civilian deaths and destruction of infrastructure).

One US Army gunner commented tellingly: 'Artillerymen would come over here and kick in doors. That's not what we trained for, that's not what we came in the Army for.'[9]

Russia has also largely led the way in terms of integration of uncrewed aerial vehicles with artillery employment. Russian forces will use a high-altitude long-loiter UAV to identify a target before passing to a lower-altitude tactical UAV to provide real-time corrections to an artillery fire mission. One commentator noted:

> Russian forces can bring their guns to bear on the enemy within only three to five minutes of an Orlan-10 UAV spotting the target.
>
> Each commander of an axis will generally retain an orbit of Orlan-10s above the fighting to provide both information to the CP and targets for responsive and accurate fire to the assigned batteries. The artillery brigade commander also often retains several Orlan-10s, coordinated in a complex above areas of interest. Thus, Ukrainian forces often find that they are being observed from two different Orlan-10 complexes – each able to call down different effects.[10]

Counter-battery fire (sometimes called counter-fire) is a battlefield tactic employed to defeat the enemy's indirect fire elements (multiple rocket launchers, artillery and mortars), including their target acquisition, as well as their command-and-control components. Counter-battery arrangements and responsibilities vary between nations but involve target acquisition, planning and control, and counter-fire.

Most importantly, the Ukrainians have received scores of counter-battery radars from Germany, Norway, the UK and the US that spot incoming artillery shells and rockets, pinpoint the source, and cue friendly howitzers and launchers to fire back. The radars, working in conjunction with small drones, make it extremely dangerous for Russian gunners to function. They must 'shoot then scoot' to have any chance of surviving Ukrainian counter-battery fire. The Russians have their own radars and drones, too, of course – but they have been less effective.

During the war, Ukrainian artillery units were actively engaged by Russian counter-battery fires. To increase the unit's survivability and counter-fire flexibility, Ukrainian ground forces started to divide artillery batteries into firing groups which consisted of one to two guns per group. The separation of battery guns gave a huge flexibility for ground commanders to conduct counter-battery fire.

The usual practice is that artillery batteries are divided into one to four fire groups. The first group of guns conducts a deception fire mission to provoke Russian artillery counter-fire and immediately changes position to a secondary firing point. During this time, two or three other artillery fire groups from separate locations, supported by UAVs, engage to destroy the now 'unmasked' enemy artillery battery.

The implementation of UAVs by Russian artillery forces falls under their strategy known as the reconnaissance-fire complex. The reconnaissance-fire complex connects ISR – from both UAVs and ground-based sensors – with artillery fire control to speed up the kill-chain, resulting in faster fire missions in response to changing conditions on the battlefield.

One of these sensors is artillery radar, which can identify and register enemy indirect fire platforms to allow counter-battery fires to engage the enemy guns, mortars or MLRS assets while also tracking friendly fire missions to improve accuracy and effects on target.

The Russians also employ a deep-fires version called the reconnaissance-strike complex, which integrates cruise, ballistic and hypersonic platforms with air, sea, ground and space-based ISR to accelerate the 'kill-chain' of

WHAT IS A KILL-CHAIN?

A kill-chain is a series of discrete steps or inputs that lead to a decision to strike a target. In Western military vernacular it comprises find, fix, track, target, engage and assess.

- Find – employing ISR, including SIGINT and UAVs, to locate potential target.
- Fix – employ ISR to monitor target in real time.
- Track – maintain electronic and/or physical eyes on target if it moves.
- Target – agree a targeting solution including ordnance type.
- Engage – launch ordnance at target.
- Assess – conduct battle/bomb damage analysis to ascertain damage, exploit intelligence and inform re-targeting decision.

identifying, transmitting targeting data and finally engaging a target. The deep-fires mission for field artillery has been revolutionized by the use of the UAV, with China, Russia and a number of NATO nations, including the US, already fielding organic UAVs within their artillery units. UAVs have enabled deep fires into the enemy's rear areas and have proven indispensable in both offensive and defensive artillery operations. In the current lexicon, deep fires are also termed 'anti-access area denial', or A2AD.

Shortening the kill-chain is a key priority; Ukraine has been using feeds from UAVs beamed directly to the artillery battery, either by an organic UAV attached to the artillery or by sharing the feed from a UAV controlled by another friendly unit. The use of UAVs to improve targeting and the speed of engagement, along with their integration with artillery radar and overall battlefield management systems, will be the next stage in the evolution of field artillery.

The Russian reconnaissance-fire complex came to wider prominence via an incident in Ukraine on 11 July 2014 that gave incorrect weight to the ISR component of reconnaissance fire while neglecting some equally important signature management tactics. The incident at Zelenopillya, eastern Ukraine, is a case study in drawing the wrong lessons about Russian indirect fires capability. The incident has been accepted by the US and other militaries and used as an abject lesson in signature management. The common version of the story claims that two Ukrainian mechanized infantry battalions were located by Russian UAVs during a short rest stop. With their communications suddenly jammed by Russian tactical EW, the Ukrainians were engaged by artillery and rockets:

Suddenly, shells shrieked down from the sky as if from nowhere, unleashing a maelstrom of fire and steel rain. Brand-new thermobaric warheads and top-attack shells took a horrible toll. Vehicles, some of them still occupied, burst into flames, while soldiers outside were torn to pieces. Within the space of a minute, the field was transformed into a boneyard of smoking wreckage, the quiet morning now sundered by incoherent screaming and shouts for help. The battle was over before it had begun, and Ukraine would never again come so close to securing their border.[11]

It was this version that caused such discomfort within Western militaries. It seemed to expose a Russian capability that even the US at the time would have difficulty matching: integrated UAV reconnaissance identifying targets that are then jammed and engaged with a massive bombardment. Frightening stuff. However, it appears that this version left out several key points:

> In Ukrainian sources and according to veterans of the battle, a poorly trained force that was unprepared for heavy artillery camped in a field. Vehicles were parked next to one another as though on a parade ground for inspection, and soldiers didn't dig trenches. That encampment had been stationary for at least a day – some accounts have it there longer – making no effort to conceal itself. It was struck, and sustained heavy damage, mostly due to not having prepared for the possibility of being struck in the first place.[12]

The site itself appears to have been a forward armament and refuelling point – an ammo and fuel dump – that may have been in place for some time, possibly a number of weeks, and had been subject to Russian UAV interest.

According to Ukrainian accounts, it was poor signature management and lazy soldiering that led to the Russian fires, not a newly capable Russian Army that could integrate UAV artillery spotting and electronic jamming with a responsive and accurate indirect fires capacity measured in minutes. Despite Ukrainian accounts, the Zelenopillya incident has entered into US doctrine as an example of exactly such a Russian capability.

Ironically, although the details may be wrong and Russian attempts at a fusion of UAV, EW and indirect fires are nowhere near as effective as the erroneous version of the story claims (as demonstrated since in the 2022 Russo-Ukrainian War), it has proven a useful 'bogeyman' to reinforce signature management principles to US and NATO troops (Ukrainian artillery units have resorted to deploying metal nets over their gun positions to catch FPVs before they impact, as their firing will immediately betray them to Russian ISR sensors).

Ukraine is, of course, the latest battlefield to be dominated by artillery and the one which reinforces its domination. Russian artillery tactics have adapted too beyond their successful implementation of the reconnaissance-fires complex, including use of Western 'shoot and scoot' drills to avoid counter-battery fires. Their traditional reliance on massed artillery has not changed, however:

> Fire is not only used to strike Ukrainian defensive positions but also, vitally, to blunt assaults. If the Russians learn that an assault is being prepared, the area is often saturated with fire to prevent its execution. Another common tactic is for the Russians to withdraw from a position that is being assaulted and then saturate it with fire once Ukrainian troops attempt to occupy it.[13]

The CAESAR or *Camion Équipé d'un Système d'Artillerie* 155mm self-propelled artillery gun operated by Ukraine. The manufacturer states that the platform has had an unusually high survival rate thanks to its ability to fire six rounds in a minute before rapidly moving location. (Photo by SAMEER AL-DOUMY/AFP via Getty Images)

They have also developed a 'come-on ambush' style drill to target Ukrainian artillery assets:

> A fire mission is conducted to deliberately provoke counter-battery fire. The firing position is detected and plotted by counter-battery radar, EW or uncommonly by sound-ranging... Lancet loitering munition UAVs, long-range guns or attack aviation are then used to attack the firing point. Speed, obviously, is the key as Ukrainian guns are practiced at dispersal and concealment.[14]

But not all is rosy. Russian Battalion Tactical Groups theoretically have one to three integrated self-propelled artillery batteries per BTG. In Ukraine it was found that many did not and instead relied upon mortars and older towed artillery. Brigade and divisional commands jealously guarded control of the more modern self-propelled guns in centralized artillery tactical groups.

BTG artillery during much of 2023 had to rely upon unencrypted mobile phones to call for and assess fire missions. As we have noted elsewhere, this phenomenon was not only constrained to the artillery, with infantry similarly using their personal phones and helicopter crews using commercial GPS apps on their iPhones for mapping.

The number of rounds expended by Russian guns is astounding and a fact that caught Western planners unaware. At the rates Russian artillery have been firing, most NATO countries would run dry within days: 'The rate of Russian fire during the first quarter of 2023 fluctuated between 12,000 and 38,000 rounds per day.'[15] In comparison, around 34,000 rounds were fired by US artillery in the three weeks of the invasion phase of Operation *Iraqi Freedom* in 2003.

During 2024, the number of rounds dropped due to several factors: the supply of ammunition, barrel wear, and the supply of sufficient propellent charge bags, which affects the range that artillery can reach (the larger the charge, the greater the range). In the words of one Russian gunner, 'We really had problems, only not with shells, but with charges. Moreover, with distant ones. We could not shoot at full range, we had to drive as close as possible to the positions and try to reach the targets.'[16]

The barrels of Russian artillery platforms are wearing out at a vastly accelerated rate, contributing to inaccuracy, and adding yet another challenge to an already overloaded logistics system. Ukraine is facing the same issue, and NATO armies are learning that in a conventional fight, artillery will fire far more than typically estimated and barrels will wear out more quickly due to this accelerated rate.

In the later months of 2023, Russian artillery tended not to exceed 24,000 rounds daily across the theatre and began to prioritize their artillery allocation, with targets that would have been previously engaged by 152mm or larger now serviced by 120mm mortars as the sting of ammunition resupply hit the frontline batteries.

Andrew Michta of the US-based Atlantic Council thinktank drove this core lesson home:

> The overarching lesson from the unfolding war in Ukraine is simply the scale of what's required to fight a modern state-on-state war. No Western military has prepared for such levels of weapons and munitions consumption and force attrition. No NATO ally today – save for the United States – has the armour or munitions stocks that could last longer than a few weeks or months at best on Ukraine-like battlefields.[17]

Retired Lieutenant Colonel Brendan B. McBreen again provides a useful summary from his Russo-Ukrainian 'lessons learned' monograph for the USMC:

> Artillery kills everybody. Rockets kill. Missiles kill less often.
>
> Reports: The RUS critical capability is fires. Dumb artillery rounds are still the greatest killer on the battlefield. Over 80% of current UKR casualties are caused by artillery, over 90% during the previous eight years, 2014–2022. Although precision weapons reduce logistics requirements, they cannot replace the large volume of dumb munitions needed.
>
> Russia fired 200,000 shells per day in the summer of 2022. Barrels melted. During the battle of Bakhmut, RUS guns were reduced from firing 60,000 shells to 10,000 shells per day. To meet high artillery consumption rates, RUS transported 700,000 tons of shells in the first five months of war.

The Russian BM-21 Grad, the spiritual successor to the notorious Katyusha of World War II fame. Russia has traditionally pioneered the use of unguided MLRS weapons, while the West has relied upon precision with guided versions fired by platforms such as the HIMARS. (Photo by Muhammed Enes Yildirim/Anadolu Agency via Getty Images)

> · RUS uses massive salvos of artillery and MLRS to suppress UKR positions and support tactical advances. Plentiful RUS artillery often makes up for poorly trained infantry assault elements. To mass artillery effectively, RUS has formed artillery brigades. Most of the 110 to 136 RUS mechanized battalion tactical groups (BTG) that had invaded UKR were dissolved, and their small detachments of artillery, tanks, engineers, and air defense were reformed into full-strength units. RUS leaders recognized that ad hoc and non-cohesive BTG, with too few infantry, poor infantry-armor cooperation, and ineffective small attachments, were unsuited for the Ukraine War.
>
> Modern fires networks can see, strike, and destroy in 60 seconds. We need counter-UAS jammers to attack the kill chain.
>
> Reports: In May 2022, a RUS unit crossing the Sverskyi Donets river was detected by UKR UAS. Artillery destroyed over 70 vehicles and killed 485 soldiers.
>
> Multiple RUS UAS forward observers supported a single attack over the village of Artemivske in 2022. One UAS targeted UKR artillery outside the city, one targeted UKR reserve routes, one scouted ahead to target enemy ambushes, and a fourth flew overwatch above the assault element.
>
> Doctrinally, a RUS 'reconnaissance fire complex' uses long-range artillery and precision weapons to destroy targets identified by distant UAS. Vehicles are attacked with guided missiles, but unit positions, HQ, and logistics are struck with high-explosive artillery, which cannot be jammed.
>
> RUS UAS now send grids directly to fires commanders. This kill-chain can take less than a minute. The goal is ten seconds. Instead of ground reconnaissance units, most RUS observers are now UAS. Multiple RUS generals (many on cell phones) have been killed by UKR fires networks. 86% of UKR targets are derived from UAS. RUS artillery no longer digs in since it must move quickly after firing.[18]

Tube and rocket artillery are not the only kinds of indirect fire used on the modern battlefield. Ballistic, cruise and hypersonic missiles are now employed against high-value targets or those that are beyond the engagement range of conventional artillery fire missions.

The 2020 Nagorno-Karabakh War saw (limited) use of theatre ballistic missiles – arguably the first conventional 21st-century conflict to do so. These included legacy Soviet designs such as the Scud (SS-1C) and Tochka (SS-21 Scarab) and more recent systems such as the Israeli LORA (Long Range Attack) and Russian Iskander-E (SS-26 Stone). Both sides appear to have been conservative in the number of ballistic missiles employed, likely due to escalation fears and the small number of missiles available.

The most prolific user of ballistic missiles prior to the 2022 invasion of Ukraine was the Houthis, an Islamist insurgent group in Yemen (formerly known as Ansar Allah) fighting a Saudi Arabian-led coalition. The Houthi insurgents captured around 100 Soviet-era Scud-B and Chinese Scud-C copies in 2015, which they used to target Saudi Arabia.

According to Armed Conflict Location & Event Data Project (ACLED), they also 'converted an additional 200 V-755 surface-to-air missiles into land-attack free-flight rockets'.[19] They later developed their own variants of Iranian Burkan missiles, almost certainly using smuggled Iranian components, and have used the Zulfiqar based on the Iranian Qiam-1 ballistic missile against targets in the UAE.

The number of attacks conducted by the Houthi is surprising – between 2015 and 2022, almost 1,000 missile/unguided rocket attacks and more than 350 attacks using UAVs of varying types. The sophistication of these attacks continues to increase, with guided rockets and missiles now almost completely replacing unguided weapons. This improvement has been possible due to Iranian support and a thriving domestic industry in producing munitions.

Notably, the Houthi employ their ballistic missiles against principally strategic targets located in Saudi or UAE to pressure those governments rather than in a traditional battlefield sense. The Houthis also fired a large number of cruise and ballistic missiles against commercial shipping in the Red Sea in 2023/24, but as a largely naval engagement this is outside of our scope.

RUSI comments on the limitations of such smaller state and non-state actors employing ballistic missiles:

> … short- and medium-range ballistic missiles – at least when used in small numbers – represent a relatively easy target to intercept. They follow set parabolic trajectories at altitudes sufficiently high to enable early warning and tracking, and therefore present capable air and missile defence networks with a relatively simple challenge.
>
> Larger, more sophisticated actors such as China's strategic rocket forces can derive tactical utility from ballistic missiles by firing coordinated salvos en masse and using them in tandem with other assets such as cruise missiles. For smaller actors, however, achieving comparable levels of mass and sophistication is unlikely.[20]

Media interest in recent years has centred on the hypersonic missile – that being a missile that can travel faster than Mach 5 or greater than five times the speed of sound. Along with their impressive speed, which obviously reduces the window of opportunity to intercept such missiles, hypersonics are increasingly favoured due to their manoeuvrability in flight, which makes them an unpredictable and difficult target for air defence systems.

There are two principal types of hypersonic platform: the glide vehicle and the air-breathing missile. Glide-vehicle hypersonics operate by piggybacking on a conventional ballistic missile. The hypersonic glider detaches itself from the ballistic missile once it reaches its optimal trajectory, entering the atmosphere before travelling at hypersonic speed towards the target.

Russia launched at least six hypersonic Kinzhal air-launched cruise missiles in 2023. May 2023 saw the first engagement and destruction of this Russian hypersonic platform – sort of. Engaged and successfully downed by a US-supplied and Ukrainian-operated PAC-3 Patriot, the missile was the Kh-47M2 Kinzhal, which was travelling at hypersonic speeds for a portion of its trajectory. It is not a true hypersonic as developed to avoid air defence systems but simply a big missile travelling at very high speed – a target that later-generation Patriots should, and obviously now can, engage and destroy.

Returning to more traditional (and low-tech) forms of indirect fire, the humble mortar is seeing a resurgence, primarily spurred on by the Ukrainian experience. Mortars provide another tool in the indirect fire toolbox – one that can range from short-ranged infantry carried (the 60mm Commando mortar, for instance), to organic medium (81 or 82mm) or heavy (120mm).

Mortars are relatively easy to transport and emplace, although like all non-armoured assets, they are at risk of counter-battery fire and artillery in general. Many NATO nations are now actively considering or in the process of procuring mortars mounted in protected mobility platforms that provide an under-armour mortar strike capability. Vehicle-mounted mortars also offer the advantage of being able to keep pace with other mechanized/motorized forces.

Mortars offer a range of targeting effects beyond high explosive, with obscuring smoke being perhaps the most useful. In many armies a mortar platoon is included in the support or heavy weapons company of a battalion, meaning that battalions can support their own local attacks with smoke or high explosive (HE).

Mobile mortar platforms will increase in popularity due to their inherent advantages in avoiding counter-battery fires and the aforementioned ability to keep pace with advancing vehicular elements. The wheeled Boxer – now adopted by a number of European nations including Germany, along with the UK and Australia – offers a turreted 120mm mortar that can deliver ten rounds per minute before withdrawing to cover or another firing point.

Insurgents and other non-state actors also appreciate the utility of the mortar, and truck-mounted versions have been seen in Iraq and Syria. Syrian rebels also constructed their own form of short-ranged artillery known generically as the Hell Cannon. This was simply a tube mounted on wheels which launched an unguided projectile – most often a 35kg propane or oxygen tank filled with explosive. Other variants include the Thunder Cannon, which used expended tank round casings, filled with explosive and welded shut with a rudimentary rocket motor attached to the base.

LEFT A light commercial truck mounting a 12-tube Type 63 or M-63 Plamen MLRS firing outside of Tikrit, Iraq, in 2014. (Photo by AHMAD AL-RUBAYE/AFP via Getty Images)

BELOW The Russian TOS-1A Solntsepyok based on the earlier TOS-1 Buratino. Although designed initially for direct fire use, the platform can fire 30 220mm thermobaric rockets out to 10km. (Photo by VASILY MAXIMOV/AFP via Getty Images)

WHAT IS A THERMOBARIC ROUND?

Thermobaric munitions work by initially dispersing an aerosol cloud of gas, liquid or finely powdered explosive. Known fuels such as ethylene oxide, propylene oxide 1, ammonium nitrate 2, and powdered PETN4 have been reported. This cloud flows around objects and into cavities and structures. [The cloud] may penetrate small openings, such as openings in buildings, bunkers and engine bays of armoured vehicles, before being ignited.[21]

Thermobaric munitions are launched from the Russian RPO-A Shmel handheld launcher, and thermobaric warheads are available for the RPG. Most well known is the TOS-1 Buratino Multiple Rocket Launch System that fires 220mm thermobaric rockets.

The Russians also operate a unique system called the Buratino, or more formally, the TOS-1, TOS-1A and TOS-2 Solnitsa/Solntsepyok 220mm thermobaric launchers, which were combat-trialled in Syria. This is a multi-barrel launch system that is designed to be employed against defensive positions or buildings. The TOS-2 entered service in 2022 and has been deployed to Ukraine. The TOS-2 is wheeled and far more resembles the US M142 HIMARS (High Mobility Artillery Rocket System) than its earlier T-72 based TOS-1 incantation.

Perhaps surprisingly, the Buratino is primarily a direct fire platform (although it has been employed in short-range low-angle indirect fire mode in Ukraine). It is unguided and thus not known for its particular accuracy, although the thermobaric rounds it uses cause horrendous wounds among targeted personnel.

As noted, the TOS-1A is not optimized to provide indirect fire support. Indeed, the vehicle is equipped with an optical sight, a laser rangefinder and a ballistic computer to provide firing solutions for targets visible within the 6km range of its rockets, which are otherwise unguided. In Ukraine, Russian forward observers and special operations have provided adjustments to the fall of shot when the TOS-1A is employed against targets not visible to the launcher crew.

The platform was used to horrifying effect against the besieged defenders of the Azovstal Iron and Steel Works plant. The US Army's Training and Doctrine Command noted its use in the 1990s in another urban environment – Chechnya: 'Despite the seeming short range, the weapon was effectively used in Chechnya to disable defenders within a specific sector just prior to an assault, to halt assaults, and to level buildings.'[24]

Although more typically used in an offensive role, the TOS-1A has also been employed in the defence in Ukraine: 'In the aftermath of the Ukrainian rout of Russian troops in Kharkiv Oblast, Russian Ground Forces switched its focus to defensive operations, utilizing the TOS-1A in final protective fires roles, often at very close ranges, in last-ditch efforts to halt Ukrainian assault forces and prevent significant breaches of Russian lines.'[25]

Guided multiple launch systems have been increasingly supplementing and, in some cases, replacing traditional tube artillery. The most well-known is the American HIMARS, which is a truck-mounted rocket system that can launch either six GMLRS rockets or one ATACMS (Army Tactical Missile System).

HOW EFFECTIVE IS THE ATACMS?

ATACMS or 'attack-ems', the MGM-140 series of Army tactical missiles, has proven a controversial weapon platform in the Russo-Ukrainian War. Washington resisted requests for months based on the fear that Russian homeland targets would be hit, until the platform was finally supplied sometime late in 2023.

The variant sent to Ukraine appears to be the MGM-140A, a shorter-range version with a range of around 160km. The Ukrainians apparently first employed the ATACMS in October 2023, striking two Russian air bases with what looked like the M39 or M39A1 cluster warhead variant – very effective at destroying exposed targets and cratering airstrips.

'The inertially-guided ballistic missiles streaked right through Russia's frayed air-defense umbrella and, as they neared the ground, scattered a thousand grenade-size submunitions apiece across the Berdyansk airfield's aprons, reportedly destroying at least nine Russian helicopters,' *Forbes* journalist David Axe reported.[22]

As far as is known, the Ukrainians do not (yet) have the unitary warhead, the M57 and M57E1 warheads, which would be more useful in targeting hardened locations such as fixed headquarters or hardened aircraft shelters. What ATACMS does, in any variant, is increase the 'danger zone' for Russian forces, forcing them to deploy further away from the front lines, degrading effectiveness.

The ATACMS was also employed during Operation *Desert Storm* in 1991 and in 2003 during Operation *Iraqi Freedom*. General David Petraeus reported:

> We did use them very effectively out in the desert, both west of Karbala and northwest of Karbala, packaged with our Apaches for both suppression of enemy air defenses enroute to our battle positions and then once our Apaches were in those positions. As I mentioned earlier, those missiles clear a grid square, a square kilometer. And so, those are incredibly lethal and were absolutely devastating against those targets in which we employed them.[23]

Unfortunately, a version that might have proven very useful in countering Russian armoured assaults was cancelled by the Pentagon back in 2003. The Brilliant Anti-Tank Munition (BAT) was to be delivered by ATACMS, with 13 packed into each missile; the warhead would airburst over an advancing enemy tank company, and each BAT would use its sensors to hone in on a target. What made BAT 'Brilliant' was the ability of the munition to preferentially distinguish between low-value targets, say a light vehicle like a BRDM2 reconnaissance vehicle, and high-value targets like a tank or air defense SPAAG.

An American M142 HIMARS operated by a Ukrainian crew launches a Unitary or DPICM GMLRS rocket. (Photo by Serhii Mykhalchuk/Global Images Ukraine via Getty Images)

The latest extended-range variant of the GMLRS can reach out to 150km, while the ATACMS (pronounced 'attack-ems') doubles this. This long-range capability of the ATACMS has been a sticking point in providing the missile to Ukraine, with the US concerned that the Ukrainians would conduct strikes against targets in the Russian homeland (which they have already conducted with drones, making the argument somewhat moot).

The standard GMLRS rockets fired from HIMARS can also vary in type. The standard M31 Unitary Warhead is designed as a precision-strike munition with reduced fragmentation, making it less than ideal against infantry or similar targets. For such targets, the M30A1 Alternative Warhead can be used. The M30A1 can be set to detonate as an airburst. Range for the standard M31 is 70km, compared with half of this for most conventional towed or self-propelled 155mm artillery platforms.

The six-wheeled chassis of the HIMARS allows the system to avoid counter-battery fire by rapidly relocating. It is also relatively lightweight, meaning it can be transported in a C-130 Hercules transport aircraft. Australia, which has 20 HIMARS on order, is looking at developing techniques to allow so-called 'fire raids' – flying into an airstrip in the enemy's rear, unloading the HIMARS and launching a salvo before recovering the truck and flying back out. USMC trials of the concept indicate such a 'fire raid' can be accomplished in sub ten minutes from touchdown to take-off.

Initially, the system was employed almost exclusively against static targets such as Russian command and control nodes and resupply dumps. HIMARS rockets have also been employed to effectively strike infrastructure targets, including bridges spanning the Dnipro River.

For HIMARS to strike accurately, it needs the GPS coordinates of a target, something easier to do with a stationary target. Increasingly, however, with the employment of Ukrainian UAVs to identify and track moving targets, HIMARS has been successfully employed against moving enemy concentrations, including AFVs and dismounted infantry.

The Russian equivalent of the HIMARS is the 9A52-4, a truck-mounted system that can launch up to six 300mm rockets out to a range of 90km. Like contemporary Western systems, it is fitted with an automated laying and fire control system, meaning that targeting data can be transmitted directly from a command vehicle. The Russians have long been proponents of MLRS platforms, and their rocket artillery forms a large part of their artillery forces. Crucially, though, Russian MLRS is unguided, making it very much an indiscriminate area effect weapon.

Increasingly, artillery will offer longer range and more accuracy. They may also deploy their own payloads, including UAVs. They already can deploy their own submunitions, such as anti-tank mines.

The Ukrainians deployed American RAAMs or Remote Anti-Armor Mines – a 155mm artillery round containing nine anti-tank mines – during the battle of Vuhledar. Although the mines are not large enough generally to cause a catastrophic kill, they can easily immobilize a tank by blowing a track, making the suddenly static vehicle an easy target for ATGMs or opposing tanks.

The US have been producing the XM1156 Precision Guidance Kit, which turns a 'dumb' artillery round into a guided munition in a similar way as JDAM (Joint Direct Attack Munition – guided aerial bomb) kits do with unguided 'dumb' aerial bombs. The XM1156 can be paired with a handheld Joint Effects Targeting System, which a US Army official said could turn a howitzer 'into a giant sniper rifle', with a forward operator marking a precise target and the round hitting the GPS coordinates.

Accuracy and range are key challenges for all artillery. The further away a gun is from its intended target, the less accurate the rounds become. Gunners calculate the area into which rounds will land as the circular error probable, or CEP. At the maximum range of a standard 155mm shell, half of the rounds fired would impact within a 250-metre circle. Use of the XM1156 would reduce this CEP to 30 metres.

A Hell Cannon being loaded by members of the Free Syrian Army in Aleppo. The Hell Cannon used cooking gas bottles filled with explosives and scrap metal as ammunition. (Photo by Saleh Mahmoud Laila/Anadolu Agency/ Getty Images)

An extremely unusual image of an FSA Hell Cannon firing its propane cannister round seemingly mounted or attached to a tractor or ATV in Aleppo, 2015. (Photo by Salih Mahmud Leyla/Anadolu Agency/Getty Images)

Excalibur is probably the best known of GPS-guided precision artillery rounds. One problem with GPS-guided rounds, however, is that a moving target may change location by the time the round arrives. Laser-guided shells are considered more accurate, as they hone in on a target illuminated by a laser designator. The Excalibur-S variant has the option of using a semi-active laser, as does the Vulcano. The laser offers further improved precision with respect to pure GPS guidance.

Furthermore, employing laser-guided artillery rounds is more effective against an enemy that actively uses electronic warfare capabilities (and is of more utility in GPS-denied environments if the enemy is jamming or spoofing GPS signals). Ukrainian ground forces learned the lesson that

Vulcano and Excalibur S are far more resilient to enemy electronic warfare capabilities and should be used while engaging high-value targets.

Ukraine has also received BONUS and SMArt 155 rounds, which deploy submunitions that float down under parachutes or small wings, hunting for the infrared signatures of armoured vehicles. When one is spotted, the submunition waits until it is aimed properly, then fires a shaped charge into the top of the target.

Off-the-shelf technology has caught up with sophisticated (and costly) military systems for calling in artillery. Iraqi CTS (Counter Terrorist Service) during the battle of Mosul in 2017 used Google Maps on smartphones to plot Islamic State positions. These details were then communicated to Coalition strike-cells that controlled Coalition artillery and air power.

HOW DOES EXCALIBUR WORK?

Excalibur uses GPS guidance and steering fins to hit targets as small as 3 metres in size up to 40km away. The gun's crew puts known GPS coordinates into the shell – likely provided by a UAV. After launch, the fins pop out, allowing the shell to adjust its trajectory to hit the designated location. The Excalibur shell can reportedly strike within 2 metres of a target.

NATO partners have also provided other precision rounds to Ukraine, such as Vulcano. The Vulcano has a range of about 70km and is accurate to within 5 metres. The shell is GPS guided, though it can also be guided to its target by a semi-active laser illuminator.

A similar example is the use of smartphone ballistic computer apps and their iPhones' integral compass function by warring factions in Syria. The commercial products enabled them to accurately launch mortar and Hell Cannon strikes at a rate not far off that of professional mortar and artillery crews from Western armies.

In Ukraine, a system known as GIS Arta employs GPS and bespoke digital mapping to keep track of the location of friendly artillery. When a target is fed into GIS Arta, the system uses algorithms to decide which artillery battery is most suitable in terms of location and type of weapon versus the target.

Russia employs the Strelets fire control system that 'allows multiple feeds from ground-based sensors or detections by reconnaissance troops to be programmed and transmitted through a wide range of bearers, which are then integrated into Russian digital fire control.'[26]

The immediate near future of indirect fire will be a focus on sensor integration in the manner of the Russian reconnaissance fires complex, with a range of space, ground and air sensors increasing the accuracy and speed of artillery fire missions. It will also see the death of the towed artillery piece, to be wholly replaced by wheeled and tracked vehicles to enable rapid relocation to avoid counter-battery fires. In addition, there will be further research and development into extending the range of common artillery calibres and extending their smart capabilities, turning all artillery into precision-guided munitions (although care must be taken to shield such guided rounds from enemy electronic countermeasures).

For instance, the LRPF or Long-Range Precision Fires is the most important pillar in the US Army's modernization programme – a view only reinforced by the war in Ukraine:

Long-Range Precision Fires is designated as the foremost priority among the modernisation portfolios, largely as a reaction to Russian and Chinese progress in long-range tube and rocket artillery. Both the 155mm Extended Range Cannon Artillery (ERCA) designed to deliver enhanced rocket-propelled shells onto targets 70km distant, and the Long-Range Hypersonic Weapon (LRHW) with an initial 2,800km capability, are scheduled to equip their respective first batteries [in 2023].[27]

A new version of the Excalibur is also entering service which, incredibly, allows precision strikes against moving targets. Excalibur S is the enhanced version that allows laser designation by ground or air units, including UAVs. A further version is under development that will feature a ramjet engine to increase range. Another development is Rheinmetall's Velocity Enhanced Long-Range Artillery Projectile (V-LAP), which has a reported range of 76km.

With the dissolution of the Intermediate Range Nuclear Forces (INF) Treaty in 2019, the US is developing platforms that would have previously been banned under the treaty – namely missiles that can reach between 500 and 5,000km. Russia, although a signatory, has long ignored the Intermediate Range Nuclear Forces Treaty, while China was never a signatory and thus the US is now playing catch-up.

US Army Futures Command is focusing on improving LRPF capabilities by 'upgrading current artillery and missile systems, developing new longer-range cannons and hypersonic weapons, and modifying existing air and sea-launched missiles and cruise missiles for ground launch.'[28]

LRPF in the American context is envisioned to include four key pillars: Extended-Range Cannon Artillery (ERCA), the Precision Strike Missile (PrSM), the Long-Range Hypersonic Weapon (LRHW) and Strategic Mid-Range Fires (SMRF).

The US's next-generation self-propelled artillery to replace the M109A7 platform will likely be the M1299 ERCA, which increases its range by the use of an extended barrel – a whopping 9 metres – and by using the 155mm XM1113 rocket-assisted round which currently offers a 70km capability, more than double that of a conventional 155mm round. The M1299 will allow targets to be prosecuted by artillery rather than by more expensive and harder to replenish tactical missiles.

The platform has faced technical challenges seemingly around the provision of an autoloader to speed up its rate of fire and excessive wear and tear on the barrel – likely a result of the rocket-assisted ammunition. Other options are being investigated, including using advanced ammunition such as the XM1115-SC, which extends the range of the legacy M109A7 Paladin, and the XM1155, which offers a guided munition designed to engage moving targets both at sea and on land.

The PrSM (pronounced "Prism") is designed to replace the MGM-140 ATACMS of Ukraine fame. The PrSM can be launched from both M270A1 MLRS and M142 HIMARS platforms and will be capable of striking targets beyond 500km and potentially out to 1,000km.

The LRHW is a 'land-based, truck-launched system... armed with hypersonic missiles that can travel well over 3,800 miles per hour. They can reach the top of the Earth's atmosphere and remain just beyond the range of air and missile defense systems until they are ready to strike, and by then it's too late to react,' according to the US Army.[29]

A speed of 3,800mph equates to five times the speed of sound. The Army further defines the LRHW as 'a strategic attack weapon system to defeat Anti-Access/Area Denial (A2/AD) capabilities, suppress adversary long-range fires, and engage other high payoff/time critical targets'.[30]

SMRF uses modified SM-6 and Tomahawk Land Cruise Missiles launched form a truck-mounted launcher to engage targets sitting at ranges between PrSM and LRHW capabilities – namely over 500km and up to 1,500km.

In conclusion, the LRPF covers short to medium range with the ERCA, medium range with the PrSM, medium to long range with the SMRF, and long-range strategic targets with the LRHW. Tactically, LRPF reduces the reliance on strike aircraft, an important objective on a future battlefield facing intense Chinese or Russian air defence networks. It also supports efforts to deliver area denial assets to the Indo-Pacific; PrSM, for instance, could be delivered to an island or atoll by C-130 and fired by a HIMARS to deny access to PLAN warships, a mission the USMC is, as of 2022, actively developing and training for.

The drone may be taking the headlines, but it will not replace artillery (and missiles), at least in the near term. Drones are an enabler that improve artillery effectiveness but do not replace the humble big gun. For one, they cannot provide anywhere near the same effects on target. As one Ukrainian official noted, 'You cannot replace a 155 [mm] shell. It's like replacing a Kalashnikov with a small gun [pistol].'[31]

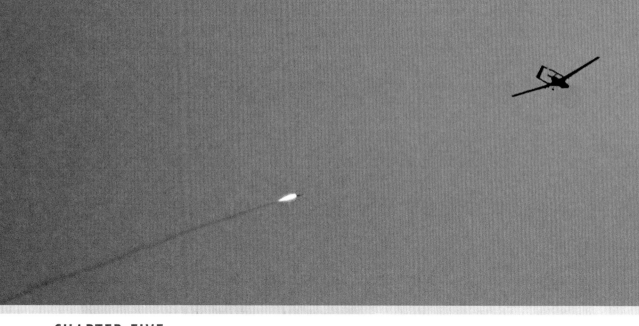

CHAPTER FIVE
UNCREWED PLATFORMS AND ELECTRONIC WAR

'Overwhelmingly, the weapon of choice has been First Person Viewer (FPV) drones'

Natasha Karner,
Australian Institute of International Affairs[1]

For many, the 2020 Nagorno-Karabakh War between Armenia and Azerbaijan served as a rude introduction to the technology of loitering munitions or suicide drones (now termed 'one-way attack' drones by the Pentagon). Many media commentators proclaimed that this 'new' method of warfare was revolutionary and would spell the end of armoured vehicles, artillery and infantry, in increasingly hyperbolic tones.

Colonel Scott Shaw, former head of the US Army's now defunct Asymmetric Warfare Group (AWG), noted when discussing the Nagorno-Karabakh War that the advent of cheap unmanned technology would change the parameters of what non-peer and non-state-based actors could achieve on future battlefields:

> What's clear in that conflict is that a less funded nation can do combined arms warfare. You don't have to be the United States or

ABOVE An iconic Ukrainian TB-2 drone about to meet an inauspicious end over Kyiv in May 2023 – shot down by a Ukrainian SAM after control was lost over the TB-2. (Photo by SERGEI SUPINSKY/AFP via Getty Images)

Russia. The price point to entry into combined arms warfare is lower than initially thought. You don't need something like the United States Air Force, a superbly trained, spectacular capability, in order to conduct potentially a local air-to-ground or air-to-air activity. In this view, the challenge posed by UAVs, be they unmanned aerial systems, naval vessels, or ground robots are profound.[2]

The truth is that the use of drones, and specifically loitering munitions in this case, was more evolutionary than revolutionary. Azerbaijan had in fact employed these suicide drones during the last conflict with Armenia in 2016. The country has been stockpiling a range of Israeli-designed and manufactured drones for a number of years, including the Harpy, Harop and Orbiter 1K (according to some reports, Azerbaijan employed modified Soviet-era An-2 Colt biplanes by remote control to trigger Armenian air defences, allowing them to be targeted both by artillery/ MLRS and by UAVs, including the now iconic Turkish-produced TB2).

The Azeri even employed truck-mounted launchers that appear strikingly like the classic MLRS, the modern ancestor of the infamous Katyusha of World War II Red Army infamy. These vehicles can launch up to 36 of the Israeli Harops, a veritable drone swarm of loitering munitions.

In the 2020 war, the Azeri employed their loitering munitions to target Armenian air defence networks and the radars that guide them – a technique known by the US Air Force as SEAD, or Suppression of Enemy Air Defenses. It was arguably the first such instance of killer drones being used in this manner.

The Center for Strategic & International Studies (CSIS) provided a balanced overview of the success of Azerbaijani UAVs, particularly useful when considering the impact of drones in the Russo-Ukrainian War:

> Azerbaijani UAVs provided significant advantages in ISR as well as long-range strike capabilities. They enabled Azerbaijani forces to find, fix, track, and kill targets with precise strikes far beyond the front lines. UAVs were operationally integrated with fires from manned aircraft and land-based artillery but also frequently used their own ordnance to destroy various high-value military assets.
>
> Open-source reporting suggests that UAVs contributed to disabling a huge number of Armenian tanks, fighting vehicles, artillery units, and air defences. Their penetration of Nagorno-Karabakh's deep rear also weakened Armenian supply lines and logistics, facilitating later Azerbaijani success in battle.[3]

Weaponized drones are not a new thing. The US Air Force and CIA have been flying armed Predators and later Reapers over the world's conflict zones since just before the attacks of September 11, 2001. In fact, the first armed Predator was deployed in the hunt for Usama bin Laden.

ABOVE An MQ-9 Reaper of the US Air Force pictured in 2007 equipped with Hellfire anti-tank missiles and GBU-12 precision-guided bombs. The MQ-9 can also carry signals intelligence pods that allow it to track mobile phones or radios, and the R9X variant of the Hellfire. The R9X carries no explosives and instead relies upon a number of blades that fold out during flight to eviscerate the target, minimizing collateral damage. (Photo by Ethan Miller/ Getty Images)

RIGHT A Chinese Tengden TB-001 MALE (medium-altitude long-endurance) unmanned combat aerial vehicle (UCAV) nicknamed the Twin-Tailed Scorpion. (Photo by VCG/VCG via Getty Images)

The Predator and Reaper are what are known as theatre-level drones – exquisitely capable but equally eye-wateringly expensive. It was the democratization of the armed drone that caused all those column inches. Suddenly, developing nations could have their own fleet of killer drones. This ignored the fact that non-state actors like Hezbollah and Islamic State had been employing cheap, weaponized, commercial drones since the mid-2010s.

Hezbollah is generally credited for the first use of a UAV dropping munitions onto a ground target – in Aleppo, Syria, in August 2016. As we detailed in Chapter 3, commercially available drones with jury-rigged munitions were even used in an attempt in 2018 to assassinate the leader of Venezuela.

Weaponized drones are clearly nothing new. However, we need to examine the differences between unarmed UAVs and their roles, and the different types of armed drone available to both state and non-state actors. Will they revolutionize warfare?

NATO has assigned UAVs three distinct categories based largely on weight and correspondingly size and capability, as the heavier the UAV, the larger it generally is and the more it can do. Class I indicates a weight of up to 150kg without payload (and payload here could be sensors or weapons). Class II is up to a maximum weight of 600kg, while Class III is any UAV over the 600kg mark.

Class III, typically a strategic or theatre-level asset (think of the Predator and Reaper and even bigger platforms like the Global Hawk), controlled by a higher headquarters than the troops on the ground, is also further subdivided into three types – MALE (medium altitude, long endurance), HALE (high altitude, long endurance) and Strike/Combat UCAV – based on their capabilities and/or intended role.

Class I and II are also sometimes referred to as Small UAVs (sUAV) or Tactical UAVs (TUAV). There are even further subclassifications of sUAVs to differentiate size, such as Micro and Mini (these might be the miniature drones used by counterterrorism teams, for instance). Although the NATO classification types are widely used, there is surprisingly no agreed international standard or naming convention.

The US Air Force has its own categorization system for UAVs that is confusingly distinct from the NATO system: 'Group 1 (mini and micro systems) through Group 5 strategic-level assets. Groups are based on speed, operating altitude, and weight. In general, the larger the platform the more robust the capabilities'.[4]

Most military drones are designed for surveillance and are equipped with cameras to provide real-time feeds of an area or individual point/person of interest. Some are more specialized and carry EW payloads to jam enemy communications or even enemy drones. Others are primarily signal intelligence platforms, scooping up electronic emissions and tracking targets by radio or phone.

(The US has two platforms in development that offer a glimpse into the future. The Future Tactical Unmanned Aerial System is designed to replace the RQ-7 Shadow as a brigade-level ISR asset offering the advantage of vertical take-off, while Launched Effects is a programme developing small UAVs that can deliver kinetic or EW effects while being launched from larger mothership airframes, either crewed or uncrewed.)

Finally, there are the dedicated weapon platforms; these generally also carry their own sensor array and a suite of electronic warfare or electronic countermeasures to assist in their own survival as well as for delivering their ordnance on target.

In the Middle East and Ukraine, we have seen the widespread militarization of commercial off-the-shelf drones; in fact, in Ukraine, the vast majority of platforms are commercial drones rather than dedicated military models. Commercial drones tend to suffer badly from electronic countermeasures; they can be easily jammed, as their electronics have not been hardened to protect them.

Even in Ukraine, most drones are ISR platforms. We have discussed previously how ISR drones have become an essential component for Ukrainian and Russian artillery. A 2023 report for the Croatian Armed Forces explained how they are being used to locate Russian artillery batteries:

A fully equipped UAV (with a camera, transmitter, receiver, etc.) is operated by an operator from a base towards a predetermined point where it flies over Russian positions, records them, and returns to the base. The recorded data is read on computers in the base. Then the process of identifying the locations of Russian vehicles and bases begins. Artificial intelligence, which can also recognize square artificial objects, is primarily used to find Russian positions and equipment, even if they are well camouflaged. Even small deviations from the environment indicate a possible target (e.g. dry leaves in a certain area compared to the surrounding fresh leaves). After discovering the target, the command decides which targets the artillery units will shoot at. Before firing, operators fly again to make sure the target is still in the same place. This double confirmation serves to avoid wasting Ukraine's limited artillery ammunition. During the firing, the command directly monitors the firing of targets and communicates with the artillery unit as needed for fire coordination.[5]

For the Russians, drones have seemingly taken over much of the physical reconnaissance function. RUSI documented that Russian infantry conducting ground reconnaissance is a relative rarity in Ukraine, with a heavy reliance on UAVs rather than traditional foot or vehicle-mounted patrols:

> … the Russians make very little use of observation or listening posts pushed forward of their main positions. Active reconnaissance, other than advancing to contact with disposable troops, is largely carried out by UAVs. Indeed, Russian troops appear to be reluctant to expose themselves through reconnaissance. Even when reconnaissance units work forward, it is usually to launch UAVs. It is typical for there to be between 25 and 50 UAVs from both sides operating over the contested area between the forward line of own troops (FLOT) and forward line of enemy troops (FLET) at any given time for each 10km of frontage.[6]

A Ukrainian truck-mounted 23mm ZPU-23-2 cannon from a mobile air defence group targets Russian drones. At night and without radar tracking, and with insufficient numbers of night-vision and thermal optics, this is a challenging proposition. (Photo by Kostiantyn Liberov/Libkos/ Getty Images)

ABOVE An Aviation Systems of Ukraine ASU-1 Valkyrja reconnaissance drone. (Photo by Lev Radin/ Pacific Press/LightRocket via Getty Images)

RIGHT A rare image of a Ukrainian FPV quadcopter carrying an RPG warhead. (Photo by Khrystyna Lutsyk/ Global Images Ukraine via Getty Images)

Brendan McBreen notes how the prevalence of drones has changed the battlefield, using Ukraine as the prime example:

> The battlefield is totally transparent. UAS are everywhere, all the time. We need to disperse, camouflage, and move to survive.
>
> Reports: During the battle of Bakhmut, in August 2022, there were 50 UAS in the sky at all times.
>
> In addition to continuous ISR, armed UAS killed tanks, artillery, and aircraft. Under this threat, UKR units have learned to disperse HQ, C2, ammunition, logistics, and aircraft. Dispersing is difficult, but more effective than concealment. 'There is no sanctuary' says U.S. Army General J. Rainey.[7]

He also mentions the increasingly disposable nature of tactical UAVs, something that RUSI have also warned of. Production of armed drones, in particular the FPV type, will become as important as artillery shell production for near-future wars. '90% of UKR drones are disposable – lost after an average of six flights. UKR may be losing 10,000 drones per month. All types of units on both sides are using expendable drones, loitering munitions, and counter-UAS capabilities. When RUS formations cannot hide and cannot mass, they cannot achieve surprise, and are therefore denied an important tactical advantage.'[8]

Ukraine has led the refinement and widespread employment of weaponized sUAVs. Although, as mentioned, Hezbollah and Islamic State largely invented the tactic in 2015/16, it has been the Russo-Ukrainian War which has seen it enter the military mainstream. Ukrainian crews even manufacture and 3D-print fins and tail assemblies to attach to RPG rounds or grenades to improve their accuracy when dropped from above by modified sUAVs.

A US Army Palletized Load System (PLS) Vehicle using an autonomous navigation kit. In the near future, all such logistics vehicles will be autonomously operated. It is one of the first relatively 'easy wins' in military autonomy. (US Army Reserve photo by Captain Katherine Alegado)

Along with the purely tactical effect of attacks by sUAVs dropping munitions, there is a huge psychological or morale effect. Russian troops can be seen desperately trying to shoot down sUAVs with small arms before the inevitable explosion. The audio signature of the sUAV hovering above likely adds to the terror.

The surprisingly common phenomenon of Russian troops shooting themselves in the head when isolated on the battlefield also may owe something to these weaponized sUAVs (and FPV loitering munitions) – rather than await their impending doom, these servicemen decide suicide is preferable.

Shashank Joshi in *The Economist* references analyst Franz-Stefan Gady, who has spent time on the ground with Ukrainian units:

> The appeal of FPV drones is that they offer cheap, accurate firepower. Unguided artillery shells cost anywhere between $800 and $9,000. A GPS-guided shell is closer to $100,000, and a Javelin anti-tank missile around twice as much again. A simple FPV drone costs perhaps $400.
>
> A typical Ukrainian assault group of 12 to 16 soldiers is now accompanied by almost the same number of drone operators, of whom half a dozen are FPV pilots. (The rest fly other sorts of drones, for tasks such as reconnaissance.)[9]

For loitering munitions, rather than quadcopter-style platforms that drop munitions such as grenades and mortar bombs, a key question has been autonomy. Besides any ethical dilemmas around the elimination of the 'human in the loop' in a lethal endeavour, fully autonomous platforms that use machine learning/AI to generate and then prosecute their own targets also need to be developed to operate within legal frameworks, including the Laws of Armed Conflict (LOAC) along with any national caveats from the operating nation state.

Consider, for example, how a fully autonomous platform could reliably recognize an enemy combatant that is *hors de combat* and thus cannot be legally further engaged. According to a UN report on the civil war in Libya, fully autonomous UAVs may have already been employed, noting the STM Kargu-2 (a quadcopter with an explosive charge) and similar platforms 'were programmed to attack targets without requiring data connectivity between the operator and the munition: in effect, a true "fire, forget and find" capability... Unlike Bayraktar TB2 or Israel's Harpy loitering munition, the Kargu-2 is designed to be an anti-personnel weapon capable of selecting and engaging human targets based on machine-learning object classification'.[10]

Teaming of FPVs with ISR has been perfected by both Ukraine and Russia. FPV attack drones work in tandem with an ISR drone operating as a spotter. The spotter drone also performs what is termed BDA, or bomb damage assessment, determining the effect of the attack drone on the target and whether the target needs to be re-engaged with another drone.

There is a natural confirmation bias occurring with the widespread recording of successful FPV attack drone strikes that perhaps overemphasizes their role, and particularly their role as a standalone weapon not in concert with indirect fire. Indeed, we know next to nothing about certain attack drones. The US Phoenix Ghost and Switchblade 600 have never been recorded in action, or at least videos of the platforms have never made it onto the internet.

Several analysts have highlighted the impact of the high-definition camera footage gleaned from Azerbaijani TB2s and other UAVs on the propaganda war during the 2020 conflict. In many ways, the Azerbaijani effort informed later Ukrainian information operations which showcased the TB2 as a 'hero of Ukraine' conducting seemingly innumerable strikes against the Russian invasion forces.

What was not known at the time was the carefully stage-managed process of releasing UAV kill footage onto social media; it now appears likely that the majority of TB2 successes (and footage) were in the first two to three days of the invasion, before Russian air defence caught up with their advance units. The Russians may also have been hesitant to engage other aircraft in the initial days to avoid fratricide, assuming that they would quickly gain air superiority if not supremacy. This, like so many Russian assumptions, was short-sighted. Ukrainian information ops masterfully released UAV footage over the course of the first several weeks, giving the impression of a veritable army of TB2s and cementing the Bayraktar as an early icon of the war.

Are FPVs as revolutionary as the carefully curated videos released by Ukrainian forces suggest? *The Economist* spells out the likely impact:

> The more common view is that drones will indeed revolutionise warfare, but alongside artillery rather than instead of it. A trio of artillery pieces might fire two or three rounds per minute for an entire hour, with each round delivering 10kg of high explosive with a blast that is lethal within a radius of 50 metres. Delivering that much firepower by an average FPV would require dozens of drones, each with their own pilot.
>
> Drones require a line of sight back to their operators. That is less of a problem in the flatter parts of Ukraine, such as Kherson and Zaporizhia, but a bigger issue in hillier regions such as Donetsk. And artillery can still fire in high winds or heavy rain – or in the cold, which can sap a drone's battery, and therefore its range.[11]

A recovered Russian ZALA Lancet loitering munition. Note that it is missing its lower wing pairs that form a distinctive X. (Photo by Thierry Monasse/Getty Images)

'Achilles', a Ukrainian drone commander interviewed by the magazine, explained:

> It is the combined firepower of artillery and drones that is powerful. FPVs – as well as more conventional mines or fire from armoured vehicles – can be used to paralyse a vehicle and force its crew out, he says. Artillery then hits the position and either kills them outright or forces them into shelter.
>
> If the soldiers make it into cover, the drones go back to work. Skilled pilots can guide them into underground shelters that artillery cannot reach. 'Even if the enemy survives the explosion, there won't be enough air to breathe. So they start coming out. And as soon as they do, we hit them with mortar [fire] or artillery or a fragmentation shell.'[12]

Weather can negatively impact drone operations. One great example of this occurred during the Nagorno-Karabakh War as Azerbaijan attempted to capture the city of Shusha, as recounted by the Modern War Institute:

A Ukrainian quadcopter drone fitted with what appear to be dummy 40mm grenades with 3D-printed tail fins to improve accuracy. 3D printing has proved a boon to AFU drone teams, with parts able to be replaced close to the front line. (Photo by Scott Peterson/Getty Images)

> On November 7 2020, foggy weather struck the area. This significantly limited Azerbaijani forces' use of aerial observation and strike assets that had given them such an advantage throughout the war. The inclement weather prevented the employment of the TB2 Bayraktar unmanned aerial vehicles, enabling Armenian forces to maximize the use of their armored vehicles – T-72 tanks, and BMP-2 infantry fighting vehicles – for counterattacks inside the city.[13]

The Azerbaijanis used Israeli and Turkish UAVs and loitering munitions. The primary Russian loitering munition that has come to prominence in Ukraine is the Lancet-3. Target acquisition is typically conducted by an Orlan-10 ISR UAV before vectoring in the Lancets for the strike. According to RUSI, 'Lancet has also been used extensively, along with FPV UAVs, to strike lead elements of Ukrainian units. Flown in complexes with ISR UAVs, these effects provide precision.'[14]

The Lancet carries a 3kg warhead in its larger Lancet-3 configuration, while its smaller Lancet-1 cousin carries a 1kg charge. Both are constructed from plastic, making them difficult to detect on radar, and are highly manoeuvrable.

Along with dedicated loitering munitions and the larger armed Group 4/5 drones such as the Reaper, the armed drone that has seen the most use in Ukraine and the Middle East has been the weaponized commercial UAV.

In Syria, non-state actors, including Islamic State, employed commercial hobby drones in a similar manner to Western armies – for the cost of several hundred dollars, an insurgent or militia group could suddenly have a capability that largely matched many of the far more expensive military drones employed at the tactical level. Insurgent drones were used to correct indirect fire, to conduct aerial reconnaissance, and as an offensive tool.

Early attempts were crude, using hand grenades or light mortar bombs, and were very hit or miss. The systems were refined, however (using certain types of grenades that were better suited for aerial bombing and even adding fins to improve accuracy), until 'weaponized' commercial UAVs became a legitimate tool on the Syrian battlefield. Insurgents could now field a capability that approximated Western loitering munitions like the Switchblade.

Iraqi and Coalition Forces faced armed drones during the campaign to oust Islamic State and during the battle for Mosul. General Raymond Thomas commented at the time:

> This last year's most daunting problem was an adaptive enemy who, for a time, enjoyed tactical superiority in the airspace under our conventional air superiority in the form of commercially available UAVs and fuel-expedient weapons systems, and our only available response was small arms fire. About five or six months ago, there was a day when the Iraqi effort nearly came to a screeching halt, where literally over 24 hours there were 70 UAVs in the air. At one point there were 12 'killer bees,' if you will, right overhead and underneath our air superiority.[15]

The Ukrainians have further developed the concept with 3D-printed fins and mounting brackets, again improving accuracy and reliability. A casual search on the internet will reveal hundreds of videos filmed from the point of view of the drone as it attacks Russian ground targets.

The R-18 Baba Yaga developed by Ukraine is quadcopter based and deploys three RKG-1600 bombs. As the nomenclature suggests, these bombs were developed from the RKG-3 anti-tank grenade. The RKG-1600 features plastic tailfins for accuracy, and the RKG-3's shaped charge can penetrate the top armour of all Russian main battle tanks.

The accuracy (and skill of the drone operator) has led to the destruction of expensive and otherwise well-protected Russian tanks and IFVs by 40mm grenades and 60mm mortar bombs dropped into open turret hatches. The success of such attacks has been bolstered once again by the poor drills of Russian soldiers who often leave hatches open and exposed while the vehicle is in a static position.

A sometimes-forgotten category of UAV is the Group 1 and 2 sUAV employed for tactical ISR at the platoon level, such as the lesser-known Bayraktar Mini – a hand-launched ISR UAV – which has also proven itself during operations in Ukraine. Man-portable drones have been seen in action since the early 2000s, with infantry and mechanized units transporting and launching their own UAVs.

Most of these platforms have been used for local aerial reconnaissance for the parent unit. Efforts are well underway that will see the outputs of such UAVs plugged into a larger sensor family that will allow the battlespace commander to access what individual squads or vehicles can see in real time.

This will cut through the traditional 'fog of war' but also poses its own challenges by potentially contributing to 'information overload'; a good and competent staff team will be needed to manage the myriad data and feeds that will soon be only a click away. The Polish WB Group Fly Eye, a man-portable Group 2 UAV, has been in service with the Ukrainian military since 2015 and has proven very successful in this role; it has also been employed by Ukrainian SOF due to its range and loiter time.

WB Group also manufacture the Warmate man-portable loitering munition. A number of Warmate UAVs were actually publicly crowdsourced for Ukraine in late 2022, in a similar fashion to the crowdsourcing of a TB2 earlier in the war. The Warmate can be fitted with different heads, allowing it to function as a purely ISR tool or as a loitering munition, including a thermobaric option.

Many loitering munitions or kamikaze drones offer a two-in-one package by providing an intelligence-gathering eye-in-the-sky with an offensive capability. The American Switchblade 60 and similar Israeli systems allow an infantry squad or SOF element to literally see behind that next hill and, if enemy are sighted hiding behind that hill, engage them with the drone.

Although the kinetic effects of these tactical loitering munitions are limited due to the size of the explosive charge carried (and most are akin to a 40mm grenade fired from an underslung grenade launcher), they still provide another card in the hand of the squad leader. Such platforms will excel in urban

environments where enemy snipers can be targeted inside buildings by flying a loitering munition in through a window or door and literally hunting down the enemy room by room.

The USMC is one of the first armies to publicly detail its near-future form with its Force Design 2030. Along with controversially divesting itself of main battle tanks and reducing its field artillery holdings, the Corps is aiming to push unmanned technology down to the fire team level. Under the plan, each infantry company will have a complement of seven JLTVs mounting multi-canister launchers deploying Hero-120 loitering munitions.

At the platoon level, two JLTVs will carry a total of six Hero-120s per vehicle, while each rifle squad will be issued one to two loitering munitions. For ISR, each fire team will be issued the Black Hornet tactical UAV; at squad, platoon and company level, a longer endurance UAV will be issued at each organizational level and task organized under the headquarters element.

In the SOF world, several specialized micro-UAVs are in service that allow special operators to look inside buildings. These drones are palm-sized but still provide a high-resolution live video feed that can be monitored by tablets carried by the operators. In hostage rescue scenarios, such drones have been employed (often alongside specially trained combat assault dogs) to search out the location of hostages, terrorists and potential IEDs.

Emerging technology allows these micro-UAVs to be equipped with a visible laser that can be employed to help guide a combat assault dog once inside an enemy structure or stronghold. Consider a tiny, silent UAV deployed into a target building that can illuminate specific rooms or areas of interest for a combat dog to search. The feed from the video camera attached to the harness

A good indicator of the cargo capacity of the Milrem Robotics THeMIS uncrewed ground vehicle. The THeMIS is in service with Estonia, Germany and Norway, and examples have been donated to Ukraine. It can also be fitted with kinetic modules, including 30mm cannon or Javelin and Stugna-P ATGMs. (Photo by Mykhaylo Palinchak/SOPA Images/LightRocket via Getty Images)

of the dog can be viewed alongside the feed from the micro-UAV to ensure the dog is heading in the right direction.

Throw-bots are also in use – particularly in the counterterrorism environment with some resembling a pair of wheels on a central 'axle'. A camera and other sensors are mounted in the 'axle'. Operators can throw the device through a window and the drone will propel itself around the room, beaming back live footage.

As Timothy Thomas notes in his superbly comprehensive 'Russian Lessons in Syria: An Assessment', it is not just Western forces who are experimenting with ISR 'bots':

In Syria a 'shock-resistant ball robot' was tested. It can withstand being thrown or dropped from a height of 5 meters, after which it adjusts itself to vertical. With four video cameras and a light-emitting diode (LED),

A pair of Russian Uran-9 UGV combat vehicles – perhaps tellingly on a trailer rather than operating under their own steam. Although equipped with a 30mm autocannon and a brace of ATGMs, the Uran-9 UGV performed poorly during combat trials in Syria. (Photo by Mikhail Svetlov/Getty Images)

a microphone, and transmitter, it can transmit images from a 360-degree view. The ball is known as the Sfera intelligence-gathering suite (referred to as the roly-poly in the army) and is used to reconnoitre tunnels.[16]

Besides ISR and attack drones of all shapes and sizes, there are both communications and electronic warfare variants. The Russian Udlintel UAV is one such unusual platform – a signal repeating/extending UAV that extends the control range of FPV and other sUAVs.

As we have seen in previous chapters, along with uncrewed aerial vehicles, near-future battlefields will feature numerous uncrewed ground vehicles of UGVs, some of which are already in, or about to enter, service.

The US Army has a major development programme to develop RCVs or robotic combat vehicles. These are distinct from the optionally crewed tanks and IFVs also under development. RCVs are built from the ground up as autonomous or semi-autonomous platforms that require minimal or no human direction.

Again, as we have mentioned in our discussion on autonomous loitering munitions, RCVs and similar UGVs that mount a lethal capability will likely remain firmly under the control of a human operator, at least when making shoot/no-shoot decisions by Western militaries. It is doubtful Russia and China would respect a similar morality.

The RCV programme initially required three platforms: RCV-Light, RCV-Medium and RCV-Heavy, divided into weight classes like their aerial brethren. The Army has since revised the requirement to a single class that sits somewhere between RCV-Light and Medium following trials.

A US Army spokesperson noted:

> … the outcome of the experiment [found] we really need a modular platform that kind of falls in between the two. It can be a little bit bigger than we were allowing the light to be, but it doesn't need to be as big as we were expecting the medium to be because what we found is the available options for payloads that exist in the defense industry right now could… fit on that smaller platform.[17]

Additionally, testing of the armed RCV-Heavy variant has been discontinued as it was discovered that firing a heavy calibre weapon on such a platform was 'a very, very difficult problem'. This was likely related to stabilizing the weapon enough to guarantee a level of accuracy. Stabilization can also affect the reliable functioning of an automatic weapon. The new RCV may see a lighter weapon such as an M240 medium machine gun mounted, but the Army is no longer looking at the likes of 30mm cannon as a potential armament.

That is not to say that heavy UGVs mounting such weapons won't appear soon; they will, but it will require more technological innovation to develop. The Russian Uran-9 that was combat tested in Syria proved disappointing, with frequent mechanical and control issues. Even when these technical issues are solved, combat UGVs attempting to survive in the direct fire zone will face challenges.

A UK Titan Strike demonstrator UGV from QinetiQ and Milrem Robotics. This variant mounts a remote weapons station with M2 .50cal. (PA Images/Alamy Stock Photo)

David Johnson, writing for *War on the Rocks*, makes this critically important point concerning UGVs: 'it is important to understand that, in all likelihood, the robot will be just as vulnerable to ATGMs and UAVs as manned systems. To be able to maneuver on the battlefields of the future, a solution that enables ground maneuver against enemy weapons is the key requirement.'[18]

Despite the reduction in size of the RCV programme, the US Army still intends to restructure its combat divisions using five templates to ensure commonality across the divisions. The Armor Division (Reinforced) – formerly known as the Penetration Division – will include a Robot Combat Vehicle Platoon in each of its Armored Cavalry and Division Cavalry Troops. Each Cavalry Troop will also have a Cross Domain Troop, which is expected to be responsible for deploying new technology, including UAVs and UGVs.

Russian social media in early 2023 loudly touted the deployment of the Marker UGV to eastern Donbas. The Marker was developed as a technology demonstrator, with two tracked and three wheeled versions known to have been produced. According to Russian reports, the Marker can be equipped with its own organic loitering munitions and has an on-board counter-UAV ECM capability. Modular weapons packages can be fitted, including a turret mounting a medium machine gun and a pair of ATGMs. Tellingly, since the initial furore on Russian Telegram channels, there has been little evidence of the platform seeing action.

The Russian defence industry has produced a bewildering number of UGVs in all shapes and sizes, some tracked, some wheeled. Most are armed, although typically this takes the form of a PKP medium machine gun slaved to a video camera. 'This is the problem with most of Russian UGV development,' noted Samuel Benett of the Center for Naval Analyses. 'They have many different projects. They have many different concepts. But they exist as single prototypes, or maybe in the case of "Marker," there are five of them instead of one.'[19]

The Israelis have deployed a robotic patrolling sentry called the Jaguar to Gaza. A six-wheeled UGV mounting a medium machine gun and a range of optics and sensors, the Jaguar 'is fitted with a self-disabling device so that, in the event one falls into the hands of hostile forces, they won't be able to recover any sensitive components. It also can transmit its coordinates so that it can be tracked and presumably destroyed by an orbiting UAV.'[20] The IDF reportedly plans to deploy the Jaguar with its conventional units as a reconnaissance and force protection tool.

UGV teaming will see ever more specific variants produced for different battlefield tasks – reconnaissance UGVs would be little more than a set of sensors with perhaps a light cannon or heavy machine gun for protection. Perhaps they will be completely unarmed and designed to be disposable. See the Israeli-manufactured Guardium 'Loyal Partner' reconnaissance vehicle – a wheeled set of sensors that can triangulate enemy fire. Imagine a similar platform but in an armoured, tracked shell.

ABOVE A US Army MaxxPro MRAP-based Electronic Warfare Tactical Vehicle, which provides radio jamming using a system based on the successful AN/VLQ-12 CREW DUKE IED jammer. (Photo by Mark Schauer, US Army, DVIDS)

RIGHT The BTR-based Infauna (RB-531B) 8x8 Amphibious Electronic Warfare System has been employed extensively in Ukraine, where it can jam radio signals. It has also been deployed to Syria, where it served as a counter-IED jamming system for Russian vehicle movements. (Photo by mil.ru)

Armed UGVs will also follow their aerial colleagues and operate in swarms to overwhelm the enemy's capability to respond in a timely and decisive manner. Indeed, armed UGVs operating as a swarm could also feature a 'suicide bomb' feature, allowing them to detonate when their human handlers or on-board proximity sensors decide they are within range of a valid target.

There are already examples of this kind of design principle, such as the Australian-designed GaardTech Jaeger-C, which includes variants that operate as the modern equivalent of the infamous German Goliath remotely controlled tracked bomb.

The Goliath was designed as an engineering tool to clear obstacles but soon found use against fortified positions. Its principal deficiency was in the trailing command wires needed to detonate the device. These could be easily cut by mortar or artillery fire, rendering the device immobile and incapable of detonation.

UAVs and UGVs are and will continue to be challenged by electronic warfare (EW). EW has also been employed to jam or distort communications and sensors such as air defence radars. Essentially, anything that operates or has devices on-board that operate on the electromagnetic spectrum are susceptible to EW.

Lockheed Martin provides a useful and clear definition of EW: 'Electronic Warfare (EW) represents the ability to use the electromagnetic spectrum – signals such as radio, infrared, or radar – to sense, protect, and communicate. At the same time, EW can disrupt, deny and degrade the adversaries' ability to use these signals.'

Further they divide EW into three major areas: 'Electronic Attack – disrupt, deny, degrade, destroy, or deceive. Electronic Protection – preventing a receiver from being jammed or deceived. Electronic Support – sensing of the electromagnetic spectrum.'[21]

Closely aligned to EW is SIGINT, or signals intelligence, and offensive and defensive cyber operations. Signals intelligence ranges from handheld scanners to intercept and listen in to unsecured communications (the I-Com scanner used during the Afghan campaign to monitor Taliban radio transmissions is one such example) to the use of aerial or even space-based platforms to vacuum up radio and mobile phone transmissions in a particular area of interest (something that would be conducted by the likes of the RQ-4 Global Hawk UAV with its Airborne Signals Intelligence Payload).

Offensive and defensive cyber operations involve computing power typically centred on 'intelligence gathering, harassment, subversion, and sabotage'.[22] An example was Russian attempts to paralyse the mobile phone network in Ukraine, which was also attempted on a more localized basis by EW jamming.

The IDF, along with a number of Western militaries including the US, has been computerizing its communications more and more in an attempt to create a networked force. If successful, this new technology will dramatically speed up the transfer of reports and commands, creating rapid responses with fire or manoeuvre to every new situation or target.

However, this technology is also more susceptible to cyber-attack and is also less mobile. The Ukrainian computerized command and control system was disrupted by a Russian cyber-attack on the first day of the war. In practice, Kyiv had prepared for this eventuality by maintaining older systems that were less susceptible to such interference.

TOP LEFT Ukrainian Kvertus KRAKEN-M jammers on display, which can jam most drone types, including FPVs, out to 800 metres in area mode or can be directed to jam specific directions out to 1,500 metres. The Russians have adapted a counter-IED jammer known as the Lesochek to mount on AFVs to jam FPVs. (Photo by Viktor Fridshon/Global Images Ukraine via Getty Images)

TOP RIGHT Another Kvertus design, the AD COUNTER FPV jammer, is produced in a manpack version that provides a jamming umbrella of around 300 metres against FPV drones. (Photo by Viktor Fridshon/Global Images Ukraine via Getty Images)

RIGHT A US Recon Marine trains with the Switchblade 300 loitering munition, monitoring its real-time feed through a ruggedized Panasonic tablet. (US Marine Corps photo by Lance Corporal Anna Higman)

This enabled the Ukrainian Army to continue to function effectively, if less efficiently. In general, to date, Russian cyber operations have not significantly affected the conflict, perhaps proving the somewhat flippant quote by British General Sir Patrick Sanders: 'You can't cyber your way across a river.'[23]

Another excellent example of offensive cyber action was the rumoured US Operation *Olympic Games*, which targeted the Iranian nuclear programme with the infamous Stuxnet virus from 2006. This operation is widely considered the 'first formal offensive act of pure cyber sabotage by the United States against another country, if you do not count electronic penetrations that have preceded conventional military attacks, such as that of Iraq's military computers before the 2003 invasion of Iraq.'[24]

Incidentally, near-future combatants will be forced to grapple with the thorny questions of at what point do offensive cyber actions cross the threshold of war, and what is a proportionate response, particularly in terms of a kinetic response.

Heading back to drones, the rise of FPV drones has also meant a rise in countermeasures that aim to stop them. They are obviously susceptible to EW jamming, and EW is considered the safest and cheapest counter-UAV method. The near future will see all AFVs equipped with some kind of jammer, and a war similar to that waged between the Joint Improvised Explosive Device Defeat Organization (JIEDDO) and insurgents constructing IEDs in Iraq will be inevitable. As soon as an effective counter is developed, manufacturers will develop a new method to avoid the jamming.

But there are, of course, countermeasures to the countermeasures. Drones can have their electronics hardened to resist jamming, though that increases the price. Some newer FPV drones are being delivered with swappable radio chips, making it easy to change the frequencies on which they operate. 'If the FPV drone is set up properly with the right software, and with the antenna at the right angle... you can't stop the drone,'[25] insists Pavlo Litovkin, an instructor at KazhanFLY, a drone training school near Kyiv. And precisely because the jammers emit so much electromagnetic radiation, they are easy-to-spot targets in their own right.

Counter-EW technologies are already deployed with theatre-level UAVs, but the technology is increasingly being pushed down towards the tactical level. A new technology that shows promise is autonomous object recognition (AOR), which uses object/landmark recognition to allow a jammed UAV to complete its mission essentially on autopilot. It also works in so-called GPS-denied environments; the Russians, for instance, routinely jam GPS signals and militaries must have means in place to operate without GPS.

Two systems that are being deployed by US forces are the Mounted Assured Positioning, Navigation and Timing System, or MAPS, and the Dismounted Assured Positioning, Navigation and Timing System, or DAPS. Both systems work on the same principle, using inputs including a global navigation satellite system (GNSS), which 'is a general term describing any satellite constellation that provides positioning, navigation, and timing (PNT)';[26] inertial sensors, on-board map data and assured GPS (so protected from spoofing or jamming). DAPS also includes data from the footfall of the individual soldier to mark location.

According to *The Economist*:

Object recognition is already available on expensive drones, like America's Switchblade 300, which costs $53,000. Russia's Ovod (Gadfly) FPV has supposedly used a similar AI-based 'terminal guidance' system since last summer. But drone advocates argue that

A US Navy SEAL training with the Switchblade 300 Lethal Miniature Aerial Munition System (LMAMS). (US Navy Photo by Mass Communication Specialist 1st Class Chelsea D. Meiller)

this too can be done on the cheap. The Ukrainian Scalpel drone, for instance, costs $1,000 and can lock onto a target designated by its pilot. So does the AirUnit, a prototype drone whose final version aims to be cheaper still.[27]

Drones will also have to contend with other drones equipped with EW systems. The US Multifunction Electronic Warfare Air Large, for example, offers sophisticated airborne EW – both offensive and defensive – from a pod mounted under the MQ-1C Gray Eagle UAV, which could be employed against aerial and ground targets.

In Ukraine, improved Russian EW systems have destroyed about 10,000 Ukrainian drones a month, and they have also intercepted and decrypted Ukrainian tactical communications in real time. They also have learned to intercept GPS-guided rockets fired by Western-supplied launchers such as the American-made HIMARS, which had previously embarrassed the Russians and inflicted major damage.

Reports in mid-2023 indicate that HIMARS has been successfully jammed by the Russians by attacking its GPS uplink, meaning that rockets will decrease in accuracy. The HIMARS has an inertial guidance system that still allows accurate targeting although not to the exacting accuracy of GPS (some analysts believe accuracy decreases from sub-15 metres with GPS to a circle of probable error of 60 metres or more).

Even JDAMs have been jammed by Russian EW. Jamming can affect most smart munitions, including guided artillery rounds – essentially anything that relies upon GPS for accuracy. GPS jamming has seen Ukrainian Army units revert to physical maps and fall back on, in some cases, runners to pass messages, as tactical radios are consistently jammed.

Russian EW units have proven proficient in both intercepting and jamming Ukrainian radio transmissions, including those conducted on secure systems such as the Motorola radios with 256-bit encryption commonly employed by Ukrainian Army units. This jamming and SIGINT monitoring can extend up to 10km behind the Ukrainian front line.

A Russian theatre-level EW platform, the Krasukha-4, which is designed to jam aircraft, drone and low-orbit satellite-based radars. A Krasukha-4 was foolishly abandoned by retreating Russian forces in early 2022 and turned over to NATO for exploitation. (Photo by Vitaly Kuzmin, CC BY-SA 4.0, https://creativecommons.org/licenses/by-sa/4.0/)

According to RUSI, the Russians have also been operating heliborne EW systems: 'There are believed to be eight Russian Mi-17s with EW suites operating in southern Ukraine. These are being utilised to some effect for the purposes of electronic attack against Ukrainian command and control, and through their altitude are able to do so in greater depth than is achievable by comparable systems based on the ground.'[28]

RUSI has also reported:

… Ukrainian forces note that the presence of attack aviation is often heralded by the lifting of GPS jamming among Russian formations, reflecting the need for precise navigation in order to coordinate strikes, given that both armies are using many of the same platforms. Russian helicopter groups are also often flying with an EW-equipped helicopter for defensive purposes, equipped with directional pods aimed at targeting radar.[29]

In the earlier Nagorno-Karabakh War, the Armenians lacked effective air defence against the Azerbaijani UAVs. Reportedly, a Russian-delivered Polye-21 (Field-21) EW system was successful in jamming the TB2s in the short term. Such EW platforms, which can be betrayed by their own electronic signature, became priority targets, as they later did in Ukraine. Air defence assets that could potentially target UAVs were themselves targeted by loitering munitions due to their electromagnetic emissions in the opening phase of the war.

We'll perhaps leave the last word on EW once again to Brendan McBreen, on the impact of EW in Ukraine:

Every signal is a target. The AO [area of operations] is electromagnetically transparent. We need to reduce emissions and mask our signals.

Reports: UKR units now view all emissions as targetable. UKR soldiers avoid cell phones. When UKR units stop cell phones and start paper-based comms, RUS sensors lose their ability to track UKR emissions. RUS brigade HQ pull back from the front line and seek protection underground in reinforced structures. Units need the capability to measure their own signals.

Jamming GPS is more effective than jamming radios. We need backup methods for navigation and targeting.

Reports: RUS jams GPS to interdict UKR UAS. Between 2018 and 2020, RUS EW disabled at least 150 UAS. In 2019, RUS neutralized 60 drone-and-missile attacks against a single air base. RUS jams GPS to counter precision weapons.[30]

In summary, as we have detailed previously, the inevitable consequence of experience with UAVs in Syria, during the Nagorno-Karabakh War and during the Russo-Ukrainian War is that every ground combat unit in the near future will require its own dedicated counter-UAV system. Most manufacturers of armoured vehicles are now offering optional add-on counter-UAV platforms mounted on the vehicle.

Like Active Protection Systems (some are being developed to target aerial drones), these counter-UAV suites are largely split between 'hard' and 'soft' kill capabilities. 'Hard' kill will see the enemy drone targeted by a kinetic platform that will shoot it out of the sky, while 'soft' kill systems focus on jamming or otherwise interfering with the drone's control mechanisms and/or its data link to its controller.

In Ukraine, we have already seen the deployment of Stinger and similar MANPADS to protect artillery and MLRS batteries against Russian UAVs (the Russians and Ukrainians use UAVs to both spot enemy artillery and in some cases attack them directly by loitering munition UAVs). The Stingers have been reasonably successful but will be obviously overwhelmed when faced with a swarm of aerial drones. For that scenario, a dedicated anti-aircraft platform designed to counter large numbers of UAVs will be required.

The US has provided 'mobile c-UAV laser-guided rocket systems'[31] to Ukraine, developed at record pace to engage Iranian-supplied Shahed-136s. The system is believed to use BAE's APKWS laser-guided rockets and is paired with both a medium machine gun and an EW system that can 'hijack' commercial non-hardened UAVs.

The US is already fielding a platform that could excel in such a role – the M-SHORAD based on the Stryker platform (which we discuss in more detail in Chapter 3). It can keep pace with wheeled or tracked self-propelled artillery or MLRS and provides an umbrella of protection against drone threats. The US is also fielding the M-LIDS, which can be mounted upon light vehicles such as the JLTV or even the venerable HMMWV.

Drones themselves will continue to adapt to stay one step ahead of the countermeasures. A Ukrainian-designed and produced UAV called the Atlas PRO offers a capability that will soon be commonplace across all UAVs – a frequency-hopping system that identifies which frequencies are being disrupted by the Russians and locks on to open frequencies which are not being actively jammed.

Atlas PRO is also conducting pioneering work in enabling a mesh radio network between UAVs. Simply put, this allows UAVs to communicate with each other without requiring constant connectivity with the UAV controller – only a single UAV requires a radio link back to the controller. The other UAVs in the swarm receive their guidance commands via its closest partner who is 'passing on the message'.

Again, as we have noted, in future conflicts, participants must be prepared to operate within a GPS-denied environment where the enemy is either jamming or actively engaging friendly satellites and thus negating systems that

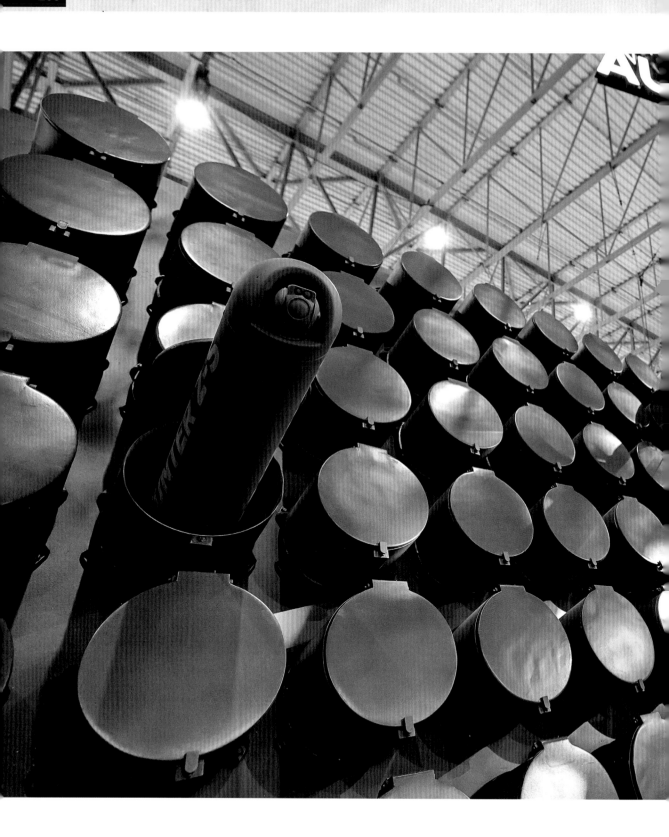

A drone swarm multi-launcher for the Emeriti-designed and produced Hunter 2-S, with a warhead up to 2kg and a 50km range. (Photo by GIUSEPPE CACACE/AFP via Getty Images)

The notorious Russian but likely Iranian-produced Shahed 136 attack drone in the skies above Kyiv. The Shahed 136 has now also been produced in Russia with Iranian components where it is known as the Geran-2. (Photo by SERGEI SUPINSKY/AFP via Getty Images)

rely upon GPS which, in most advanced militaries, is almost everything. NATO has recognized this and is implementing platforms that can operate in such environments, such as the Theatre Positioning System (TPS) that doesn't rely upon GPS satellite data.

Systems that rely upon GPS will also be susceptible to 'GPS spoofing', an EW technique that 'spoofs' or sends a false signal to a GPS receiver. Satellites may be directly targeted. China is also reportedly developing directed energy (laser) weapons to target satellites. The US have been developing similar platforms.

According to a number of leaked US documents, the Russians may have been experimenting with using their Tobol-1 satellite EW defence system to conduct EW attacks against SpaceX Starlink satellites. Satellites can be attacked in space by uplink jamming, which sees the attacker distorting the signal from the satellite to the ground receivers, leading to incorrect location information displaying on GPS receivers.

Attacks against ground receivers, known as downlink jamming, jam the signal by transmitting on the same frequency as the satellite and are more like traditional radio jamming. Starlink units in Ukraine have suffered from localized downlink jamming as well as uplink jamming, which has restricted the use of audio and has slowed the process of a Starlink connecting with a satellite.

Russia is pushing 'directional jammers and arrays for hijacking UAVs'[32] down to the platoon level. Some reports also note that Russia is upping its counter-UAV game by employing specialist UGVs to target aerial drones. A previously unknown platform developed specifically for the war in Ukraine comprises a 'remotely controlled combat module (RSWM) with an automatic guidance system and tactical augmented reality goggles, specifically to tackle the threat of small UAVs. The new system would integrate remote control, automatic aiming, microwave detection, tracking and suppression, via a low-power laser and MANPADS, all within a common mission management module.'[33] As with a number of Russian systems (the Armata series of next-generation AFVs, for example), the RSWM may yet turn out to be vapourware.

BELOW A Ukrainian tank crewman points out a counter-drone jammer on what appears to be a Polish-supplied T-72M1R. (Photo by Andre Luis Alves/ Anadolu via Getty Images)

NEXT PAGE Ukrainian forces employing SpaceX's Starlink satellite internet system, which allows sharing of real-time ISR feeds and enables communications when radios and mobile/cell phones are jammed by Russian EW. (Photo by Maxym Marusenko/NurPhoto via Getty Images)

CHAPTER SIX
INFANTRY

'… to close with the enemy by means of fire and maneuver. Its purpose is to destroy or capture him, to repel his assaults by fire, close combat, and counterattack, or all of these…'

US Army FM 3-21.20 (The Infantry Battalion)[1]

The core of any army is the infantry. They exist to capture or destroy the enemy and seize and hold objectives. The Australian and British armies employ a similar definition of the role of the infantry: 'to seek out and close with the enemy, to kill or capture them, to seize and hold ground, repel attack, by day or by night, regardless of season weather or terrain.'[2]

This role remains unchanged in the 21st century: physical objectives cannot be held unless infantry are sitting on it with their 'boots on the ground'. All manner of technology will assist in that endeavour, but no drone, robot tank or hypersonic missile can hold territory. For that, the infantry reigns supreme. And for that reason, there will always be a need for the humble foot soldier.

Along with taking and holding that terrain, be it a strategically placed hill, city or bridgehead, the infantry conducts a wide range of tasks that enable employment of other 'teeth arms' (the combat elements of an army). Logistical supply convoys need to be protected from ambush; forward refuelling and rearming points require securing; buildings and terrain features need to be cleared of enemy; civilians protected, and aid

ABOVE US Army soldiers in Syria, with one carrying the disposable AT-4 (M136) anti-tank rocket. Note the Bradley IFV in the background. (Photo by DELIL SOULEIMAN/AFP via Getty Images)

Russian soldiers in Mariupol, Ukraine, 2022. Note the 'Z' invasion patch and optics and rail-equipped 5.45mm AK-74Ms. (Photo by ALEXANDER NEMENOV/ AFP via Getty Images)

provided… In fact, it is difficult to consider any ground task or objective that doesn't require the infantry. They are the tactical glue in land warfare.

Of course, in a recurring theme, the infantry cannot operate in isolation. They must be part of that combined-arms approach that sees infantry supported by artillery, armour and air power, let alone the dark arts of electronic warfare, cyber and information operations.

For the infantry to triumph on the battlefield, all components of this combined-arms approach must work in concert. Russian efforts to seize the Ukrainian capital of Kyiv in March 2022 are illustrative of what happens if these disparate but interconnected arms do not work hand-in-glove.

The Russian Army suffered from a lack of infantry within their BTGs; the infantry units assigned to these larger Battalion Tactical Groups were severely undermanned due to recruitment and retention problems that have plagued the Russian military for years.

Even if the requisite training had been completed for the Russian infantry to operate in close concert with their armour (it had not), the motor rifle units in particular were chronically short of soldiers – a consequence of high casualties in earlier wars in places such as Chechnya and Georgia, along with their bloody ten-year Afghanistan commitment.

Indeed, in the initial 2014 Russo-Ukrainian War, the 'lack of infantry causes BTG commanders to prefer to isolate urban infantry strongpoints for prolonged sieges instead of assaulting to reduce them… Instead of combined-arms maneuver to overpower inferior Ukrainian forces, Russian BTGs preferred to… employ fires.'[3]

While it is true that no army ever goes to war with a full and complete table of organization and equipment (former US Defense Secretary Donald Rumsfeld famously but accurately quipped, 'You go to war with the army you have, not the army you might want or wish to have at a later time'), the Russian Army were understrength to an alarming degree, indeed a degree which actively conspired to see Russia's overly optimistic (some would argue fantastical) ambitions of a three-day operation to capture Kyiv in early 2022 fail spectacularly.

Numerous observers commented on this lack of coordination, coupled with understrength motor rifle units: 'BTG infantry cannot prevent Ukrainian mechanized and light infantry anti-tank hunter/killer teams from attriting their AFV, IFV, and SP artillery. This is the primary job of infantry in tank units.'[4]

Conversely, the US Army in the invasion of Iraq, Operation *Iraqi Freedom*, was far better manned and trained in infantry-armour coordination. Mechanized infantry carried in Bradley infantry fighting vehicles would dismount to provide a defensive cordon against RPG and ATGM teams and established forward security for the necessarily long logistical chain that kept the tanks and IFVs running as they advanced on Baghdad.

The Second Battle of Fallujah (Operation *Phantom Fury/Al-Fajr*) in 2004 also provides an illustrative counterpoint to the Russian experience in February 2022. In Fallujah, US Marine and Army infantry units worked closely and highly effectively with their armoured brethren. US tactics in clearing city blocks within Fallujah infested with diehard jihadists were glaringly more successful than Russian efforts at urban warfare in contested Ukrainian cities (and in Chechen cities several decades earlier).

Ukrainian National Guard troops training with BTR-4 Bucephalus infantry fighting vehicles. Note the suppressor (silencer), angled foregrip, red dot optic and extended 40-round magazine on what appears to be a captured Russian 5.45mm AK-12. (Photo by Stringer/Anadolu via Getty Images)

ABOVE A US Marine during a partnered presence patrol in Ramadi, Iraq, 2008. Note the AK-armed Iraqi Police behind the Marine. The Marine carries the 5.56mm M16A4, fitted with ACOG optic, PEQ-2 laser illuminator, and forward grip. The M16A4 has since been replaced withthe M27, a version of the HK416. (Photo by Cpl Casey Jones, DVIDS)

So it is clear that to undertake any ground operation infantry is the key component. For much of the first two decades of the 21st century, Western infantry has been employed in counterinsurgency. Consider Iraq and Afghanistan – wars of choice certainly, but ones where the West's overwhelming technological and qualitative advantages could not prevail alone.

COIN requires old-fashioned infantry patrolling, outside of armoured vehicles and able to 'meet and greet' the locals to dissuade them from the attractions of the insurgents. Again, like holding physical objectives on a conventional battlefield, this cannot be accomplished by any other element of the combined-arms matrix.

COIN will only have a chance of success (and there are many wider arguments whether modern COIN can ever be truly successful) by employing light infantry in the dismounted patrolling role.

The preponderance of COIN and Support and Stability Operations (SASO) during the noughts and 2010s saw an obvious reduction in emphasis on peer or near-peer conflict (and thus conventional warfighting skills) and a focus instead on more COIN-focused tactics by US and NATO armies. Arguably this did not affect the capabilities of the infantry as much as it did other combat branches.

RIGHT US Marines seen practising shotgun breaching with the issue Benelli M1014 semi-automatic shotgun. Elite units like the Rangers and Delta Force continue to rely on pump/slide-action shotguns rather than semi-automatics as they more reliably feed low pressure shells like specialist breaching rounds. (US Army photo by Staff Sergeant Armando R. Limon, 3rd Brigade Combat Team, 25th Infantry Division)

Syrian militiamen of the Faylaq al-Rahman Brigade carrying craft-produced 12.7mm anti-materiel sniper rifles, pictured in 2017. The weapon, known as the Nimr-2, appears to have been created using the barrels from Chinese W-85 heavy machine guns and cheap Chinese optics. Similar craft 12.7mm and even 14.5mm have been manufactured by various irregular groups, including the Kurdish YPG and Islamic State. (Photo by ABDULMONAM EASSA/ AFP via Getty Images)

COIN and SASO require solid patrolling drills, competency in building clearance and breaching, and a renewed focus on force protection ('preventive measures taken to mitigate hostile actions,' according to the US military) of units and facilities. Many of these skills are equally useful in more conventional warfare.

Russian infantry were involved in operations that could be very loosely interpreted as SASO during the 1990s in Chechnya and later during the 2008 Russo-Georgian War with the annexation of Abkhazia and South Ossetia. Many of their tactics, however, relied upon traditional Russian warfighting means – massed rocket and artillery fires and a brutalist approach to urban combat. It appears few lessons were learned institutionally by the Russian Army in their employment of infantry during these conflicts, as many of the same issues re-emerged during the 2022 Russo-Ukrainian War.

Traditionally, Russian-supported armies such as the Syrian Arab Army theoretically followed Russian infantry tactics but were generally poor performers, at least against any Western standard. They also exhibited poor coordination between infantry and armour, although the quality of opposition forces meant that they often triumphed despite themselves.

The PLA is the great unknown. China hasn't been involved in a conventional war since a limited conflict with Vietnam in the late 1970s. All indications are that Chinese infantry will exhibit quality levels closer to Russian infantry than US or NATO armies. They will follow a staunch and restrictive command and control system that actively discourages individual initiative and consequently any form of mission command, a concept that makes Western armies so much more effective.

The unusual Chinese QLZ-87B, a semi-automatic high-velocity 35mm grenade launcher. (Photo by Costfoto/NurPhoto via Getty Images)

Where infantry of different nations have more in common is in their structure. The basic building block of most modern infantry units is the fire team. This fire team is typically composed of four soldiers, each with their own defined tactical role within the subunit: the team leader; the grenadier carrying an underslung grenade launcher attached to his assault rifle; the gunner equipped with a light machine gun; and a rifleman.

Two to three such fire teams make up a squad (or section in Commonwealth armies like the British or Australians). Three (or occasionally four) such squads make up a platoon. As noted, however, armies are rarely if ever at full strength, so understrength platoons are the norm. In Afghanistan this resulted in the British Army and Royal Marines operating as 'bricks', a term that originated from operations in Northern Ireland.

A 'brick' saw two sections as its core manoeuvre element while often reinforced with members of the company's support platoon (general-purpose machine guns and sniper rifles, for example). The support platoon would act as a fire support group overwatching the manoeuvre elements ('overwatch' being a tactic that sees one unit providing a 'look-out' for another, ready to interdict by fire any enemy movement that threatens the manoeuvring element).

The Russians, of course, do things differently, with infantry structure based around the transport capacities of their BMP and BTR vehicles. A Russian squad is typically six soldiers strong, including a machine gunner equipped with the PKP and an RPG gunner. The Russians do, however, often form combat groups for a specific function or operation, harking back to similar assault groups formed during urban fighting in World War II.

Timothy Thomas, again writing for the MITRE Center for Technology and National Security, detailed one such example grouping used in Syria by Russian forces conducting urban warfare:

> To force terrorist forces out of their positions, maneuvering assault teams became the primary means of attack. Applying some criteria from World War II's lessons learned fighting under urban conditions to the Syrian experience, Kiselev noted that each team usually included seven assault riflemen, five combat engineers, three or four light and heavy machine crews, and two antitank riflemen.
>
> The engineer teams determined if minefields were present and disarmed them when possible. Artillery or direct fire was then opened against one corner of a building, then against another to create openings for assault teams. Engineers used explosives to expand the breach, with riflemen shooting at fleeing terrorists. Tanks were employed behind the advancing assault teams, but they were used sparingly, usually only when broad maneuver was allowed.[5]

Most armies continually experiment with structure, and the infantry is no different. The USMC has added a squad systems operator to each squad who will manage uncrewed platforms and ECM/EW and an assistant squad leader who will handle fires. The Marines have now added two Marines to each squad, bringing them up to 15.

A Ukrainian soldier firing the Russian 7.62mm PKP Pecheneg, a modernized variant of the PKM medium machine gun. Note the blue tape on his helmet, a common identification friend or foe measure. (Photo by Jose Colon/Anadolu Agency via Getty Images)

EXO-SUITS AND LIQUID ARMOUR

Despite several attempts, there are no true 'exo-suits' (in the sense of sci-fi movies like *Edge of Tomorrow*, where powered armour suits are controlled by the wearer). The most likely success in this area will be weight-bearing exoskeletons that allow the soldier to carry more weight over longer distances for longer periods of time.

US Army Futures Command predicated that a true armoured battle-suit-style exoskeleton – dubbed the 'Warrior Suit' – won't become a reality until the 2040s as technology matures. A similar project headed up by US Special Operations Command, for instance – the TALOS, or Tactical Assault Light Operator Suit – was shelved in 2019 after issues integrating differing technologies and ensuring a viable power source.

The Russians have been parading their own suit, the Ratnik-3, for several years, but it is yet to be seen on an actual battlefield (although, like many Russian systems, there are untested claims that it was trialled in Syria). The Ratnik-3 also suffers from power supply problems, with a reported four-hour battery life.

German firm Mehler Protection, well known for its body armour products, is developing the ExoM Up-Armoured Exoskeleton, which is a non-mechanical full-body armour exoskeleton that uses a titanium frame to redistribute its weight, allowing users to wear the suit for longer. It's really a heavy body armour suit and best suited for breachers (it is being co-developed with French counterterrorism unit GIGN).

In terms of next-generation body armour, a Polish company are working to perfect Shear-Thickening Fluid (STF) – a liquid that hardens when impacted and spreads the force of the impact over a wide area while reducing the indention caused by the projectile. It appears to hold great promise for use in body armour.

The British Army's Experimentation and Trials Group have been working on the ideal structure for an infantry section designed for urban combat. Under Urban Phalanx, so-called Next-Generation Combat Teams were formed of two infantry platoons of three ten-person sections, with each platoon supported by a Manoeuvre Support Group. Each Phalanx platoon also has a small HQ, a UAV/UGV system operator and an anti-armour component.

The dissemination of support and anti-armour weapons, UAVs/UGVs and countermeasure systems against IEDs and UAVs adds further weight to the infantry platoon, who must man-pack all of their kit into action after dismounting from their battle taxis. Afghanistan proved an excellent example of how overloaded modern infantry can be. British infantry routinely struggled under 40–60kg loads, indeed so much so that some Taliban wits allegedly referred to them as donkeys on their iCom radios.

Despite much of this weight being 'protective' in nature – the body armour with plates, the helmet, the electronic countermeasures kit, the Vallon mine

detector and all the rest – it ironically means that the infantry is often less effective and arguably less protected. The heavy loads mean that their nascent capability to physically manoeuvre on the battlefield – the basics of being able to move quickly, go prone (and quickly get up again) and patrol over extended distances without heat exhaustion setting in – is significantly impacted.

British mechanized soldiers in Basra, Iraq, 2006. Note the short-lived Kestrel body armour with collar protection. (Photo by Daniel Berehulak/ Getty Images)

An obvious solution would be to try to reduce this weight to improve manoeuvre – the so-called 'fight light' concept, carrying only equipment that is likely to be of immediate use during an operation. Of course, the obvious challenge of the 'fight light' idea is determining exactly which pieces of equipment will be needed and which can be left at the forward operating base. Australian experiments in the concept saw infantry carrying only four magazines for their rifle, for example – arguably sufficient for COIN in a semi-permissive environment, but for facing the might of the PLA in a regional peer conflict…?

There is also a moral component here. What platoon leader will knowingly reduce protections for his infantry, to rightly reduce weight and thus improve manoeuvre, at the risk of having to write that awful letter to the soldier's parents explaining that he or she was killed as they were not wearing back plates in their combat body armour? Or that the ECM kit that could've prevented the detonation of that remotely detonated IED was left behind? Or that the soldier ran out of ammunition, and his or her position was overrun because they were only carrying four magazines of ammunition?

Although they are generally not getting any lighter, infantry small arms today are more accurate and deadly than ever before thanks to the widespread adoption of combat optics, from red dot sights to magnified scopes by Western armies. Russia has lagged behind NATO, with a far smaller percentage of their general-issue rifles featuring optics of some kind.

RIGHT The Russian 5.45mm AK-12 assault rifle fitted with a red dot holographic weapons sight. The AK-12 and its 7.62 cousin the AK-15 have been adopted by the Russian Army to supplement the AK-74M; however, only relatively small numbers of AK-12s have been recovered in Ukraine. (Photo by AFP via Getty Images)

BELOW RIGHT A French soldier of the 13eme BCA (*Bataillon de Chasseurs Alpins*) armed with a 5.56mm Minimi, equipped with sound suppressor and EOTech holographic weapon sight, in Afghanistan, 2010. (Photo by JOEL SAGET/AFP via Getty Images)

An upgrade to all AK-74M rifles and AK-12 was planned but, like so much within the Russian military, the programme was beset by delays and corruption. Today, it is still comparatively rare for Russian rifles with optics to be encountered in Ukraine, for example.

In the West, optics have become standard for all assault rifles and most light and medium machine guns. They tend to fall into two categories: non-magnified and magnified. Non-magnified optics are typified by the likes of the EOTech or Aimpoint, which project a red dot within the optic itself (unlike the visible red lasers seen in the movies); the shooter aligns the red dot on the target. Red-dot optics speed up engagement times (quicker to get on target at short ranges) but do not provide a magnified view of the target.

Magnified optics are more akin to the traditional 'sniper scope'; the target is magnified within the optic, allowing more accurate shooting at longer range. The most popular of this type of combat optic is the Trijicon ACOG, or Advanced Combat Optical Gunsight, which provides a 4x magnification of the target.

There are also a number of optics that combine both magnified and non-magnified. EOTech and Aimpoint both market optics that include a 'swing-out' magnifier that can be flipped out of the way for close-range shooting using just the red dot. Others offer a mini red dot sight that is mounted on top of or to the side of the main optic.

Weapon calibres have remained largely focused around the traditional 5.56x45mm (as fired from the M4A1 and SA80A3, for example), the 5.45x39mm (the AK-74), and the 7.62x54mm and 7.62x51mm (used in Russian and Western medium machine guns and marksman rifles respectively). In recent years, the US has embarked on a number of programmes to develop a new standard round for its issue rifle and squad automatic weapon. This resulted in a 2022 announcement that the US Army would adopt a new calibre – the 6.8x51mm under the Next Generation Squad Weapon (NGSW) programme.

The new calibre was the result of a number of still contentious assumptions around what was termed 'overmatch', which in this context claimed that US forces were out-ranged by enemy armed with longer-range weapons (the 7.62x54mm SVD marksman rifle and PKM medium machine gun).

This idea gained currency during the war in Afghanistan but didn't take into account a number of factors: the poor marksmanship of the insurgent enemy; the actual number of wounds and deaths caused by enemy small-arms fire; and the concept's applicability in other parts of the world (most infantry firefights in Ukraine, for example, are still short ranged).

The Next Generation Squad Weapon – Rifle (NGSW-R) for the US Army: the 6.8x51mm XM7 developed by SIG. The 6.8x51mm round features a hybrid case manufactured of steel and brass, allowing extremely high chamber pressure which results in the ability to fire a heavy projectile at a very high velocity, even from relatively short-barrel carbines. (US Army photo by Jason Amadi, DVIDS)

It also didn't consider that the two weapon types that were claimed to be overmatching US capabilities were already in US inventory: each US Army squad has a designated marksman with a scoped 7.62x51 rifle able to engage targets out to 500 metres and beyond, and each platoon has access to M240 7.62x51mm medium machine guns that are attached as needed.

The second reason given for the switch to the new calibre was a concern about penetration of Russian and Chinese body armour and helmets. The initial requirement for the new round was the ability to consistently penetrate Level IV body armour plates at 600 metres – Level IV armour is proofed against multiple strikes by 7.62x51mm and 7.62x39mm (the calibre of the AK-47) armour-piercing ammunition.

The new weapons designed to fire the 6.8x51mm are the XM7 rifle and the XM250 automatic rifle. Both are designed and manufactured by SIG Sauer. It is still open to question at the time of writing whether the new weapons will ultimately replace the M4 and the M249 and/or be adopted by other NATO nations. The plan is currently to equip infantry and airborne units with the new weapons while non-combat arms will retain the M4A1.

The cost of adopting a new weapon is far larger than simply the purchase of the new guns and, in this case, ammunition (introducing a new ammunition type obviously leads to its own logistical challenges). The largest cost is in retraining everyone who will use the new weapons and those who are tasked to maintain said weapons.

The NGSW does come as a system, however, and the new M157 fire control system, which is perhaps the most useful element, combines a variable magnification optic, a laser rangefinder, and an on-board ballistic computer that will automatically adjust aiming points to account for bullet drop at extended ranges.

Additionally, the M157 is designed for integration with enhanced or augmented reality devices, such as

THE M7

The biggest change in the 2020s has been led by the US military and its development of the M7 assault rifle. Designed by SIG, the M7 fires the 6.8x51mm XM1186 round. The calibre is impressive in that it outperforms the 7.62x51mm but in a lighter package.

The secret sauce is the casing itself – a hybrid that uses a stainless-steel base rather than a fully brass casing, enabling significant increases in pressure. This means that the round has an extremely high velocity, even in short-barrel carbines which traditionally see a significant velocity bleed.

The M7 is expected to replace the legacy 5.56x45mm M4A1 carbine in the hands of infantry, air assault and airborne units. It will be paired with the M250 automatic rifle in the same calibre – a replacement for the M249 squad automatic weapon series. Both the M7 and the M250 will feature a sophisticated day/night sight with laser rangefinder, which is expected to improve both the situational awareness and accuracy of the average shooter.

The 5.56mm Zbroyar UAR-15 in Ukrainian service, a domestically produced M4-style assault rifle featured here with suppressor and optic. A 7.62mm version, the UAR-10, is also produced. (Photo by Elizabeth Servatynska/Azov Media/ Global Images Ukraine via Getty Images)

Israeli reservist infantry armed with the 5.56mm bullpup X-95 Tavor assault rifle. The machine gunner in the foreground carries the iconic 7.62mm FN MAG58 general purpose machine gun. (Photo by Amir Levy/Getty Images)

the US Army's Integrated Visual Augmentation System. With the goggles or future variants built into ballistic protection eyewear, infantry can mark items or areas of interest through their goggles and weapon optic, and automatically share this with fellow squad or platoon members (think of an NCO pointing out a potential enemy firing point, no verbal directions required). Navigational waypoints can also be added to visually show avenues of advance or attack.

Along with the US 6.8x51mm, there have been a number of programmes in recent years looking to lighten the weight of the medium machine gun and increase its range and lethality. One success story is the SIG MG 338, officially the Lightweight Machine Gun – Medium (LMG-M), adopted by US Special Operations Command and now in the running for wider adoption across the US Army and potentially USMC.

The LMG-M both reduces the weight burden compared with the issue M240 family and increases the range of the platform to 1,800 metres. The .338 Norma Magnum round it fires is also heavier hitting than the legacy 7.62x51mm of the M240. The LMG-M will likely serve as the template for other NATO nations who wish to upgrade their 7.62x51mm machine guns.

There has also been a move away from the integrated combination rifle/ grenade launcher typified by the M4/M16 with underslung M203 40mm launcher attached under the rifle's barrel. Standalone launchers have been found to be more accurate and less unwieldy than the combination underslung versions, and the US Army is issuing the M320 in a standalone form along with a mounting kit should the soldier prefer the underslung configuration.

The US Army is also experimenting with the Grenade Launched Unmanned Aerial System (GLAUS), which as the name implies, gives every soldier a camera-equipped UAV that can be launched from the standard-issue M320 grenade launcher. Other developments include laser-guided 40mm grenades and rounds that are 'dialable', allowing the soldier to choose an airburst option, for instance, if faced with enemy behind cover.

Although there have been a number of attempts to introduce a successful magazine-fed grenade launcher into NATO armies, such as the XM25 Punisher, the only platform that has gained some acceptance is the Milkor M32 series, which looks like a revolver on steroids. The M32 has been adopted by the USMC and US Special Operations Command.

Rheinmetall is developing a new grenade launcher at the time of writing called the SSW40 (Squad Support Weapon 40), which is a magazine-fed semi-automatic launcher and which can fire both low-velocity and medium-velocity 40mm ammunition (medium-velocity rounds offer greater range and a lighter velocity).

The war in Ukraine has also refocused attention on mines as a means of channelling the enemy or denying access to territory. A standard from the Cold War has re-emerged after its successful employment by Ukrainian infantry: the off-route mine.

Off-route mines more resemble a remote anti-tank rocket than a traditional land mine and are triggered either by a vehicle crossing over a concealed 'breakwire' or by command wire detonation (i.e., by a soldier hidden nearby). The advantage of off-route mines is that they can be angled to attack the (usually thinner) sides of an enemy armoured vehicle.

The USMC is one of the first organizations to widely field suppressors on all small arms. The Corps is even adding suppressors to the M240B medium machine gun. The advantage to the user in terms of hearing protection is obvious; less obvious are other advantages, such as not spooking civilians and being able to clearly communicate while firing. Suppressors also make it more difficult for the enemy to pinpoint the source of incoming fire. (US Marine Corps photo by Sarah N. Petrock, 2nd Marine Division Combat Camera)

Ukrainian Territorial Defence Force soldiers riding atop a BTR-80 series armoured personnel carrier (note distinctive digital camouflage). Because of poor underbody protection against mines and the generally poor survivability of Russian APC and IFV designs, soldiers commonly ride on top. In Ukraine, however, this proves its own challenge as numerous videos of APC-borne infantry being engaged by FPV drones or artillery show. (Photo by Maxym Marusenko/NurPhoto via Getty Images)

Modern off-route mines are also programmable so can be set to activate or deactivate remotely. When triggered, the mine launches a HEAT warhead. Their low angle of attack also means that they may not trigger a response from an enemy APS. In another sign of the growing recognition of the importance of mine warfare in any future conventional war in Europe, the German Bundeswehr delivered some 1,600 MBDA Panzerabwehrrichtmine (PARM) off-route anti-tank mines to Ukraine in 2022, ordering more in 2023 to replenish their own stocks.

The Russians have employed mines to a staggering degree in Ukraine. They have also reverted to other traditional defensive measures, such as anti-tank ditches and dragons' teeth (normally cement constructions that are difficult for vehicles to cross). RUSI examined Russian defensive TTPs in their 2023 *Russian Tactics* report:

Russian defensive positions generally comprise two to three lines, depending on the context. The first line, along the line of contact, comprises the fighting positions made by the infantry. The second constitutes properly made trenches – as compared with fox holes in the first – and concrete firing posts where possible.

Several obstacle belts are laid in front of these positions, usually formed with a 4-m-deep and 6-m-wide anti-tank ditch, dragons' teeth and wire track entanglements. The trench positions are usually structured as company fighting positions in wood blocks and on ridge lines, placed to cover areas of open ground with fire, rather than as contiguously occupied front lines. The depth of the defence line is usually 5km from the first, and each belt of physical defences tends to span between 700m and a kilometre, so that the entire obstacle series is covered by fire.

The third line usually comprises fall-back fighting positions and concealed areas for reserves, with positions dug for vehicles. Command posts (CPs), meanwhile, tend to be subterranean and fortified with concrete. The overall depth of defensive fortifications exceeds 30km on some axes. Minefields are another element of the Russian defence line. These rarely follow a discernible pattern and are seldom marked. Ukrainian forces note that the Russians have no shortage of mines, creating mixed fields containing both anti-tank (AT) and anti-personnel (AP) mines.

The report goes on to say that Russian infantry and engineer units indeed display:

> ... a strong preference for mining the approaches to natural choke points. In some cases, an AP mine may be placed directly on top of the AT mine. Initiation mechanisms are also often mixed. It is common for AP mines, for example, to be initiated by a seismic sensor and to have an immediately adjacent mine initiated by wires, which are laid out in a cross from the device. The Russians have also made extensive use of magnetically activated AT mines delivered via multiple launch rocket systems (MLRS). Although Russian forces have been successful in tracking the routes through their own minefields, they have performed less well in breaching mine belts laid by the AFU [Armed Forces of Ukraine].[6]

Non-state actors have employed mines and IEDs in similar ways: 'In Sangin, Afghanistan, the Taliban invested significant resources into putting out a high volume of relatively unsophisticated antipersonnel IEDs. This tactic was successful in limiting the operational mobility of British forces, who were effectively hemmed into the district center by IEDs. When [US] marines took over in 2010, operational mobility was restored only at the cost of significant casualties.'[7]

Light anti-tank capabilities are also being refined by Western armies. The US Army aims to replace its fleet of M72 series, M136 AT4, M136A1 AT4 (Confined Space) Light Anti-Tank Weapons, and the M141 Bunker Defeat Munition with a new Shoulder-Launched Munition known currently as the XM919 Individual Assault Munition. The new platforms aim to incorporate capabilities across the spectrum of previous LAW types, including the ability to fire from within enclosed spaces (typically the explosive backblast makes launching LAW or RPG type weapons dangerous from within rooms or other confined spaces).

Javelin anti-tank guided missile fired by US troops during an exercise in Syria. The Javelin benefits from a top-down attack mode targeting the much thinner top armour of enemy AFVs. (Photo by DELIL SOULEIMAN/AFP via Getty Images)

UPDATING THE RPG

The PG-29V rocket fired from the RPG-29 Vampir features a tandem-charge warhead that has defeated the armour of Challenger 2 and Merkava IV MBTs. The Vampir, which weighs in at a hefty 18kg, can also fire the TBG-29V thermobaric and the OG-29 anti-personnel round.

An updated variant, the RPG-29-2003, features a folding tripod and an integrated laser rangefinder and day/night optic. Iran has produced a copy, the Ghadir. The PG-7VR Resume rocket is a tandem-charge warhead for the ubiquitous RPG-7 platform, improving its ability to attack and defeat ERA and applique armour.

Modern ATGMs like the Javelin and Ukrainian Stugna-P employ tandem-charge warheads. These were developed to counter Russian explosive reactive armour (ERA), such as the older Kontakt and more recent Relikt. ERA was initially designed to defeat shaped-charge warheads, such as the historically ubiquitous HEAT, and thus is susceptible to tandem-charge ATGMs.

Tandem-charge warheads work on the principle of using a smaller explosive precursor which detonates the target's ERA before a larger follow-on explosive penetrator defeats the armour of the enemy vehicle. In simple terms, the top/front part of the tandem-charge warhead clears the way through the ERA for the armour plate to be attacked directly by the molten metal jet of the penetrator.

A Ukrainian soldier firing the iconic RPG-7. Note the stabilization fins that have deployed on the rocket which increases accuracy. (Photo by Muhammed Enes Yildirim/Anadolu Agency via Getty Images)

TOP LEFT Ukrainian anti-tank gunners launch a Kornet (AT-14 Spriggan) ATGM against Russian positions. The Kornet is relatively rare in Ukrainian service, with the domestically produced Stugna-P much more widely employed; the Stugna also allows remote but tethered firing. (Photo by Laurent Van der Stockt for Le Monde/ Getty Images)

CENTRE LEFT A superb image of current-generation infantry anti-tank weapons. From the top: the 84mm Carl Gustav M3, the Saab-Bofors Dynamics Next-generation Light Anti-tank Weapon (NLAW), and the AT4/M136. All have been employed to great effect against Russian armour and fighting positions in Ukraine. (Photo by Erika Gerdemark/Bloomberg via Getty Images)

BOTTOM LEFT The famous NLAW provided to Ukraine by the UK. The single-use NLAW has a top-attack option to attack the weaker top armour of AFVs and operates by predicted line of sight (PLOS), which requires the operator to keep the target in their sights for several seconds before launch. Once fired, the NLAW warhead follows the target in 'fire and forget' mode. (Photo by AFP via Getty Images)

The British Army, perhaps witnessing the effectiveness of the Carl Gustav M3 in Ukraine (a Carl Gustav famously destroyed a T-90M in May 2022 near Stary Saltiv), announced in 2023 that they would be adopting the lighter M4 variant of the recoilless rifle.

The Carl Gustav has a long history with British forces and was first adopted in 1963, becoming a mainstay as the section anti-tank weapon during the long Cold War years before being retired in favour of single-shot launchers, culminating in the NLAW.

Saab, manufacturer of the Carl Gustav, now offers a wide range of warheads for the M3 and M4, including the HE 441E Programmable Round, which delivers airbursts out to 1,500 metres; the ADM 401, which is filled with flechettes to target infantry or soft-skin vehicles in the open; and the HEAT 751, which 'neutralizes explosive reactive armour (ERA) tiles fitted to a target. It then initiates the HEAT warhead to penetrate the target's main armour.'[8]

Platforms like the Carl Gustav will continue to see a resurgence in Western armies and will likely be pushed down to the section/squad level as an organic support weapon capable of engaging light and heavy armoured vehicles, and urban structures and defensive positions.

Infantry and cavalry units will increasingly be equipped with their own organic ATGM capability mounted on light vehicles that can provide anti-tank overwatch for their fellows. The UK Brimstone in Light Forces variant offers 'a salvo launch option to achieve coordinated effects on multiple targets during a single mission and includes line-of-sight or non-line-of-sight engagements [and] third-party targeting',[9] meaning that a single vehicle could incorporate its own UAVs for spotting purposes.

Counter-drone technology has also seeped down to the infantry section. 'Drone Buster' guns that jam the transmission of commands and GPS data from and to small UAVs are already commonplace. Body-worn detectors are also being introduced that will alert infantry to the presence of tactical UAVs, providing them hopefully enough early warning to combat the drone with either jamming or a more kinetic response. Most of these devices have a range of 2–3km.

The US Air Force's 'Small-Unmanned Aircraft Systems Guide & Reporting Procedures' helpfully notes, 'sUAS can be loud due to their rotors cutting through the air, the rotors cause a distinct, high-pitch buzzing noise. Sound is a good indicator that the drone is close enough to see. This noise can be heard within a couple hundred meters of your location.'[10] Unfortunately, in combat with all of the attendant noise, sound is not a good indicator.

Shotguns have proven useful in Ukraine against small drones and may see them return to limited issue (shotguns are still used for breaching doors with specialist ammunition). The British Army has purchased the Israeli-designed Smart Shooter SMASH x4 optical sight, which employs image-processing software to track and predict the movement of the UAV; once the firing solution is generated, the sight fires the rifle when the likelihood of a hit is highest.

A British Army trainer noted:

> Our current option to target a drone is to just shoot at it, and they are small and mobile targets that are very hard to hit. The Smash sight increases the probability of a hit, reducing the amount of ammunition used. It's about efficiency, and it also offers a surveillance capability to detect drones that soldiers might not have spotted.[11]

The SMASH system has already been used in combat by the IDF and US Special Operations Forces in Syria.

Western infantry will soon be equipped with a range of devices that will significantly increase their situational awareness. The Integrated Visual Augmentation System (IVAS) is the US Army's effort to develop a smart goggle using Microsoft's HoloLens display. HoloLens is a see-through lens that can be used to project data, including real-time video, to the user – for instance, the feed from a UAV or UGV or even from a camera mounted on another soldier's weapon.

As the US military becomes increasingly networked, other data may be fed (and be visible) via weapon optics or goggles; for example, drones overhead may be able to provide 3D mapping of terrain out of line of sight to the infantry or highlight a concealed enemy position that can be engaged – perhaps with the infantry squad's own loitering munitions – before the enemy have a chance to engage advancing friendly forces.

In the near term, IVAS will offer integration with the current issue Black Hornet squad-level UAV, allowing fledgling capability to look beyond the next hill. When integration with the likes of the AeroVironment Switchblade 300 or its successors occurs, the infantry will have the ability to also strike beyond that hill.

In common with all such technological advances, equal effort must be made to ensure such devices and inputs are hardened

INFANTRY DRONES

UAVs used by the infantry range from Group 1 micro-UAVs, such as the Black Hornet that transmits video to the soldier's ATAK tablet, to larger Group 3 drones, such as the RQ-21A Blackjack operated by the USMC. Increasingly, they are also operating loitering munitions such as the Switchblade or Russian Scalpel.

An Australian innovation allows a UAV to be launched from a grenade launcher. The DefendTex Drone40 is, according to the company's datasheet, an 'autonomous, loitering grenade deployed from either a 40mm grenade launcher or hand launch'. The strength of the system is that it democratizes both ISR and loitering munition capability, pushing it down to the infantry fire team level, and is lighter and easier to operate than the Switchblade.

Soldiers can carry several Drone40s, but these will likely be grouped with the squad's systems operator, who will monitor feeds and agree kinetic employment of the munition with the squad or fire team leader.

The Drone40 gives the infantry a platform that can conduct aerial reconnaissance before the infantry must traverse the terrain on foot. If enemy are spotted, they can then be engaged as the Drone40 becomes, in the words of the Pentagon, a 'one-way attack drone'.

against enemy hacking and exploitation. As the possible hacking of US drones by Iranian cyberwarfare units shows, every such new technology is at risk of exploitation by a technologically savvy opponent. A hacked augmented reality weapon optic could be disastrous, as it feeds nefarious information to the user – perhaps spoofing their location, messing with range-finding data and using the user's own technology to highlight their presence to enemy forces.

Communications systems are also being integrated into augmented reality systems like IVAS. One challenge in urban environments has been maintaining consistent radio communications due to the level of interference caused by the concrete and rebar of structures.

The Mobile Ad Hoc Network (MANET) only requires connection to a soldier's closest teammate to provide access to the MANET network, which will assist in maintaining communications through building complexes, for example. Soldiers could conceivably act as relay stations; such systems could also prove to be the solution for the problem of maintaining communications underground while navigating sewers.

The Android Team Awareness Kit (ATAK) is also being incorporated into IVAS. ATAK is a smartphone/tablet-based software that incorporates mapping and communication, and one which talks to battlefield management systems, displaying the location of friendly and enemy forces.

The US Army development of augmented reality via 'smart' day/night goggles will continue apace, as the capability gains are simply too potentially impressive to ignore. AR integration allowing infantry to utilize sensors mounted on future AFVs will be the next step, vastly increasing situational awareness of soldiers who have been traditionally 'blind' to the immediate battlespace while travelling in IFVs or APCs.

'The goal of platform integration… is to not only ensure that Soldiers equipped with IVAS don't lose their enhanced situational awareness while mounted, but to also take advantage of the on-board platform sensors that enable them to see what the combat vehicle sees,' explained a spokesperson for the IVAS programme during a demonstration of IVAS augmented reality integration with the Bradley IFV in 2021.

> With this integrated technology, they can get map, mission, and intel updates enroute. They can see what is around them to strategically position the Bradley and then drop the ramp where they are not in direct fire and execute immediately. In World View [an AR setting which gives the user a wider view of the battlefield], they can also know where their brother and sister platforms are, so they can work together, cover more ground, and make informed decisions and ad hoc changes on the move all while buttoned up in the Bradley.[12]

KNOW YOUR NIGHT VISION

Night vision is classified by generations, with first generation obviously being the oldest and third generation being the latest and greatest. All generations work on the same principle: amplification of ambient light. If there is little to no ambient light available – in a tunnel, for example – an external infrared light source is needed.

With each generation there was a step-change both in image quality and in life expectancy of the tube(s) in the night-vision device (and in cost). Much of Russia's night-vision technology is still second generation, for example, primarily down to cost and Russia's engineering base. Modern Western night vision is typically classed as third generation or third generation +. These are typified by the four-tube 'quad-eye' GPNVG-18 goggles, which drastically increase the field of vision by employing quad tubes.

Infrared lasers (the green lasers seen in Hollywood productions and the *Call of Duty* franchise) can only be seen by someone using night vision, making them ideal to mark positions. Less commonly seen in the movies but widely employed by Western units are infrared torches or flashlights, whose beam is only visible through a night-vision device.

With any such technology, the risks of information overload remain. At what point does the user become effectively paralyzed as they attempt to process and make decisions based on the myriad feeds available to them? It's also worth considering countermeasures for such technology, as it will eventually fall into the hands of the enemy.

A good example of this is the spread of night-vision technology among non-state actors such as the Taliban and Syrian militias. This has meant that the overwhelming advantage once held by Western forces is fast eroding. Techniques such as reducing the use of infrared lasers to only when a target is being 'painted' (and thus limiting the possibility of the enemy spotting the laser and using it to 'track-back' to the user) are of some assistance, but it is a worrying development.

The L3Harris GPNVG-18 (Ground Panoramic Night Vision Goggle) in use by German special forces. The GPNVG offers a 97-degree panoramic field of view and was originally intended for aviators. (Jens Büttner/ dpa-Zentralbild/ZB/dpa/ Alamy Live News)

Infantrymen and special operators fear non-state actors getting their hands on infrared strobes used to identify friendly units on the ground to overhead assets. This would effectively hamper close air support at night as air assets would be unsure of the nature of those wearing the strobes – friendlies or enemy. The proliferation of such technology will reduce another traditional advantage of Western militaries (namely, owning the night on the battlefield).

CHAPTER SEVEN
SPECIAL OPERATIONS FORCES

'Russia's Federal Security Service (FSB) said on Thursday that Britain's Special Boat Service had been operating in Ukraine and helping Ukrainian forces carry out attempted operations against Russian forces.'

Reuters,
11 April 2024[1]

Long before they came to worldwide notoriety thanks to their role in Ukraine and their later failed rebellion against Putin, the Russian private military company Wagner Group came face to face with the elite of the US military. And came off second best.

The battle occurred in February 2018 in eastern Syria, when Wagner mercenaries supported by pro-Assad militiamen and Syrian government forces attempted to wrest control of the Conoco gas plant. All told, the force numbered somewhere between 300 and 400 fighters supported by T-55 and T-72 tanks. Next to the plant was a small American special operations Mission Support Site manned by around 30 special operations forces (SOF) soldiers from the US Army's Delta Force and Ranger Regiment.

As the enemy forces took the site under effective fire, the Americans, supported by a Green Beret Quick Reaction Force, called in artillery and

ABOVE A 75th Ranger Regiment soldier armed with a 7.62mm Mk17 SCAR battle rifle, pictured in Afghanistan in 2019. The 5.56mm SCAR was not popular with the Rangers, as it offered little over their M4A1 carbines, but the 7.62mm has supplemented the M110 as a designated marksman rifle. (US Army photo by Specialist Jonathan Bryson)

massive amounts of close air support, decimating the opposition. The operators and Rangers also engaged with their own Javelins, machine guns and sniper rifles. When the dust settled, somewhere between 68 and several hundred of the enemy force had been killed and a number of armoured vehicles destroyed.

The battle – known variously as the battle of Khasham (named for the town close to where the incident occurred) or the battle of Conoco Fields – gives a glimpse into the shadow battlefields where modern SOF operate. Although the concept of unconventional or irregular warfare can be traced back to the French and Indian War (the birth of the Ranger lineage), it was not until World War II that modern special operations came into their own.

Small bands of soldiers formed into often derided 'private armies', such as the Special Air Service (SAS) and Long-Range Desert Group (LRDG), along with their contemporaries on the intelligence side of the house, the Special Operations Executive (SOE) and the Office of Strategic Services (OSS), developed the template for today's SOF. These originators specialized in what would later be recognized as core SOF skills: reconnaissance, raiding, targeted killing, and raising and supporting resistance forces behind occupied lines.

The Global War on Terror (GWOT) was perhaps the first war that saw SOF being the supported command rather than supporting conventional forces. During the early years of operations in Afghanistan, SOF led the campaign. Later, in Iraq, SOF were instrumental in conducting shaping operations for conventional forces during the invasion and ushered in the now controversial era of 'kill/capture' – targeting of insurgent and terrorist targets.

'Kill/capture' has been discredited by some as a valid counterinsurgency tool, with the argument alleging that killing insurgents simply produces more recruits, particularly if civilians are inadvertently harmed during such operations. Others say that 'kill/capture' denies an insurgency the technical knowledge and leadership of senior leaders, as they are taken out of the game. Certainly, in Iraq, both theories could be true. SOF largely dismantled al-Qaeda in Iraq only for it to re-emerge as the fledgling Islamic State.

When SOF are employed correctly as a strategic asset, they act as a force multiplier and can provide an impact on the battlefield far outweighing their size. Reports from March 2023 indicate that Russian forces are employing Spetsnaz units as a form of light infantry, heavily equipped with anti-tank weapons, as a reserve force behind static lines of defence to act as a 'fire brigade' to blunt Ukrainian breakthroughs.

One battle in mid-March illustrated this tactic, with a Ukrainian armoured and mechanized infantry force in T-72 main battle tanks and YPR-765 APCs breaching the first line of Russian defences (likely manned by 'mobilized' troops, i.e., conscripts). Ukrainian ISR had failed to detect a GRU Spetsnaz Brigade behind the conscripts, which promptly stopped the advance with ATGMs, artillery and air support.

NEXT PAGES An Australian-produced but British-crewed Bushmaster Protected Mobility Vehicle (PMV) seen in Syria in 2022. This Bushmaster is operated by UK Special Forces, in this case 22 Special Air Service (SAS). (Photo by AFP via Getty Images)

WHAT IS THE ROLE OF SOF?

The best summary of the myriad of SOF missions is perhaps not surprisingly proved by USSOCOM, the Special Operations Command of the US military who list the following as Core Activities of US SOF on their website:

- **Direct Action:** Short-duration strikes and other small-scale offensive actions employing specialized military capabilities to seize, destroy, capture, exploit, recover, or damage designated targets.
- **Special Reconnaissance:** Actions conducted in sensitive environments to collect or verify information of strategic or operational significance.
- **Unconventional Warfare:** Actions to enable a resistance movement or insurgency to coerce, disrupt, or overthrow a government or occupying power.
- **Foreign Internal Defense:** Activities that support an HN's [host nation's] internal defense and development (IDAD) strategy and program designed to protect against subversion, lawlessness, insurgency, terrorism, and other threats to their internal security, and stability, and legitimacy.
- **Civil Affairs Operations:** CAO enhance the relationship between military forces and civilian authorities in localities where military forces are present.
- **Counterterrorism:** Actions taken directly against terrorist networks and indirectly to influence and render global and regional environments inhospitable to terrorist networks.
- **Military Information Support Operations:** MISO are planned to convey selected information and indicators to foreign audiences to influence their emotions, motives, objective reasoning, and ultimately the behavior of foreign governments, organizations, groups, and individuals in a manner favorable to the originator's objectives.
- **Counter-proliferation of Weapons of Mass Destruction:** Activities to support USG [US government] efforts to curtail the conceptualization, development, possession, proliferation, use, and effects of weapons of mass destruction (WMD), related expertise, materials, technologies, and means of delivery by state and non-state actors.
- **Security Force Assistance:** Activities based on organizing, training, equipping, rebuilding, and advising various components of Foreign Security Forces.
- **Counter-insurgency:** The blend of civilian and military efforts designed to end insurgent violence and facilitate a return to peaceful political processes.
- **Hostage Rescue and Recovery:** Offensive measures taken to prevent, deter, preempt, and respond to terrorist threats and incidents, including recapture of U.S. facilities, installations, and sensitive material in overseas areas.
- **Foreign Humanitarian Assistance:** The range of DOD [Department of Defense] humanitarian activities conducted outside the US and its territories to relieve or reduce human suffering, disease, hunger, or privation.[2]

During the Nagorno-Karabakh War in 2020, Azerbaijani SOF were employed in a more strategic role to support a conventional thrust to capture the city of Shura. Several hundred SOF infiltrated covertly into the area largely on foot through inhospitable mountain and forested terrain. Their mission allowed conventional forces to retake the city.

The Russians have employed their SOF in more strategic tasks; for instance, during the annexation of Crimea and the Donbas, they were employed in covert action tasks (earning the infamous nickname Little Green Men due to their lack of identification and sudden arrival posing as separatists) and in special reconnaissance and direct-action missions. Many of these were tasked by the GRU, Russian military intelligence.

In Donetsk in 2014, for example, the Ukrainian government managed to negotiate with the local separatists to surrender their position holding the local town hall. As Russia learned of the agreement, Little Green Men in unmarked uniforms arrived and convinced the separatists of the error of their ways and the deal was cancelled.

The GRU's Spetsnaz is the most recognized of Russian SOF; they date back to the 1950s and fuelled many a NATO planner's nightmares. During the Cold War they were tasked with behind-the-lines activity, including assassination of NATO leadership and sabotage missions against industrial and military targets. Despite their popular image, they are not directly comparable to Western SOF, being more an elite light infantry unit that can conduct a limited range of SOF tasks. In Western parlance, they would be a Tier Three or possible Tier Two SOF entity.

An MH-6M Little Bird flown by the US Army's 160th Special Operations Aviation Regiment during a hostage rescue demonstration in 2024. Operators ride on the external bench seats and can use the Fast Rope Insertion/Extraction System (FRIES) to fast rope onto an objective if it is unsafe for the Little Bird to touch down. Note the swing-arm mounted M240L medium machine gun to provide suppressive fire. (Photo by Luke Sharrett/Getty Images)

SOF TIERS

During the GWOT, the classification of SOF began to be defined by tiers. Initially, this was likely related to US military funding and the source of that funding: Tier One units were funded by JSOC (Joint Special Operations Command), while Tier Two were paid for by US Special Operations Command. Later it became somewhat lazy shorthand for the operational capabilities of SOF units.

There is to this day no hard and fast rule as to what constitutes a particular tier capability, but it is generally accepted that units such as Delta Force, 22 Special Air Service, Naval Special Warfare Development Group (SEAL Team 6), the Special Boat Service and the Russian SSO are regarded as Tier One. Tier One units tend to be focused on counterterrorism and strategic national missions.

Tier Two units are what many would consider traditional SOF – units such as the US Army's Special Forces (the famous Green Berets) and 75th Ranger Regiment, the US Navy SEALs, and UKSF (UK Special Forces) units, such as the Special Reconnaissance Regiment and the Special Forces Support Group.

Rarely used as a term, Tier Three is typically related to conventional units that have some special operations capability – normally airborne (paratroopers), Marines, or airmobile (helicopter-borne) units that can support SOF units or conduct limited SOF-like tasks such as non-combatant evacuations or airfield seizures.

Along with Spetsnaz, Russia has the SSO, an organization established in 2013 and directly modelled on US and UK Tier One units. It is, in simple terms, the Russian JSOC (Joint Special Operations Command). The SSO is even structured into five divisions or squadrons. Like their Western equivalents, SSO conduct more sensitive missions and covert actions. Russia's domestic intelligence agency, the FSB, also has two SOF units: Alfa and Vympel. The former provide a national counterterrorism response function while the latter are a specialist protection force guarding high-value facilities.

As mentioned, Russia has employed the GRU's Spetsnaz in conventional operations in Ukraine, but SSO have also been tasked with such missions as the attempt to kill key Ukrainian leadership targets during the first days of the 2022 invasion. Thankfully, due to incompetence by the GRU and their informer network, along with US-supplied intelligence to the Ukrainians, these missions failed.

The Ukrainians have their own SSO who have been very active against Russia. They are typically employed on nationally strategic missions, such as deep penetration raids into Russia itself, the destruction of targets such as radar and EW sites (famously they seized an oil platform in the Black Sea captured by the Russians to enable a successful strike against a Russian radar unit), and rumoured overseas operations (in 2024, stories of Ukrainian SOF operating against the Wagner Group in Sudan, for instance, surfaced).

In the West, SOF have been the 'go-to' force for the last two decades, resulting in deep experience and increased budgets but at a terrible cost to many of the soldiers and their families in both physical and mental scars. As mentioned, it has also seen the rise of allegations of war crimes by US, UK and Australian units; some argue that the repeated deployments against a nebulous foe in campaigns with sometimes hazy strategic objectives such as Afghanistan have contributed to this malaise.

Despite this, SOF continue to grow and transform to meet battlefield challenges. As we have seen with a number of Western armies (most prominently the USMC), squad and platoon infantry organization is changing to facilitate the addition of both EW and unmanned systems operators. A similar change is occurring within Western SOF.

Traditionally, SOF have operated with a large number of 'enablers' – operators who have not necessarily completed the same level of selection required for the 'badged' operators. Originally a distinction made by UKSF and Australian SASR (Special Air Service Regiment), this divided SOF personnel between those who have completed selection and been presented with the famous winged Excalibur – the 'badged' – and the 'enablers' who have completed a shortened tactical course that teaches some of the fundamentals but who are relied upon to bring specialist skills to the unit.

LEFT Members of the Ukrainian special purpose unit of the Main Directorate of Intelligence, Shaman Battalion. Note the M4 style carbines and Minimi light machine gun. Shaman have conducted successful deep penetration raids and assassinations within the Russian homeland. (Photo by Serhii Mykhalchuk/ Global Images Ukraine via Getty Images)

BELOW A rare shot of Shaman Battalion special operators boarding one of their own organic UH-60 Blackhawk helicopters. (Photo by Serhii Mykhalchuk/Global Images Ukraine via Getty Images)

Green Berets of the US Army's 5th Special Forces Group near Al Tanf in southern Syria. Vehicles include the GMV (Ground Mobility Vehicle) 1.1 and the Polaris MRZR all-terrain vehicle. Note also the Jordanian Blackhawk helicopter in the background. (US Army photo by 1st Sergeant Jacob Connor, DVIDS)

Instead of this division, organizations like the US Navy SEALs and the US Army's Green Berets are looking to expand the size of their subunits to include operators trained in cyber, electronic warfare and unmanned systems. Both units are expanding the number of billets within their subunits to accommodate extra specialists.

In the US Army Special Forces, the plan calls for a reduction of the number of ODAs (Operational Detachment Alphas, the storied Green Beret 'A-Teams') per company from six to four but with an increase in personnel per ODA from the traditional 12 to 16. A similar change is being considered within SEAL platoons.

Another big change in recent years has been the shifting of counterterrorist responsibilities away from specialist commands to wider SOF. The best example of this is in the provision of the much-heralded 'over the horizon' (OTH) counterterrorist capability that was put in place following the departure of Coalition Forces from Afghanistan.

Rather than basing SOF (and drones) in Afghanistan or in neighbouring Pakistan, US Central Command decided upon an OTH option that would see missions planned and executed from regional hubs. The US now runs counterterrorism operations, mainly by Reaper drone, in (and over) Afghanistan from Qatar.

Another example is in the shadow war in Yemen. Long the preserve of JSOC and SEAL Team Six, the US has quietly replaced the JSOC 'shooters and sensors' with Naval Special Warfare Unit 3, under the command of Special Operations Command Central (SOCCENT).

Naval Special Warfare Unit 3 is composed of 'white' SEAL platoons, Special Warfare Combatant Crew who man specialized watercraft to infiltrate and exfiltrate SEALs, and SEAL Delivery Vehicle sailors who manage submersibles (mini-submarines). The task unit is supported by the Army's 160th Special Operations Aviation Regiment who, along with specialist helicopters, also have a squadron of armed Reaper drones.

Increasingly, as JSOC is re-tasked towards operations in support of Great Power Competition, longstanding counterterrorism commitments are being transferred to 'white' SOF units. The CIA, long responsible for strikes in non-

US Navy SEALs in Raqa, Syria, 2016. Both wear SEAL-specific AOR2 pattern uniforms. The lead SEAL carries a 5.56mm MK18 suppressed carbine while the second SEAL carries a 7.62mm MK17 battle rifle. (Photo by DELIL SOULEIMAN/AFP via Getty Images)

declared operational areas such as Pakistan, will also likely increasingly handle drone strikes. For example, the killing of al-Qaeda luminary Al Zawahiri in July 2022 was conducted by the CIA rather than the military, which has conducted most such strikes in the past two decades in Afghanistan.

SOF are also seeing a large-scale swing away from Direct Action (DA) to more traditional skill sets such as Unconventional Warfare and Foreign Internal Defense. The GWOT fostered Direct Action almost to the exclusion of other roles, with some arguing that the US Army's Green Berets, for instance, had lost touch with their traditional roles.

Although many SOF units were tasked with Foreign Internal Defense duties training Afghan and Iraqi partner forces, some have been criticized as only paying lip-service to such efforts, to the extent of engineering opportunities to conduct Direct Action operations themselves rather than by and through their local partners.

The increasing threat from China and Russia began a resurgence in SOF skills that focused on training and facilitating those partner forces and looking again at how to raise and support a guerrilla army within a contested environment. Strategically, SOF sees the Great Power Competition as the future. As units which traditionally have had to struggle to survive and thrive during periods of relative peace, SOF leaders have seen the writing on the wall with the drawdowns in Iraq and Afghanistan and refocused on more traditional threats.

Ukrainian special operations forces firing the domestically produced 5.56mm Malyuk or Vulcan-M assault rifles, the closest to the camera fitted with a sound suppressor. The Malyuk is a bullpup configuration like the British SA80A3, meaning the magazine and working parts are located behind the pistol grip, allowing for an overall shorter length of the weapon. (Photo by GENYA SAVILOV/ AFP via Getty Images)

Soldiers from an Iraqi Regional Commando Battalion in Iraq, 2010. Both carry 5.56mm M4A1 carbines with Aimpoint optics, PEQ-2 laser illuminators and foregrips integrating a tactical light. They wear the unique Iraqi Special Forces Digital Camouflage Uniform produced from Chinese Type 07 fabric. (Photo by US Navy Petty Officer 1st Class Shawn D. Gentile)

Direct Action, most commonly in the form of counterterrorism operations, will still continue but at a vastly reduced pace; consider that some units were conducting multiple raids per night for three to four monthly rotations during the height of the GWOT. Although Islamic State still exists, it has, at the time of writing, been vastly reduced in numbers and capability. The same can be said for al-Qaeda.

Delta Force ran the classified SOF campaign against Islamic State under the name Task Force 9 and a targeting programme called Talon Anvil. The structure and roles of Task Force 9 are instructive of how SOF will prosecute any future action against non-state actors. The *New York Times* explained:

> The unit was called Talon Anvil, and it worked in three shifts around the clock between 2014 and 2019, pinpointing targets for the United States' formidable air power to hit: convoys, car bombs, command centers and squads of enemy fighters.
>
> The strike cell was run by a classified Special Operations unit called Task Force 9 that oversaw the ground offensive in Syria. The task force had multiple missions. Army Green Berets trained allied Syrian Kurdish and Arab forces. Small groups of Delta Force operators embedded with ground forces, and an assault team of Delta commandos were on call to launch ground raids on high-value targets, including the Islamic State leader, Abu Bakr al-Baghdadi.

The cell used tips from allied ground forces, secret electronic intercepts, drone cameras and other information to find enemy targets, then hit them with munitions from drones or called in strikes from other coalition aircraft. It also coordinated air support for allied Kurdish and Arab forces fighting on the ground. The task force had a second strike cell that worked with the C.I.A. to hunt high-value Islamic State leaders.[3]

Tier One SOF will retain their national counterterrorist responsibilities but are also increasingly reorienting towards operations in support of the Great Power Competition. Although unknown at the time of writing and likely to remain forever classified, JSOC elements are almost certainly conducting operations in support of Ukrainian forces.

These operations would likely include embedding liaison personnel within Ukrainian headquarters elements to facilitate the provision of US and NATO intelligence, and the distribution of lethal and non-lethal aid provided by the US and NATO partners. A leaked although unverified PowerPoint slide from 2023 showed a handful of US personnel in country and around 50 UKSF, all likely to be conducting training.

Two Iraqi Special Forces soldiers pictured in Mosul armed with an RPG-7 and an American AT-4 respectively in anticipation of an Islamic State SVBIED attack. (Photo by ODD ANDERSEN/AFP via Getty Images)

Ukrainian SSO special operators in the Donetsk region in 2014. Note the use of MultiCam and what appears to be A-TACS AU pattern camouflage uniforms and the rail-equipped AK-74s. (ANATOLII STEPANOV/AFP via Getty Images)

US Special Operations Forces, most likely Green Berets from the 5th Special Forces Group, ride in an armed Non-Standard Tactical Vehicle in Raqqa, Syria in 2016. The weapon is a 40mm Mk47 automatic grenade launcher. (Photo by DELIL SOULEIMAN/AFP via Getty Images)

The Kremlin has accused Western SOF of advising Ukrainian SOF, which it almost certainly has, although some of Moscow's more outrageous claims must be taken with a very generous pinch of salt. Western SOF (and this is the US, the UK and France and possibly Poland) are also likely providing support and training in specific technologies that will assist Ukrainian SOF on the battlefield, such as SIGINT and EW platforms.

In terms of technology, SOF are at the cutting edge. Long gone are the modified trucks, Pinzgauers and Humvees of the Iraq campaign; today's SOF use lighter, faster vehicles, including modified all-terrain vehicles like the Polaris MRZR and custom pickup trucks that can be covertly armoured or even modified with clip-on panels to alter their appearance.

The weapons carried on these vehicles have changed too. As noted previously, the 70mm VAMPIRE APKWS was first fielded by US SOF in Syria on the back of one such pickup. It has now emerged on the battlefields of Ukraine. Many of the advances in small arms owe their development to SOF: the widespread adoption of combat optics; the emergence of the .338 machine gun; and adoption of specialist calibres like the 6.5mm Creedmoor.

SOF soldiers still tend to employ 5.56x45mm carbines, with the German Heckler and Koch 416 still dominating. A new calibre and weapon was introduced during the GWOT to address the issue of needing a small, integrally suppressed weapon that could engage targets beyond the effective range of a suppressed sub-machine gun. This was the SIG LVAW (Low Visibility Assault Weapon), later termed the MCX. Chambered for the .300 Blackout cartridge, the weapon could be employed with shorter-ranged but very quiet subsonic rounds or, at the switch of a magazine, normal supersonic ammunition that could be used effectively out to 400 metres.

SOF have taken advantage of the growth in drones too – from Throwbots, which can literally be thrown into a building, to micro-UAVs that can fly into buildings unobtrusively to spy on the inhabitants. US SOF were the first users of the Switchblade drone in Afghanistan, Iraq and Syria before it became something of a household name in Ukraine.

Despite the technology and the impressive budgets, SOF are only as good as the soldiers who staff the units. With continuing recruitment and retention challenges across most NATO and Western militaries, this may be the greatest threat to the future of SOF. Additionally, they have attempted to carve out a new niche for themselves in the Great Power Competition, but how successful they will be in this brave new Cold War remains to be seen.

An Oshkosh M-ATV (MRAP All-Terrain Vehicle) employed by US Army Special Forces pictured in Syria in 2022. Note the M153 Common Remotely Operated Weapon Station (CROWS) mounting an M2 .50cal heavy machine gun. (Photo by Frederic Lafargue/Paris Match via Getty Images)

CHAPTER EIGHT
FUTURE WAR

'The nature of war is never gonna change. But the character of war is changing before our eyes – with the introduction of a lot of technology, a lot of societal changes with urbanization and a wide variety of other factors.'

General Mark Milley,
Association of the US Army Convention, 2017[1]

Any book that discusses the future will bound to be wrong – or at least only partly right! When discussing military technology and the changing face of war, the likelihood of error multiplies dramatically. Programmes get cancelled with depressing regularity. Platforms are discovered not to meet current requirements and are shelved, then are sometimes dusted off when circumstances change. And Black Swans occur.

Black Swans are events that are difficult, if not impossible, to foresee and that have a significant negative impact. The term appears to have originated from the financial sector but is now used by planners to denote any surprise event that causes a negative effect.

We have focused heavily on the reported combat experiences in the Russo-Ukrainian War, as it gives us our first look at a large-scale conventional peer conflict in modern times. Undoubtedly some of the inferences drawn, or even the early lessons learned, from these reports will be wrong.

ABOVE Militia fighters of the Sunni Islamist Liwa Tahrir al Sham wearing respirators in response to a suspected chemical weapon attack by Syrian government forces in 2013. Note the folding stock AKM and the much rarer Steyr AUG carried by the militiaman in the background. (Photo by Laurent Van der Stockt/ Getty Images Reportage)

Historians caution against examining subjects that are too close in the rear-view mirror, arguing that time is needed to contextualize and understand the dynamics of an event, or in this case, a conflict. They are undoubtedly right, but we should also be looking at how we can learn the lessons of Ukraine as quickly as possible, even if some prove incorrect. The world at the time of writing is in a very unstable place, with the threats of China, Russia, Iran and North Korea ever present.

So, what are the key early (potential) lessons, and how do they relate to the near future of land warfare? Some are obvious, others less so as one might expect. The biggest is that artillery is still the god of war. The side with the biggest and the most will retain a distinct advantage in any conventional war.

With the introduction of extended-range artillery shells (at the time of writing, Rheinmetall had announced the provision of prototype shells to Ukraine with a reported range of 100km) and the future use of artillery to deliver other technologies besides mines (a Chinese company, Chengdu Aviation, already have a loitering munition that fits within a regular 155mm artillery shell), artillery will continue to be the backbone of offensive and defensive operations.

These guns will need to be fed, and that has proven a thorny problem for Ukraine and, to a lesser degree, Russia (who are apparently happy with high-dud-rate North Korean 152mm). Western nations have recognized this challenge and are finally making efforts to increase production of consumable ordnance, not just for supply to Ukraine but also for their own war stocks. The expenditure rate of artillery ammunition has brought into sharp focus just how quickly NATO armies would run dry in a conventional war.

US Army Robotic Combat Vehicle – Light (RCV-L) prototypes equipped with CROWS-J remote weapons stations. (Photo by Savannah Baldwin, DVIDS)

Armies will increasingly look at optionally crewed artillery platforms, with wheeled self-propelled guns currently gaining wide acceptance in NATO armies (due to their ability to rapidly relocate to avoid counter-battery fires and/or FPV drones: see the British Army decision to acquire Boxers mounting 155mm guns). Automated or semi-automated reloading under armour will also be a common feature of future artillery systems. The Hanwha K9 system already uses a semi-automated process with its armoured reloading vehicle, but a fully automated platform is being developed.

The speed with which artillery can conduct counter-battery fire missions will also increase as the fusion of ISR evolves. Russian artillery dramatically improved the speed of their counter-battery fires over the period of the first two years of the Russo-Ukrainian War, and this will continue to evolve.

Artillery will need to shoot accurately and quickly and then move position before the counter-battery arrives. Jammers will also be needed to help scramble enemy ISR drones that attempt to plot the location of the battery. A future where counter-battery might involve not only enemy artillery fire but a swarm of loitering munitions tracking the signature of the just-fired friendly artillery unit is not hard to envision.

The difficult question of cluster munitions has been raised by the Russo-Ukrainian War. The US has supplied Ukraine with stocks of 155mm Dual-Purpose Improved Conventional Munition (DPICM) ammunition, which separates into bomblets covering a large impact area. Designed originally to counter massed Soviet tanks, they have proven very effective against all manner of targets but particularly so against Russian 'meat shield' human-wave attacks.

The controversy arises due to DPICM and similar cluster munitions being banned by a majority of Western nations. Russia and China have no such qualms. The West must decide what course to take, as the DPICM capability will be essential in any future peer or near-peer land war due to DPICM's ability to target large areas with a smaller number of rounds. They are particularly economical in a war where production and supply of artillery ammunition is a significant factor.

Deep fires have also been recognized as a key requirement of future conventional war: note the success of such platforms as the UK Storm Shadow and the US ATACMS. The US is slightly ahead of the curve here, but all Western armies will need some sort of deep fires capability to strike targets beyond the range of even extended-range artillery and GMLRS. This also ties in with the USMC pivot towards the Indo-Pacific; such missiles will be needed to deny PLA Navy access to key sea lanes.

Speaking of GMLRS, the HIMARS has become an iconic performer out of Ukraine. Poland and Australia have placed large orders (with other nations purchasing the South Korean competitor, the K239 Chunmoo, including Poland, who placed a supplemental order to their HIMARS purchase to

increase the numbers of GMLRS they could field in the short term). Truck mounted, and able to be rapidly transported within common military cargo aircraft, GMLRS will be a staple for many years: its versatility is its strength.

Another significant impact of Ukraine has been the realization that with the ever-present danger from artillery and FPV drones, infantry in the direct fire zone need protected mobility vehicles for all but the most specialist tasks, such as shoot-and-scoot ATGM ambushes as conducted in Ukraine by all-terrain vehicles or quad bikes. Artillery kills mainly by concussive blast and fragments, both of which a protected mobility platform like a Bushmaster can help negate.

The seemingly limitless capabilities of uncrewed aerial vehicles are also a key lesson but perhaps in ways not recognized by hyperbolic references to wars conducted solely by machines. As we have examined, drones have not replaced artillery (and other indirect fire platforms such as GMLRS) but have increased the accuracy and efficiency of artillery by working in partnership. Drones will be an essential ISR requirement for all future artillery formations.

Drones will also continue to evolve in what capabilities they can bring to the battlefield. A major growth area will be UAV-delivered EW effects. Today's theatre-level UAVs such as Reaper already carry sophisticated SIGINT pods that assist with targeting, but UAVs that can conduct offensive electronic warfare are already starting to take to the air: note the Multi-Function Electronic Warfare – Air Large (MFEW-AL) being fitted to the M-1C Gray Eagle by the US Army. This will only increase.

A destroyed Ukrainian BTR-4 IFV seen near Kharkiv in 2022. Note the slat armour around the turret. (Photo by SERGEY BOBOK/AFP via Getty Images)

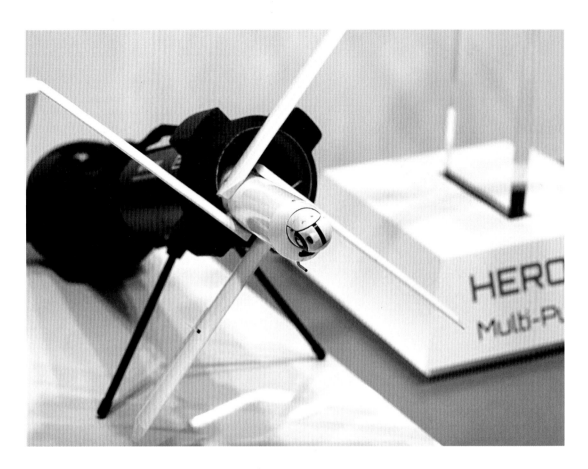

The UVision Air Hero-30 anti-tank loitering munition. Israeli designed, the drone has a 30-minute loiter time, a 10km range, and carries a 500g warhead. Its closest direct Western competitor is the Switchblade 300. (Photo by GEOFFROY VAN DER HASSELT/AFP via Getty Images)

Swarms of FPV-style loitering munitions will be accompanied by specialist drones that actively jam enemy sensors and spoof the location of the swarm. Other drones will be martyrs designed to trigger enemy air defences and allow drones carrying radiation-seeking ordnance to destroy them.

The US are also supplying a hitherto unknown JDAM variant to Ukraine known as the Home-On Jam Seeker, with the operational concept of targeting Russian EW assets to allow other GPS-guided assets to be used (think Excalibur and even HIMARS, whose accuracy as we have discussed has been significantly degraded due to Russian jamming). The next logical step is to make a similar munition that can be delivered by an uncrewed platform.

We will also likely see coordinated swarms attacking armoured vehicles, probably under the direction of a mothership drone that itself may be controlled by a human operator in another platform – an AH-64E Guardian attack helicopter, for instance. Multiple strikes by small FPVs may overwhelm any active protection systems fitted to a targeted AFV.

Other drones will move in for the kill. Again, at the time of writing, the famous Switchblade 300 loitering munition is receiving an upgrade (the Block 20, which also addresses two of the most common complaints about the platform: its camera quality and its endurance) featuring an explosively formed penetrator designed for armour penetration of the weaker top armour of Russian MBTs.

Dedicated anti-tank attack drones are also on the horizon, which will eclipse the Ukrainian ad hoc method of strapping an RPG warhead to the underside of a cheap Chinese quadcopter. The US Army has the Low Altitude Stalking and Strike Ordnance (LASSO) programme, with a focus on anti-tank capability. The first tranche of the LASSO requirement is being supplied by the Switchblade 600 with its Javelin ATGM warhead.

Man-pack loitering munitions will increasingly move out of the remit only of SOF and into the hands of regular infantry platoons. The USMC announced in May 2024 that the Corps would be acquiring the Teledyne/FLIR Rogue 1 loitering munition under its Organic Precision Fires – Light programme.

Each weighs only 5kg, with a 10km range, VTOL (Vertical Take-Off and Landing) capability and 30 minutes' loiter time. The Rogue 1 offers an anti-armour warhead or an anti-personnel version that launches tungsten cubes. This is a likely template for future infantry-carried loitering munitions.

The opportunities and capabilities loitering munitions offer must also be tempered by the fact that we all suffer from confirmation bias. Innumerable videos have been released showing successful strikes. What they don't show us are the dozens of others that are unsuccessful – either misses, jammed or otherwise intercepted by EW, or shot down. Loitering munitions and similar armed drones are an important capability, but they are not the panacea that some in the media have declared.

Counter-UAV is one of the core lessons from Ukraine (but also a largely unrecognized at the time lesson from Nagorno-Karabakh and from Syria/Iraq). Starting now, every vehicle that will be deployed in or near the direct fire zone of combat needs a counter-UAV system. An argument could be, and should be, made that logistics support vehicles should be similarly equipped. And speaking of logistics support vehicles, in the very near future, these will be optionally crewed; for convoys so-called 'follow-me' UGV capabilities seem ideal.

As noted previously, the drone/counter-drone cycle will only increase in much the same way as the counter-IED fight. UAVs will require constant upgrades to avoid/minimize counter systems such as jammers. They will also need to be hardened to make hacking more difficult and include failsafe systems should GPS signals be disrupted.

Infantry too will need credible counter-UAS. These may take the form of advanced versions of the Drone Buster and similar handheld weapons, along with detectors and man-pack jammers. Russia is experimenting at the time of writing with shotgun-like shells for their underslung 30mm grenade launchers as a measure for their infantry to combat FPV drones. If successful, this could add another capability that could be easily copied by Western armies.

Another major lesson from Ukraine has been the vital importance of mobile ground-based air defence. As we have examined, NATO has largely ignored GBAD for many years, with fatal consequences for Ukraine. Optionally crewed GBAD platforms that likely combine a number of weapons systems will be the future: long-range surface-to-air missiles, 30mm to 57mm cannon to engage larger UAVs and helicopters, and a targeted soft-kill jamming system to engage smaller UAVs. The US is already heading in this direction with its M-SHORAD Strykers and M-LIDS platforms. Other nations will have to catch up. And quickly.

Ukraine has also reinforced the need for the tank rather than announcing the death knell for the MBT. Despite omnipresent FPVs and other attack drones, tanks (at least modern Western designs) are still hard to kill. A video from April 2024 that shows a Ukrainian M1A1 Abrams being immobilized is illustrative; the tank appears to have been hit by multiple FPVs, a larger Lancet attack munition, several guided artillery rounds, and an ATGM. Even after all of this punishment, the vehicle doesn't brew up and send its turret flying as with Russian designs. Instead, the crew appear to safely escape the disabled tank.

And key NATO nations hardly think the tank is dead. France and Germany have restarted the Main Ground Combat System (MGCS), a previously stalled joint venture to develop a future MBT for both nations. Reports indicate that the MGCS will feature a counter-UAV system, a hybrid diesel-electric engine, and a main gun in a calibre between 130mm and 140mm. The MGCS design concept appears to be based on the idea of a common chassis with specialist modules bolted on.

Despite still being relatively rare, future tank designers must develop MBTs that can win the tank-on-tank engagement. This means seeing the enemy tank first and then being able to engage it with a first-round kill. For this to happen, the tank needs a sensor package that speeds up the process of acquiring the enemy. As we have discussed, there is a major opportunity for machine-learning/AI to accelerate this process.

When the inevitable happens (and it may have already occurred with the Israeli Iron Fist Light Kinetic system) near-future APS will be capable of intercepting long-rod APFSDS penetrators. What is the solution for this, when even tank main gun rounds can be destroyed or degraded before they strike the target vehicle?

Any solution will likely fall back on the tried-and-true concept of tandem warheads or, in this case, tandem rods. We may also see an EW component to the solution, jamming the APS, particularly if it is radar based. Whatever the solutions that are initially developed, just as in the drone/counter-drone battle, industry will be forced to continually evolve the solutions to keep pace with countermeasures.

We will likely also see more platforms like the American M10 Booker adopted as the need for an assault gun to support infantry has re-emerged from the Ukrainian experience. Indeed, a significant proportion of tank operations have been in direct support of infantry whether by firing indirectly or in intimate support as an assault gun. A lighter and less protected platform (if it isn't likely to go head-to-head with an enemy T-90M, why add the extra weight and expense of ERA and/or APS?), makes more sense for such a requirement than a fully-fledged MBT.

Future MBTs will no doubt be accompanied by a range of UGVs in a Loyal Wingman mix. Dedicated EW UGVs (already seen in Ukraine with multiple Russian designs) will provide a protective umbrella while UGVs with mounted cannon firing smart and/or airburst rounds will engage drones and attack helicopters directly. Other UGVs may serve as reconnaissance, with ISR sensors to scout out routes for the crewed AFVs. A tank killer UGV mounting the iconic Javelin has already been developed.

For the infantry too there will be an explosion in adoption of UGVs for the task of resupply and medical evacuation. According to Ukrainian sources, such UGVs are already in widespread use. Carrying ammunition and water, for instance, means that the infantry can carry less, a perennial problem as we have detailed in Chapter 6.

The US Army already has the General Dynamics Squad Multipurpose Equipment Transport (SMET), which is an eight-wheel platform that can be controlled via a handheld device or using 'follow me' technology. The SMET can carry the rucksacks and ancillary equipment of an infantry squad, trailing the soldiers at a distance to ensure the equipment is quickly available. These types of UGVs will be the first to be employed widely across armies, as they are suitable for many uses.

Industry is developing UAVs that can fly a medical diagnostics suite directly to a platoon medic treating a casualty on the front line. This can be integrated with a mechanical mule UGV that can transport the hopefully stabilized casualty back to a safe evacuation point. Such platforms reduce or eliminate the inherent risk in evacuating a casualty from the direct fire zone. The USMC has already ordered a resupply cargo drone known as the Tactical Resupply Unmanned Aircraft System, which can carry around 70kg of resupplies, including medical products like whole blood, into forward areas.

Another lesson, and one that applies to all elements of the force mix, is one of signature management. If it can be seen (sensed), it will be engaged and killed. From basic tactical SOPs (using camouflage nets, noise and light discipline, dispersal of force elements) to more advanced measures (spoofing or jamming enemy sensors or employing robotic decoys), the near-future battlefield will feature units that are proficient in minimizing their signature (including in the electromagnetic realm). Units that don't won't survive long enough to gain the skill.

In the air above the battlefield there will also be change. Alongside what will be a panoply of drones, there will be uncrewed or Loyal Wingman type platforms operating with an increasingly limited number of human-crewed fast jets. As the UCAV gains prominence for both strike and interception and

NEXT PAGES Ukrainian soldiers training to engage tanks the old-fashioned way – with hand grenades, after the tank has passed over a trench or fighting position. (Photo by DIMITAR DILKOFF/AFP via Getty Images)

the problems of recruitment and retention bite into every military, human pilots will be a rare commodity that will need to be jealously guarded. Most will be piloting uncrewed platforms from bases thousands of kilometres away from the battlespace.

What may also be missing from that scene is the helicopter – at least in any form we know today. Attack aviation has proven to be severely curtailed in Ukraine thanks to the triple threat of GBAD, EW and airborne interception. While true that a peer military may be able to achieve air superiority in a way that neither the Ukrainian Air Force nor the Russian VKS have been able to (and really the only contender here is the combined might of the US Air Force and US Navy), and thus be able to limit the employment of these three threats, the environment is still very dangerous for rotary platforms and in particular crewed rotary platforms.

Indeed, the US Army has decided to cancel the Future Attack Reconnaissance Aircraft programme largely due to concerns from the experiences in Ukraine. The UK, Poland and Australia are still continuing with their planned procurements of the AH-64E, but their tactics and processes will have to change to ensure survivability above the modern and near future battlespace. Will helicopters become extinct in this context?

Airmobile assaults will certainly likely never be seen again – at least without total air supremacy. In a peer/near-peer fight, transport helicopters, even with advanced countermeasures, are simply too vulnerable. Witness the failed Russian helicopter assault on Hostomel Airport in February 2022. The air assault consisted of several hundred VDV airborne troops transported in 24 Mi-8/Mi-17 Hip helicopters and escorted by Mi-24 and Ka-52 attack helicopters.

By most accounts, at least four helicopters were shot down initially by a mix of MANPADS and the intervention of Ukrainian Air Force MIG-29s. A number of others were seriously damaged. The MIG-29s kept Russian air support at bay and allowed Ukrainian Su-24s to bomb the Russian air assault force. The Ukrainian National Guard element defending the airport also downed a further three attack helicopters and another Hip.

Likewise, parachute assaults are also a thing of the past for much the same reasons. Transport aircraft are also too exposed to be employed over an active air defence environment. The US and UK still maintain a parachute capability, but in a conventional fight these troops will either parachute into a relatively safe staging area far behind the lines or arrive by other means. Special operations forces will maintain a parachute insertion capability but, in most instances, this will be used for covert infiltrations in operations other than conventional war.

In the background to all these lessons is the invisible enemy – electronic warfare. EW is already a core part of the combined-arms mix; however, this will further increase as the war for the electromagnetic spectrum evolves to a

position of primacy. Drones can be jammed or forced down, enemy ground units can be denied access to GPS navigation or spoofed into believing they are somewhere else, and even armoured vehicles can be hacked.

Related disciplines such as SIGINT or signals intelligence will also increase in importance. As we have seen in Ukraine, SIGINT (and EW) has assisted in identifying Russian C2 nodes (the fancy way of saying leadership targets), which can then be verified by UAV and engaged by artillery or long-range missiles.

Mobile phones can and are intercepted and tracked, even when turned off in some cases. Consider a roaming FPV that loiters until it locks on to an errant iPhone and then strikes. Future battlefields will see a blanket ban on such devices, and any personal electronics that emit a trackable signal (such as the humble Fitbit). Along with kinetic targeting, such items open up a vulnerability for information operations, with propaganda or worse transmitted directly to the soldier's device.

What appear to be German Army KSK special operations forces use a glass breaker to breach a window after abseiling into position during a demonstration in 2018. Hostage rescue will remain a core competency for Western special forces. (Monika Skolimowska/ dpa-Zentralbild/dpa/Alamy)

An Islamic State armoured SVBIED intercepted by Iraqi forces before it could detonate in Mosul. Islamic State maintained a number of garages specifically tasked with manufacturing SVBIEDs of varying types. They also pre-positioned them on likely lines of advance of Iraqi forces, reducing their reaction window. (Photo by Laurent Van der Stockt for Le Monde/Getty Images Reportage)

In terms of battlefield tactics, the opposed breach will again gain prominence as the calculus of advantage shifts to the defender. Armoured breaching vehicles like the M1150 Assault Breacher Vehicle, paired with armoured explosive line throwing platforms, and even armoured bulldozers, will attain vital importance in a conventional war. All of these vehicles will need systems to counter loitering munitions and APS, as they will face all manner of threats. The failure of the 2023 counteroffensive by Ukraine is a stark reminder of the importance of combat engineering.

Opposed breaching is not just a tactic for conventional fights. Consider the retaking of Mosul or Israeli operations in Gaza. In many cases against an asymmetric opponent, similar techniques and equipment are required. For instance, Iraqi forces found Islamic State in Mosul had constructed a sophisticated array of prepared defences, including concentric defensive positions with overlapping arcs of fire, IED minefields to channel attackers, tunnels to resupply and infiltrate back into 'cleared' areas, and employed human shields to counter the impressive firepower advantage provided by the US.

Mosul and Gaza, along with the city fight in Marawi in the Philippines, are a timely reminder that not all future wars will be a peer or near-peer, largely conventional conflict with Russia, China, North Korea or Iran. As mentioned earlier, Black Swan events do occur. The 9/11 attacks were one such Black Swan that saw the United States and some of its key allies entrenched in decades of counterinsurgency and counterterrorist operations.

As the world's population becomes increasingly urbanized, war will be increasingly conducted in the cities. Many of the lessons of Mosul, Fallujah and Marawi will hopefully assist in developing effective TTPs for these most difficult of operations. Littoral warfare is also coming to the fore, particularly in the Indo-Pacific.

As previously mentioned, the USMC has conducted a pivot towards the region, with the US Army largely focusing on Europe and the Middle East. Smaller militaries such as that of Australia are also tilting towards a 'strategy of denial' to keep Chinese ambitions in check across the Indo-Pacific region.

For land warfare, this will present its own unique set of challenges. Emerging USMC doctrine of Expeditionary Advanced Base Operations looks to require small elements of infantry to defend rocket or missile systems that are forward deployed to deny sea lane access by the PLAN. Resupply of these small teams will be difficult as will casualty evacuation.

Despite all of these technological developments and operational challenges, land warfare in the near future will still come down to infantry taking and holding an objective. Everything else – the drones, the artillery, the tanks, the EW – is about getting them there. As General Milley noted, the character of war is changing but the nature isn't.

A quick internet search will reveal brutal and graphic videos of Ukrainian infantry clearing Russian trenches which, apart from the gear and weapons, could be a mirror of the Somme. There should be no surprise that artillery is still the principal casualty-producing weapon on the modern battlefield; again, footage of Russian 152mm batteries firing is grimly reminiscent of World War I. And even the challenges facing tanks today – the ATGMs, the FPV drones, the EFP IEDs – are like the historical arms race between tanks and anti-tank weapons that began in 1916 with anti-tank rifles and mines. Again, the character is indeed changing but the nature remains the same.

The return of trench warfare to Ukraine – a Ukrainian infantryman of the 57th Separate Motorized Infantry Brigade near Bakhmut in 2023. Note the Ukrainian-issue digital pattern trousers which resemble legacy US Iraq-era ACU pattern. (Photo by ANATOLII STEPANOV/ AFP via Getty Images)

LIST OF ACRONYMS

AD	Area Denial
AFV	armoured fighting vehicle
AI	artificial intelligence
APC	armoured personnel carrier
APFSDS	armour-piercing fin-stabilized discarding sabot
APKWS	Advanced Precision Kill Weapon System
APS	Active Protection System
ATACMS	Army Tactical Missile System
ATGM	anti-tank guided missile
BMP	Boyevaya Mashina Pyekhoty, 'infantry fighting vehicle'
BTG	Battalion Tactical Group
CAS	close air support
COIN	counterinsurgency
CROWS	Common Remotely Operated Weapon Station
CSAR	combat search and rescue
CSIS	Center for Strategic and International Studies
DoD	US Department of Defense
DPICM	Dual-Purpose Improved Conventional Munition
DVH	double-V hull
ECM	electronic countermeasures
EFP	explosively formed projectile or penetrator
ERA	explosive reactive armour
ERCA	Extended-Range Cannon Artillery
EW	electronic warfare
FPV	first-person view (drone)
GBAD	Ground-based Air Defence
GMLRS	Guided-Multiple Launch Rocket System
GWOT	Global War on Terror
HEAT	high-explosive anti-tank
HESH	high-explosive squash-head
HIMARS	High Mobility Artillery Rocket System
ICV	infantry carrier vehicle
IDF	Israeli Defence Force
IED	improvised explosive device
IFV	infantry fighting vehicle
ISIL	Islamic State
ISR	intelligence, surveillance and reconnaissance
ISV	infantry squad vehicle

IVAS	Integrated Visual Augmentation System
JDAM	Joint Direct Attack Munition
JLTC	joint light tactical vehicle
LRPF	Long-Range Precision Fires
LRHW	Long-Range Hypersonic Weapon
MANPADS	man-portable air-defence systems
MBT	main battle tank
MCLOS	manual command line of sight
M-LIDS	Mobile – Low, Slow, Small UAS Integrated Defeat System
MLRS	Multiple Launch Rocket System
MPF	Mobile Protected Firepower
MRAP	Mine Resistant Ambush Protected
M-SHORAD	Maneuver Short Range Air Defense
NLAW	next-generation light anti-armour weapons
JLTV	Joint Light Tactical Vehicle
PLA	Chinese People's Liberation Army
PLAN	Chinese People's Liberation Army Navy
PrSM	Precision Strike Missile
RCV	robotic combat vehicle
RPG	rocket-propelled grenade
RUSI	The Royal United Services Institute
RWS	remote weapon station
SAM	surface-to-air missile
SEAD	Suppression of Enemy Air Defences
SHORAD	Short Range Air Defense
SMRF	Strategic Mid-Range Fires
SOF	special operations forces
SOP	standard operating procedure
SPAAG	self-propelled anti-aircraft gun
sUAV	small unmanned aerial vehicle
SVBIED	suicide vehicle-borne IED
TIC	Troops in Contact
TTP	tactics, techniques and procedures
TUSK	Tank Urban Survival Kit
UAE	United Arab Emirates
UAS	Unmanned Aircraft Systems
UAV	unmanned aerial vehicle
UCAV	unmanned combat aerial vehicle
UGV	uncrewed ground vehicle
UKSF	UK Special Forces
USMC	US Marine Corps
VBIED	vehicle-borne improvised explosive device
VKS	Russian Aerospace Forces

NOTES

Introduction: Current and Future Land Warfare

1 https://www.csis.org/analysis/first-battle-next-war-wargaming-chinese-invasion-taiwan

2 https://www.marines.mil/Portals/1/Docs/230509-Tentative-Manual-For-Expeditionary-Advanced-Base-Operations-2nd-Edition.pdf?ver=05KvG8wWlhI7uE0amD5uYg%3D%3D

3 https://www.politico.eu/article/vladimir-putin-russia-germany-boris-pistorius-nato/

4 A. Palazzo, *Land Warfare: An Introduction for Soldiers, Sailors, Aviators and Defence Civilians*, Department of Defence, Canberra, 2023

5 https://www.csis.org/analysis/seven-critical-technologies-winning-next-war

6 https://wavellroom.com/2021/01/01/into-the-grey-zone-airborne-operations-ukraine-parachute-uk-16brigade/

7 https://warontherocks.com/2017/05/how-the-ied-won-dispelling-the-myth-of-tactical-success-and-innovation/

8 https://www.ncbi.nlm.nih.gov/pmc/articles/PMC10344429/

9 Ibid.

10 Ibid.

11 https://www.dni.gov/index.php/gt2040-home/gt2040-deeper-looks/future-of-the-battlefield

12 *Joint and National Intelligence Support to Military Operations*, 2-01, 5 July 2017.

13 https://www.csis.org/analysis/seven-critical-technologies-winning-next-war

14 https://www.dni.gov/index.php/gt2040-home/gt2040-deeper-looks/future-of-the-battlefield

15 https://theweek.com/russo-ukrainian-war/1020438/the-weapons-helping-ukraine-fight-back

16 Ibid.

17 https://www.forbes.com/sites/davidaxe/2022/12/24/russia-electronic-warfare-troops-knocked-out-90-percent-of-ukraines-drones/?sh=4731ea38575c

18 https://mwi.westpoint.edu/the-return-of-the-tactical-crisis/

19 https://www.armyupress.army.mil/journals/military-review/online-exclusive/2023-ole/the-graveyard-of-command-posts/

20 https://www.nzdf.mil.nz/assets/Uploads/DocumentLibrary/Future-Land-Operating-Concept-2035-1.pdf

21 https://researchcentre.army.gov.au/sites/default/files/Spotlight_Brief_3_22_Russo-Ukraine%20Lessons%20Learnt_accessible_reduced.pdf

Chapter One: Main Battle Tanks

1 https://warontherocks.com/2022/04/the-tank-is-dead-long-live-the-javelin-the-switchblade-the/
2 https://www.rheinmetall.com/en/products/large-calibre/large-calibre-weapons-and-ammunition
3 https://wavellroom.com/2022/09/22/russian-tank-graveyard/
4 Ibid.
5 https://mwi.westpoint.edu/on-killing-tanks/#:~:text=The%20critical%20weaknesses%20of%20an,as%20new%20TTPs%20are%20explored
6 Ibid.
7 https://wavellroom.com/2023/02/10/armata-the-story-is-over/
8 https://static.rusi.org/403-SR-Russian-Tactics-web-final.pdf
9 Jason Conroy and Ron Martz, *Heavy Metal: A Tank Company's Battle to Baghdad*, Potomac Books, 2005
10 https://www.armyupress.army.mil/Journals/Military-Review/English-Edition-Archives/March-April-2017/ART-009/
11 https://www.theguardian.com/uk/2007/apr/24/iraq.world
12 https://www.historynet.com/interactive-u-s-tank-action-iraq-2004/
13 https://nationalinterest.org/blog/reboot/how-good-france%E2%80%99s-leclerc-tank-uae%E2%80%99s-war-yemen-offers-clues-191600?page=0%2C1
14 https://www.rand.org/content/dam/rand/pubs/perspectives/PE100/PE184/RAND_PE184.pdf
15 https://warontherocks.com/2022/04/the-tank-is-dead-long-live-the-javelin-the-switchblade-the/
16 https://static.rusi.org/403-SR-Russian-Tactics-web-final.pdf
17 https://2ndbn5thmar.com/ukr/
18 https://warontherocks.com/2022/04/the-tank-is-dead-long-live-the-javelin-the-switchblade-the/
19 https://crsreports.congress.gov/product/pdf/IF/IF11859
20 https://www.army.mil/article/246274/army_announces_divestiture_of_the_stryker_mobile_gun_system
21 Ibid.
22 https://www.rheinmetall.com/en/products/tracked-vehicles/tracked-armoured-vehicles/panther-kf51-main-battle-tank
23 https://www.knds.fr/en/our-news/latest-news/nexter-prepares-future-battle-tank-armament
24 Ibid.

25 Ibid.

26 https://euro-sd.com/2023/04/articles/31247/running-light-escaping-the-vehicle-growth-and-weight-spiral/

27 Ibid.

28 https://www.army-technology.com/features/hybrid-drive-emerges-as-key-capability-for-us-armys-omfv/

29 https://euro-sd.com/2023/04/articles/31247/running-light-escaping-the-vehicle-growth-and-weight-spiral/

30 https://www.armyupress.army.mil/journals/military-review/online-exclusive/2023-ole/the-tank-is-dead/

Chapter Two: Armoured Fighting Vehicles

1 https://www.forbes.com/sites/craighooper/2023/06/18/ukraine-shows-the-fight-to-make-the-bradley-ifv-safer-was-worth-it/?sh=3b827f974472

2 https://www.tjomo.com/article/wrong-technology-for-the-wrong-tactics-the-infantry-fighting-vehicle/

3 https://www.army.mil/article/166990/1st_stryker_brigade_combat_team

4 https://www.dote.osd.mil/Portals/97/pub/reports/FY2011/army/2011strykermgs.pdf?ver=2019-08-22-112309-643

5 https://www.popularmechanics.com/military/a2696/4253991/

6 https://www.army.mil/article/246274/army_announces_divestiture_of_the_stryker_mobile_gun_system

7 https://www.armyupress.army.mil/Portals/7/combat-studies-institute/csi-books/StrykersInAfghanistan.pdf

8 https://www.army.mil/article/148861/army_outfits_first_vehicles_with_electronic_stability_control#:~:text=To%20withstand%20the%20greatest%20underbody,higher%20propensity%20to%20roll%20over

9 https://www.armyupress.army.mil/Portals/7/combat-studies-institute/csi-books/StrykersInAfghanistan.pdf

10 Ibid.

11 https://www.army.mil/article/92154/armys_stryker_double_v_hull_is_a_resounding_success

12 https://hansard.parliament.uk/commons/2023-07-13/debates/10D2C40B-D0F6-4F32-B134-3060A2249F6F/NATOSummit

13 https://www.tjomo.com/article/wrong-technology-for-the-wrong-tactics-the-infantry-fighting-vehicle/

14 https://www.twz.com/24543/armys-newest-airborne-unit-gets-second-hand-but-air-droppable-usmc-lav-25-armored-vehicles

15 https://www.czdefence.com/article/why-we-need-new-ifvs-or-lessons-from-ukraine

16 https://euro-sd.com/2023/01/articles/29120/the-role-of-wheeled-vehicles-in-peer-conflict-and-the-tracks-vs-wheels-debate/

17 Ibid.

18 Ibid.

19 https://www.forbes.com/sites/davidaxe/2023/09/05/ukraines-2024-problem-how-to-repair-thousands-of-western-made-combat-vehicles/?sh=77a3068c7bcd

20 https://www.washingtoninstitute.org/policy-analysis/soldiers-end-times-assessing-military-effectiveness-islamic-state

21 https://hugokaaman.com/islamic-state-of-iraq-a-snapshot-of-svbied-design-use-2007-2012/

22 https://csbaonline.org/research/publications/of-ieds-and-mraps-force-protection-in-complex-irregular-operations/publication/1

23 Ibid.

24 https://csbaonline.org/research/publications/of-ieds-and-mraps-force-protection-in-complex-irregular-operations/publication/1

25 Ibid.

Chapter Three: Ground-based Air Defence and Close Air Support

1 https://www.airandspaceforces.com/ukraine-war-shows-importance-of-counter-uas-air-defense-distributed-ops-to-air-warfare/

2 https://csbaonline.org/about/news/integrated-air-and-missile-defense-early-lessons-from-the-russia-ukraine-war

3 https://www.nato.int/cps/en/natohq/topics_8206.htm

4 https://sgp.fas.org/crs/weapons/IF12645.pdf

5 https://rusi.org/explore-our-research/publications/commentary/defending-mother-russias-skies

6 https://www.businessinsider.com/fighter-jets-unable-to-provide-close-air-support-over-ukraine-2023-3

7 https://mwi.westpoint.edu/contested-skies-air-defense-after-ukraine/

8 https://www.forbes.com/sites/davidaxe/2023/04/14/ukraines-new-american-made-avenger-air-defense-vehicles-are-too-vulnerable-for-the-front-line/?sh=287c119c3dfe

9 https://euro-sd.com/2023/03/articles/30039/us-army-modernisation-a-mid-term-report/

10 https://www.pacom.mil/Media/News/News-Article-View/Article/2744229/army-to-field-laser-equipped-stryker-prototypes-in-fy-2022/

11 https://breakingdefense.com/2023/01/us-army-selects-epirus-leonidas-for-high-power-microwave-initiative/

12 https://www.washingtonpost.com/world/2023/05/19/ukraine-air-defense-systems-patriot/

13 https://euro-sd.com/2023/05/articles/31334/counter-uav-technology-and-options-of-the-us-armed-forces/#:~:text=High%2Dend%20air%2D%20and%20missile,systems%20to%20locate%20and%20impact.

14 https://www.leonardodrs.com/news/in-the-news/defeating-small-drones-the-u-s-armys-next-big-challenge/

15 https://mwi.westpoint.edu/contested-skies-air-defense-after-ukraine/

16 https://rusi.org/explore-our-research/publications/commentary/lessons-houthi-missile-attacks-uae#:~:text=Low%2Dflying%20targets%2C%20particularly%20UAVs,on%20a%20number%20of%20trajectories.

17 https://euro-sd.com/2023/05/articles/31334/counter-uav-technology-and-options-of-the-us-armed-forces/

18 Ibid.

19 https://www.trngcmd.marines.mil/Portals/207/Site%20Images/TBS/B2C0333XQ-DM%20-%20B2C0393XQ%20Six%20Funtions%20of%20Marine%20Avations%20and%20Aviation%20Employment%20Considerations.pdf

20 https://www.doctrine.af.mil/Portals/61/documents/AFDP_3-01/3-01-AFDP-COUNTERAIR.pdf

21 https://www.trngcmd.marines.mil/Portals/207/Site%20Images/TBS/B2C0333XQ-DM%20-%20B2C0393XQ%20Six%20Funtions%20of%20Marine%20Avations%20and%20Aviation%20Employment%20Considerations.pdf

22 https://www.businessinsider.com/fighter-jets-unable-to-provide-close-air-support-over-ukraine-2023-3

23 https://www.bbc.com/news/world-europe-65461405

24 https://static.rusi.org/403-SR-Russian-Tactics-web-final.pdf

25 https://www.thedefensepost.com/2023/03/23/us-combat-helicopter-operations/#:~:text=These%20losses%20are%20largely%20due,air%20and%20on%20the%20ground

26 https://www.google.com/url?sa=t&rct=j&q=&esrc=s&source=web&cd=&cad=rja&uact=8&ved=2ahUKEwiT5JL4_vqFAxXLslYBHeYgDgQQFnoECA4QAw&url=https%3A%2F%2Fcommunity.apan.org%2Fcfs-file%2F__key%2Fdocpreview-s%2F00-00-08-56-58%2F1997_2D00_12_2D00_01-Air-Operations-in-Low-Intensity-Conflict-_2D00_-The-Case-of-Chechnya-_2800_Thomas_2900_.pdf&usg=AOvVaw0xR79A5PmpbFQL1BYfpiOt&opi=89978449

27 Ibid.

28 https://nationalinterest.org/blog/buzz/will-f-16-fighting-falcon-lead-ukraine-victory-against-russia-207529?page=0%2C2#:~:text=%E2%80%9COur%20biggest%20enemy%20is%20Russian,fighter%20jets%2C%20they%20are%20mobile.

29 https://www.forbes.com/sites/davidaxe/2022/10/26/ukraine-has-shot-down-a-quarter-of-russias-best-attack-helicopters/?sh=2f2946241879

30 https://www.newsweek.com/russia-ukraine-ka52-alligator-helicopter-counteroffensive-zaporizhzhia-robotyne-1818151#:~:text=%22In%20recent%20months%2C%20Russia%20has,the%20British%20Defense%20Ministry%20added.

31 https://static.rusi.org/SR-Russian-Air-War-Ukraine-web-final.pdf

32 https://static.rusi.org/403-SR-Russian-Tactics-web-final.pdf

33 https://www.twz.com/44803/russian-attack-helicopters-are-now-wildly-lobbing-rockets-over-ukraine

34 https://warontherocks.com/2024/03/drones-the-air-littoral-and-the-looming-irrelevance-of-the-u-s-air-force/#:~:text=As%20Army%20Chief%20of%20Staff,more%20inexpensive%20than%20ever%20before.%E2%80%9D

35 https://www.usmcu.edu/Portals/218/FALLUJAH.pdf

36 https://warontherocks.com/2016/06/how-afghanistan-distorted-close-air-support-and-why-it-matters/

37 https://www.defensenews.com/air/2022/07/11/air-force-rethinks-combat-rescue-for-major-war-but-what-will-it-look-like/

38 https://www.japcc.org/articles/potential-game-changer-for-close-airsupport/

39 https://www.csis.org/analysis/russia-probably-has-not-used-ai-enabled-weapons-ukraine-could-change

40 https://www.japcc.org/articles/potential-game-changer-for-close-air-support/

41 https://mwi.westpoint.edu/mq-9s-over-sirte-unmanned-airpower-for-urban-combat/#:~:text=Flying%20at%20high%20speeds%20with,or%20to%20employ%20larger%20weapons.

Chapter Four: Indirect Fire

1 https://www.gov.uk/government/speeches/defence-secretarys-speech-on-defence-reform

2 https://www.rusi.org/explore-our-research/publications/special-resources/preliminary-lessons-conventional-warfighting-russias-invasion-ukraine-february-july-2022

3 https://cove.army.gov.au/article/future-ready-royal-australian-artillery-perspective-part-1-framing-issue

4 https://yadda.icm.edu.pl/baztech/element/bwmeta1.element.baztech-cdf73e44-7edc-4309-a0cd-ae04b4a8abaa/c/Safety_2021_3_2.pdf

5 https://finabel.org/long-live-the-king-of-battle-the-return-to-centrality-of-artillery-in-warfare-and-its-consequences-on-the-military-balance-in-europe/

6 https://static.rusi.org/403-SR-Russian-Tactics-web-final.pdf

7 https://info.publicintelligence.net/AWG-RussianNewWarfareHandbook.pdf

8 https://finabel.org/long-live-the-king-of-battle-the-return-to-centrality-of-artillery-in-warfare-and-its-consequences-on-the-military-balance-in-europe/

9 https://www.army.mil/article/212751/dropping_steel_rain_artillerymen_deter_enemy_rockets_in_afghanistan#:~:text=%22Artillerymen%20would%20come%20over%20here,of%20Soldiers%20firing%20the%20howitzers

10 https://static.rusi.org/403-SR-Russian-Tactics-web-final.pdf

11 https://my7969.com/2020/12/02/the-battles-of-zelenopillya/

12 Ibid.

13 https://static.rusi.org/403-SR-Russian-Tactics-web-final.pdf

14 Ibid.

15 Ibid.

16 Ibid.

17 https://www.atlanticcouncil.org/blogs/new-atlanticist/mass-still-matters-what-the-us-military-should-learn-from-ukraine/

18 https://tacticalnotebook.substack.com/p/ukraine-lessons-for-leaders

19 https://acleddata.com/2023/01/17/beyond-riyadh-houthi-cross-border-aerial-warfare-2015-2022/

20 https://rusi.org/explore-our-research/publications/commentary/lessons-houthi-missile-attacks-uae

21 https://jmvh.org/article/munitions-thermobaric-munitions-and-their-medical-effects/

22 https://www.forbes.com/sites/davidaxe/2023/10/17/ukraines-new-atacms-missiles-arent-bridge-killers-not-yet-at-least/?sh=59ab15fa6d77

23 https://jmvh.org/article/munitions-thermobaric-munitions-and-their-medical-effects/#:~:text=Thermobaric%20munitions%20work%20by%20initially,and%20into%20cavities%20and%20structures

24 https://www.twz.com/44479/the-truth-about-russias-terrifying-tos-1a-thermobaric-rocket-launchers-now-in-ukraine

25 https://www.moore.army.mil/infanTry/Magazine/issues/2023/Winter/pdf/9_Rivero_txt.pdf

26 https://static.rusi.org/403-SR-Russian-Tactics-web-final.pdf
27 https://euro-sd.com/2023/03/articles/30039/us-army-modernisation-a-mid-term-report/
28 https://crsreports.congress.gov/product/pdf/IF/IF12135/13
29 https://news.usni.org/2023/12/05/report-to-congress-on-army-long-range-hypersonic-weapon
30 Ibid.
31 https://foreignpolicy.com/2024/04/09/drones-russia-tanks-ukraine-war-fpv-artillery/

Chapter Five: Uncrewed Platforms and Electronic War

1 https://www.internationalaffairs.org.au/australianoutlook/fighting-drones-with-drones-learning-from-ukraine-on-the-future-of-warfare/
2 https://foreignpolicy.com/2021/03/30/army-pentagon-nagorno-karabakh-drones/
3 https://www.csis.org/analysis/air-and-missile-war-nagorno-karabakh-lessons-future-strike-and-defence
4 https://media.defense.gov/2022/Mar/14/2002956269/-1/-1/1/SUAS%20IDENTIFICATION%20AND%20REPORTING%20GUIDE.PDF
5 https://hrcak.srce.hr/file/440574
6 https://static.rusi.org/403-SR-Russian-Tactics-web-final.pdf
7 https://varabungas.camp/wp-content/uploads/2024/01/ukr-lessons-for-leaders-230904.pdf
8 Ibid.
9 https://www.economist.com/interactive/science-and-technology/2024/02/05/cheap-racing-drones-offer-precision-warfare-at-scale
10 https://lieber.westpoint.edu/kargu-2-autonomous-attack-drone-legal-ethical/
11 https://www.economist.com/interactive/science-and-technology/2024/02/05/cheap-racing-drones-offer-precision-warfare-at-scale
12 Ibid.
13 https://mwi.westpoint.edu/the-battle-of-shusha-city-and-the-missed-lessons-of-the-2020-nagorno-karabakh-war/
14 https://static.rusi.org/mass-precision-strike-final.pdf
15 https://www.defensenews.com/digital-show-dailies/sofic/2017/05/16/socom-commander-armed-isis-drones-were-2016s-most-daunting-problem/#:~:text=%22This%20last%20year%27s%20most%20daunting,small%20arms%20fire%2C%22%20Gen.

16 https://www.mitre.org/sites/default/files/2021-11/prs-19-3483-russian-lessons-learned-in-syria.pdf

17 https://www.defensenews.com/unmanned/2023/10/09/robot-army-of-one-service-focuses-on-single-robotic-combat-vehicle/

18 https://warontherocks.com/2022/04/the-tank-is-dead-long-live-the-javelin-the-switchblade-the/

19 https://www.newsweek.com/russia-marker-combat-robots-ukraine-tests-impact-1774666#:~:text=%22They%20have%20many%20different%20projects,in%20one%20expendable%20military%20mission

20 https://nationalinterest.org/blog/reboot/israel%E2%80%99s-newest-high-tech-border-guard-jaguar-robot-192061

21 https://www.lockheedmartin.com/en-us/capabilities/electronic-warfare.html

22 https://carnegieendowment.org/2023/04/18/integrating-cyber-into-warfighting-some-early-takeaways-from-ukraine-conflict-pub-89544

23 https://www.army.mod.uk/news-and-events/news/2022/06/rusi-land-warfare-conference-cgs-speech/

24 https://www.newyorker.com/news/daily-comment/the-rewards-and-risks-of-cyber-war#:~:text=%E2%80%9COlympic%20Games%E2%80%9D%20seems%20to%20be,before%20the%20invasion%20of%202003.

25 https://www.afr.com/policy/foreign-affairs/cheap-drones-are-transforming-warfare-in-ukraine-20240219-p5f5wz

26 https://www.furuno.com/en/gnss/technical/glossary#:~:text=Global%20Navigation%20Satellite%20System%20(GNSS,are%20Global%20Navigation%20Satellite%20Systems

27 https://www.economist.com/interactive/science-and-technology/2024/02/05/cheap-racing-drones-offer-precision-warfare-at-scale

28 https://static.rusi.org/403-SR-Russian-Tactics-web-final.pdf

29 https://static.rusi.org/Stormbreak-Special-Report-web-final_0.pdf

30 https://varabungas.camp/wp-content/uploads/2024/01/ukr-lessons-for-leaders-230904.pdf

31 https://www.newsweek.com/ukraine-us-c-uas-laser-guided-rocket-systems-1793015

32 https://www.france24.com/en/live-news/20230530-how-drone-warfare-has-evolved-in-ukraine

33 https://www.unmannedairspace.info/counter-uav-systems-and-policies/russia-and-ukraine-rapidly-accelerate-c-uav-capabilities-in-face-of-new-UAV-threats/

Chapter Six: Infantry

1 https://irp.fas.org/doddir/army/fm3-21-20.pdf
2 https://www.defence.gov.au/adf-members-families/honours-awards/badges/infantry-combat-badge#:~:text=The%20role%20of%20the%20infantry,commencing%20from%20the%20Korean%20War
3 https://www.moore.army.mil/armor/earmor/content/issues/2017/spring/2Fiore17.pdf
4 https://www.dupuyinstitute.org/blog/2022/04/11/some-initial-observations-on-the-russian-army-battalion-tactical-group-btg-concept/
5 https://www.mitre.org/sites/default/files/2021-11/prs-19-3483-russian-lessons-learned-in-syria.pdf
6 https://static.rusi.org/403-SR-Russian-Tactics-web-final.pdf
7 https://www.armyupress.army.mil/Journals/Military-Review/English-Edition-Archives/March-April-2017/ART-009/
8 https://www.saab.com/contentassets/4871a223666449af9aa3da9e2871d087/gcs_handbook_update_2023_print-aw.pdf
9 https://www.armyrecognition.com/news/army-news/2022/supacat-and-mbda-jointly-launch-brimstone-hmt-overwatch-demonstrator
10 https://media.defense.gov/2022/Mar/14/2002956269/-1/-1/1/SUAS%20IDENTIFICATION%20AND%20REPORTING%20GUIDE.PDF
11 https://www.forces.net/services/army/airborne-soldiers-do-some-smart-shooting-new-sight-helps-smash-drones
12 https://www.army.mil/article/253170/ivas_allows_maximum_mission_awareness_in_transit#:~:text=%E2%80%9CWith%20this%20integrated%20technology%2C%20they,direct%20fire%20and%20execute%20immediately

Chapter Seven: Special Operations Forces

1 https://www.reuters.com/world/europe/russias-fsb-says-british-special-forces-operating-ukraine-2024-04-11/
2 https://www.socom.mil/about/core-activities#:~:text=Core%20Activities,-Direct%20Action&text=Short%2Dduration%20strikes%20and%20other,recover%2C%20or%20damage%20designated%20targets.&text=Actions%20conducted%20in%20sensitive%20environments,of%20strategic%20or%20operational%20significance
3 https://www.nytimes.com/2021/12/12/us/civilian-deaths-war-isis.html

Chapter Eight: Future War

1 https://warontherocks.com/2018/04/forecasting-the-future-of-warfare/

INDEX

References to images are in **bold**.